X 11171 / BW   £6.00

Fiction

The Age of Consent (also published as *Waiting For Love*)
The Twelve Days of Christmas
Fred's First Waltz

Social History

Where Have All the Cowslips Gone?
Shadows of the Past
Echoes of the East End

Castle Howard

THE LIFE AND TIMES OF A
STATELY HOME

★

Venetia Murray

VIKING

VIKING

Published by the Penguin Group
Penguin Books Ltd, 27 Wrights Lane, London w8 5tz, England
Penguin Books USA Inc., 375 Hudson Street, New York, New York 10014, USA
Penguin Books Australia Ltd, Ringwood, Victoria, Australia
Penguin Books Canada Ltd, 10 Alcorn Avenue, Toronto, Ontario, Canada m4v 3b2
Penguin Books (NZ) Ltd, 182–190 Wairau Road, Auckland 10, New Zealand

Penguin Books Ltd, Registered Offices: Harmondsworth, Middlesex, England

First published 1994
1 3 5 7 9 10 8 6 4 2
First edition

Typeset by Datix International Limited, Bungay, Suffolk
Printed in England by Clays Ltd, St Ives plc
Filmset in Monophoto Bembo

A CIP catalogue record for this book is available from the British Library
ISBN 0-670-83379-7

For Rupert and Sophy, with love

Contents

List of Plates

Charles Howard, 1st Earl of Carlisle, by Sir Godfrey Kneller

Aerial view of Naworth Castle in Cumberland (*Country Life Picture Library*)

Charles Howard, 3rd Earl of Carlisle, by William Aikman

The three Howard sisters, daughters of the 3rd Earl, Ladies Elizabeth, Anne and Mary, by Giovanni Antonio Pellegrini

South front view of Castle Howard, by William Marlow

Nicholas Hawksmoor's initial drawings for the Mausoleum (*Photo © Three's Company*)

View of the Mausoleum in the grounds of Castle Howard (*Edwin Smith*)

Thomas Gainsborough's portrait of Isabella Byron, second wife of the 4th Earl of Carlisle

Nineteenth-century view of Castle Howard from the North Lake, by Henry Barlow Carter

The Grand Assembly Rooms in York (*York City Art Gallery*)

Entertainment at York Races, an anonymous eighteenth-century watercolour (*York City Art Gallery*)

Caroline, 5th Countess of Carlisle, by John Jackson

Georgiana, 6th Countess of Carlisle, by John Jackson

The 5th Earl of Carlisle with members of his family and household in Phoenix Park, Dublin, in 1781, by Francis Wheatley

The 5th Earl of Carlisle, with his youngest son Henry Howard, viewing a picture in the Long Gallery, by John Jackson

The 5th Earl of Carlisle with his lifelong friend George Selwyn, by Sir Joshua Reynolds

Lady Mary Howard, youngest daughter of the 6th Earl of Carlisle, by John Jackson

All plates are reproduced by courtesy of Castle Howard unless otherwise indicated.

Text illustrations are reproduced by permission of the following: Mary Evans Picture Library, pp. 13, 37, 74, 89, 105; Mansell Collection, pp. 17, 71, 103; Victoria & Albert Museum, pp. 32, 33; Castle Howard Collection, pp. 50, 51, 197; Country Life Picture Library, p. 67; Illustrated London News Picture Library, pp. 159, 164, 167.

Acknowledgements

Most of the material quoted in this book comes from the extensive archives at Castle Howard. My first thanks must therefore be to Mr Simon Howard for allowing me complete freedom of access to the archives, and for his whole-hearted cooperation in the project. I am particularly grateful to Dr Christopher Ridgeway, the librarian at Castle Howard, and to Mr Eeyan Hartley, the archivist, for their help and patience over the three years I have been working on this book. Both have also been kind enough to read the manuscript. My thanks, too, to Dame Christian Howard, who allowed me to tape-record her recollections of life at Castle Howard during the twenties and thirties.

I am greatly indebted to those scholars who have preceded me in researching the lives of the Earls of Carlisle: notably, Charles Saumarez Smith, Andrew Duncan and Diana Oliens, whose published theses on the 3rd, 5th and 7th Earls respectively have made my task so much easier. I would particularly like to thank Andrew Duncan for his kindness and generosity in allowing me to make use of his excellent manuscript 'A Georgian Country Estate – Castle Howard 1770–1820'. The former archivist at Castle Howard, Judith Oppenheimer, has provided another invaluable source in her treatise 'A Touch of Pomp and Ceremony', describing Queen Victoria's visit in 1850.

I cannot sufficiently express my thanks to Alexander Murray, of University College, Oxford, who has given me so much support and encouragement throughout, and who has also taken the trouble to read the manuscript at all the various stages of its development. I am equally grateful to L. G. Mitchell, also of University College, who has not only helped me with the section dealing with Whig politics in

Acknowledgements

the eighteenth century but has also been kind enough to read the whole book.

My thanks also to my agent, Jane Judd, who has been full of enthusiasm and support for the project from its conception, and to my editor at Viking, Eleo Gordon, for the same reasons. In 1990 I was awarded a Hawthornden Fellowship to work on this book, and I would like to express my thanks to the director and staff of Hawthornden Castle during my stay there. Among the many other people to whom I am indebted in one way or another are: Mrs Margaret Collins, John Jolliffe, and my nephew Robert Powell-Jones, who has been a constant source of encouragement and has also helped on several important sections of the book.

I would like to add a special thank you to both generations of the Toynbee family at Ganthorpe for all their hospitality while I was researching this book. It was entirely thanks to Jean, Lawrence, Rosalind and Joe that my visits to Yorkshire became a serious pleasure rather than a necessary chore.

Finally, my thanks to my family and to Rupert and Sophy, who have, as usual, provided constant moral support.

Author's note: in quoted material, contemporary spelling has nearly always been left as in the original, but punctuation and capitalization have occasionally been altered in the interests of clarity.

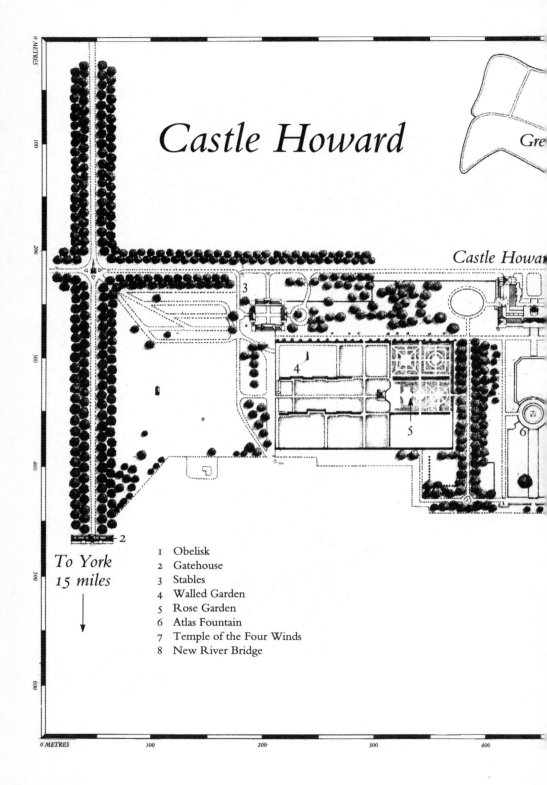

Castle Howard

Gre

Castle Howa

To York
15 miles

1 Obelisk
2 Gatehouse
3 Stables
4 Walled Garden
5 Rose Garden
6 Atlas Fountain
7 Temple of the Four Winds
8 New River Bridge

0 METRES   100   200   300   400

Ray Wood

South Lake

Mausoleum

600   700   800   900

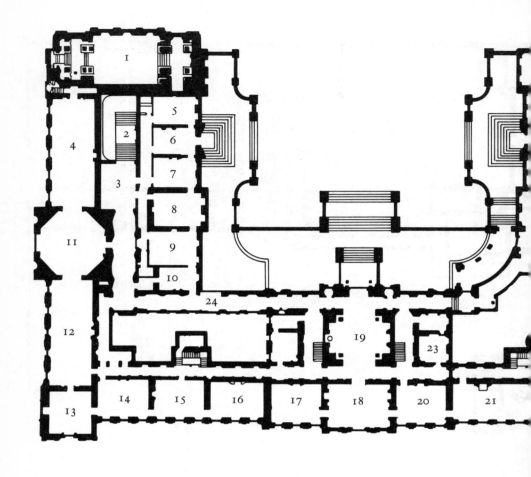

metres

0   10   20   30   40   50

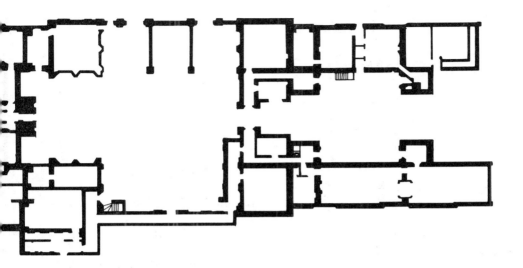

Castle Howard – The Ground Plan

The Howard Family Tree

THOMAS HOWARD
(1536–72)
4th Duke of Norfolk, beheaded and forfeited all honour [1]
= (1) MARY FITZ–ALAN, d. of Henry, 22nd Earl of Arundel

PHILIP HOWARD = ANN DACRE [2]
(succeeded through mother to become Earl of Arundel)
= (2) MARGARET AUDLEY

THOMAS HOWARD
= MARY DACRE [2]
(created 1st Earl of Suffolk)

LORD WILLIAM HOWARD
(1563–1640)
= ELIZABETH DACRE [2]
(inherited Naworth Castle through wife)

5 daughters

SIR PHILIP HOWARD
(1581–1616)
= MARY CARRYL

9 sons

3/4 daughters

SIR WILLIAM HOWARD
(1603–44)
= MARY EURE

2 sons

5 daughters

CHARLES HOWARD
(1629–85)
(created 1st Earl of Carlisle, 1667)
= ANNE HOWARD

4 sons

3 daughters

EDWARD HOWARD
(1636–92)
2nd Earl of Carlisle
= ELIZABETH UVEDALE

2 sons

4 daughters

CHARLES HOWARD
(1669–1738)
3rd Earl of Carlisle, builder of Castle Howard
= ANNE CAPELL

4 sons

HENRY HOWARD
(1694–1758)
4th Earl of Carlisle
= (1) FRANCES SPENCER
= (2) ISABELLA BYRON, d. of William, 4th Baron Byron

ELIZABETH HOWARD
= (1) NICHOLAS, Lord Lechmere
= (2) SIR THOMAS ROBINSON,
architect of West Wing

1 son

4 daughters

[1] The great-great grandson of the
4th Duke of Norfolk was restored
as 5th Duke in 1660.

[2] Three sisters.

FREDERICK HOWARD
(1748–1825)
5th Earl of Carlisle
= MARGARET CAROLINE LEVESON–GOWER,
d. of Granville Leveson–Gower, 1st Marquess of Stafford

4 daughters

GEORGE HOWARD
(1773–1848)
6th Earl of Carlisle
= GEORGIANA DOROTHY CAVENDISH,
d. of William Cavendish, 5th Duke of Devonshire

3 sons   6 daughters

GEORGE WILLIAM
FREDERICK HOWARD
(1802–64)
7th Earl of Carlisle

REVD WILLIAM
GEORGE HOWARD
(1808–89)
8th Earl of Carlisle

EDWARD GRANVILLE
GEORGE HOWARD
(1809–80)
created Baron Lanerton, 1874

CHARLES WENTWORTH
GEORGE HOWARD
(1814–79)
= MARY PARKE

2 sons   6 daughters

GEORGE JAMES HOWARD
(1843–1911)
9th Earl of Carlisle
= ROSALIND FRANCES STANLEY, d. of John, 2nd Lord Stanley of Alderley

CHARLES JAMES
STANLEY HOWARD
(1867–1912)
10th Earl of Carlisle
(inherited Naworth Castle, Cumbria)
= RHODA ANKARAT L'ESTRANGE

HON. GEOFFREY WILLIAM
ALGERNON HOWARD
(1877–1935)
(inherited Castle Howard, York)
= ETHEL CHRISTIAN METHUEN

4 sons   5 daughters

GEORGE JOSSELYN HOWARD
(1895–1963)
11th Earl of Carlisle

GEORGE ANTHONY
GEOFFREY HOWARD
(1920–84)
created Baron Howard
of Henderskelfe, 1983
= LADY CECILIA BLANCHE
GENEVIEVE FITZROY

ROSEMARY
CHRISTIAN HOWARD
(1916–)
created D.B.E., 1986

CHARLES JAMES
RUTHVEN HOWARD
(1923–)
12th Earl of Carlisle

HON. HENRY HOWARD
(1950–)

HON. NICHOLAS HOWARD
(1952–)
= (1) AMANDA NIMMO
= (2) VICTORIA BARNSLEY

HON. SIMON HOWARD
(1956–)
= ANNETTE,
Countess Compton
née Smallwood

HON. MICHAEL HOWARD
(1958–)
= LINDA LOUISE MCGRADY

2 sons   1 daughter

GEORGE FULCO GEOFFREY HOWARD (1985–)

ARABELLA BLANCHE   GRANIA HOWARD
GENEVIEVE HOWARD (1986–)   (1988–)

'A Passion for Heiresses'

In 1725 the Earl of Oxford, journeying through the north of England, stopped off to visit Castle Howard, which was still in the process of construction. His verdict on the enterprise was this:

To take a view of this place, to consider the climate, the situation, the nature of the soil, one would scarce think it was possible for any man in his senses to have begun a work of the nature this is, and to have been drawn into the expense this man has been let into.

The visitor today may well feel the same. Confronted for the first time with the magnificent splendour of this great house, with its elegant gardens and sculptured park, it is difficult indeed not to wonder about the man who conceived it and about the generations who followed him, to whom Castle Howard was their natural home. The imagination peoples those great rooms with figures in fancy dress: was this where they dined? was that where they danced? How did they get through their day, these gilded creatures who had so many servants they never had to lift a finger? Were they bored, those sheltered young ladies? Did they cultivate their minds and elevate leisure to a form of art? How did the mistress of so vast a household manage? She, at least, must have had a busy life. Which were the children's quarters? And which were the servants'? Was money ever a problem to these fabulously rich men? And what did they spend it on anyway? Were they good landlords, on easy terms with their tenantry? Or were there constant problems with the estate? How did the commune — for that is what an estate of such size amounted to — fare from one generation to the next? How did it all start? And, above all, who were they exactly, and what were they like, these grandees who lived their daily lives in such sumptuous style?

Castle Howard was built at the beginning of the eighteenth century by Charles Howard, 3rd Earl of Carlisle, and has been lived in by his descendants ever since. By the time the Earl began to dream of building a great house in Yorkshire, his family's position had already been established as one of the very richest and most powerful in England.

The Carlisle dynasty was founded in the sixteenth century by Lord William Howard, the third son of Thomas, 4th Duke of Norfolk. The family wealth and title derived from the previous century, when John Howard was created the first Duke of Norfolk in 1485, as a reward for his loyalty at Bosworth. By the time Thomas inherited the title, the family had become not only one of the richest in the country, with enormous estates, but also one of the most influential at Court, thanks to the Duke's position as titular head of the Catholic faction. Like most magnates of his age, the Duke was an opportunist, always on the look-out for ways of advancing the family interests – and the spectacular route he chose to achieve his ends created a legend, even in his own lifetime.

Thomas Norfolk was addicted to heiresses. He married three, in quick succession; but it was over his final attempt, on finding himself a widower once more, that he lost his head, quite literally, as subjects of the Tudors normally did when they aimed too high. With sublime arrogance, not to mention stupidity, Thomas set out to capture the young Mary, Queen of Scots, as his fourth wife. The dowry this time included a dangerous claim to the throne of England – and Queen Elizabeth was already both suspicious of the Norfolk family's political influence and covetous of their estates. The Duke's presumption that he could gain even greater power by marrying into the Royal family was the last straw: under the usual contemporary charge of treason the Queen had him executed.

2

Before his death, however, the Duke had cannily foisted his passion for heiresses on to the next generation. He was well situated to do so. Heiresses were important political assets in the sixteenth century, and the crown, therefore, took a considerable interest in their marriages. The Tudors had created a 'Master of the Court Wards', to oversee their welfare – and Thomas Norfolk secured this office for himself. From this vantage-point he was able to manoeuvre his own family into a strong strategic position. The Duke's third wife had been the Dowager Lady Dacre, of Gilsland in Cumberland. She was by far the richest of his wives, the owner of vast estates spread all over the north of England. Lady Dacre had an added attraction; her only son had been killed in a freak accident as a child, falling off his toy wooden horse and thus bringing the Dacre line to an end – but she had three small daughters. The Duke, as Master of Wards, acted swiftly. He arranged betrothals between his own three young sons, by his earlier marriages, to the three Dacre heiresses. Of course arranged marriages were the rule at the time, rather than exceptions, and alliances were always a matter of financial negotiation. A bride's dowry, not her face, was her fortune; a girl without a 'portion' was usually doomed to spinsterhood, as one of the 3rd Earl's daughters was later to discover.

Lord William Howard, the third and youngest of the Duke's sons, was formally engaged to Lady Elizabeth Dacre at the age of eight – just in time, as it turned out. His father, the Duke, was executed the following year. Despite this disgrace the marriage went ahead as soon as it was decently, and physically, possible. The groom was fourteen at the time, and the bride even younger. It was a happy choice for Lord William: the marriage settlements brought him estates all over the north of England, including Naworth in Cumberland, Morpeth in Northumberland and Henderskelfe – where the 3rd Earl of Carlisle was later to build Castle Howard – in Yorkshire. The wealth of the Carlisle Howards therefore stems directly from Elizabeth Dacre's dowry. It was an inheritance which was to elevate this cadet, junior, branch of the Howard family to the position of one of the major aristocratic dynasties in the land.

It was, however, to be twenty-five long, traumatic and highly dangerous years before Lord William could finally benefit from his wife's inheritance. The very fact of their success made the whole Howard family anathema to Queen Elizabeth – though political expediency had previously forced her to cooperate with them. Not only did they have far too much secular power for Elizabeth's peace of mind but they were also the leading Catholic family in the country, at a time when the Protestant settlement was still young. It was hardly surprising, therefore, that when two of the heiresses' uncles, on the Dacre side, decided to dispute the inheritance they found a formidable ally in the Queen. Elizabeth saw an opportunity to kill two birds with one stone. She abandoned the Dacres altogether and claimed the property for the Crown, thus both crippling the Howards and adding very considerably to her own coffers. Lord William and his brother Philip were thrown into the Tower on a charge of treason – as Catholic noblemen they were suspected of sympathizing with Philip II of Spain, who was already planning the Armada. Philip died in prison, but William was eventually released and permitted an allowance of just £400 a year. He was imprisoned again in 1585 on yet another charge of treason. Ultimately the Queen relented – on amazing terms. The Dacre sisters were granted Royal permission to buy their own land back from the Crown for the preposterous sum of £10,000 each. Not quite the scenario the avaricious Duke of Norfolk had had in mind when he arranged his dynastic marriages.

Thereafter Lord William steered clear of the Court. He had been an unwilling pawn in his father's political scheming and was far too shrewd a man to seek further trouble. In any case, as a Catholic, he was effectively barred from Government office. Lord William opted for a more constructive life.

The couple settled at Naworth, a medieval border castle in Cumberland, lying just south of the Scottish border. Naworth is a beautiful and romantic fortress, looking to the north over Hadrian's

Wall and the wild fell country and surrounded to the south by dark forest. Lord William felt passionately about Naworth, as, indeed, did subsequent generations of his family. In fact, even after Castle Howard was built, demoting Naworth to the status of a *maison secondaire*, the latter continued to be greatly treasured by all the Howards and to play an important part in their lives. In later years it became a favourite retreat for the family when they wished to escape from the grandeur of Castle Howard, a place for summer holidays and splendid Christmas gatherings. Moreover, the Cumberland estates (up until the twentieth century, when the Carlisle inheritance was broken up on the death of Rosalind, wife of the 9th Earl) provided a large part of their income, and at least one of their hereditary 'rotten boroughs'.

Naworth, which had been crenellated by the first Lord Dacre of Gilsland in 1335, was also – indeed first and foremost – an important defensive stronghold. During the Middle Ages life had been an almost constant drama, dominated in the north by the Border Wars. For centuries the northern counties had been subject to sudden invasions by marauding Scots, bent on pillage and plunder. Naworth thus provided an important bulwark, and in the Dacres' time, a necessary haven for the local people. However, after the last Lord Dacre's death, and before Lord William Howard had been able to assume his inheritance, there was a period of some thirty years when the castle was abandoned. During the interim Naworth fell into decay.

Lord William's first concern was, therefore, the restoration of the castle. His initials first appear on one of the pipes in 1602; in 1619 he tackled the important work of repairing the great Dacre tower which dominates the castle. Next he put in new windows, replastered galleries, remodelled the Howard tower and created new, more convenient suites of apartments. The interior was modernized (by contemporary standards, that is) without interfering with the beautiful architecture of Naworth. The crenellated battlements, great towers and thick walls stand virtually undamaged today.

At the same time Lord William embarked on the truly formidable task of imposing law and order on the countryside. It was not only the Scots whom he had to subdue; Border brigands, known as 'moss troopers', had banded themselves together and ranged all over the north devastating the land. They attacked at random, stealing the cattle and setting fire to the homesteads; the farmers lived in terror, and profitable agriculture was at a standstill. Lord William had already been made Warden of the West March, an office which authorized him to raise his own army, in the King's name, to defend the peace in the immediate neighbourhood. At the head of a considerable force he set forth to quell the countryside – with such success that he became known as 'Bauld Willie', 'the Civilizer of our Borders'. (His wife, incidentally, acquired the nickname of 'Bessie of the Broad Acres', in deference to the size of her inheritance, not her figure.) There is a list, in Lord William's own handwriting, still in existence, of 'the felons taken and prosecuted by me, for felonies in Gilsland and elsewher, since my abode ther'. In his first ten years at Naworth the total comes to twenty-nine, nearly all of whom were summarily executed.

Having restored at least a modicum of peace, Lord William was at last able to concentrate on improving his own estates. He introduced a number of agricultural reforms, cleared the land and built new farms. Confidence returned to the estate – and the Howard fortunes prospered accordingly.

Lord William was a civilized man with a cultivated, scholarly mind. His friend Camden, the historian and antiquarian, refers to him as 'a singular lover of valuable antiquity and learned withal'. Hadrian's Wall, only a mile or so from Naworth, yielded the basis for a notable collection of Roman artefacts, altars and inscriptions carved on stone, which he housed in the Naworth gardens. He was a passionate bibliophile, who had been collecting books and manuscripts since his youth, and founded a valuable library at Naworth, a small part of which remains today.

The flavour of life in the north in the seventeenth century remained predominantly medieval in character. Naworth, in Lord William's day, must have been a cauldron of activity. In *Life in the English Country House*, Marc Girouard, describing the great medieval household, points out that though 'exorbitantly large by our standards . . . it was essentially functional; everything in it, including the element of conspicuous waste, had a practical purpose'. It was 'a mixture of office, barracks, court and hotel'. The structure of the household was like a pyramid:

... its lord floated in splendour at its apex, but was supported by widening layers of gentlemen, yeomen and grooms, approximating in function and status to officers, N.C.O.s and other ranks in the army today ... households were not only pyramidal in organization; they were power blocks as solid as pyramids in the front which they presented to the world, and the weight which they gave to their members. The fact that an entire household, whether related to its lord or not, was described as his family accurately expressed its close-knit nature. It was a mutual benefit society, which worked not only for the power and glory of its lord but for the advantage and protection of everyone in it.

Naworth is not a particularly large castle but it was certainly an important and powerful focal point in the Border country. It must have been crammed to bursting point. Apart from the immediate family, room would have to have been found for large numbers of functionaries – clerks, tutors, governess, chaplain, comptroller, auditor, the gentlemen and gentlewomen in waiting, and pages. There would have been a veritable legion of servants, all necessary to the running of the resident household alone, from the aristocratic, liveried steward down to the sweaty little scullery boys who did all the really unpleasant work. In this kind of household the grander 'servants' would still have been drawn from the upper classes of society: younger sons of the gentry, or even of the nobility, who often began their career in the service of a great landowner. Service was a recognized means of gaining an education, of making contacts and of observing at close quarters the machinations of power.

In addition to the resident household the castle would have had to cope with a constant stream of visitors, each accompanied by his own, private, 'satellite' servant. 'Where I dines I sleeps' was once an accepted maxim. The distances between neighbours could be a matter of days, and the state of the roads was such as to make any journey an arduous, if not distinctly hazardous, undertaking. And, of course, there was always the northern climate to complicate visiting even further. Those who came to Naworth, whether on business or for pleasure, nearly always had to be put up for the night.

Hospitality, in fact, was an essential ingredient of the feudal creed, '*noblesse oblige*' – and it was a much more spontaneous example of generosity than the later, calculated, philanthropy of the Victorians. It was the custom among the aristocracy to keep a virtually open house. Anyone who came to the door, whatever their class or business, would be offered refreshment, no beggar refused alms, or traveller sanctuary. The purpose of the 'conspicuous waste' was simply that more provender than was necessary for the Lord's table and household was always on hand, so that the left-overs could be given out to the poor who waited daily at the castle gates. Catering for a permanent household of at least 200 must alone have entailed staggering quantities of food. The most spectacular amounts recorded were those of a gargantuan feast given at Cawood Castle in Yorkshire by the Nevilles, close friends of the Howards. At this event, to which some 2,500 people were invited and which lasted for several days, the list of food consumed included 1,000 sheep, 113 whole oxen, six wild bulls, 2,000 geese, 2,000 pigs, 2,000 chickens and twelve porpoises.

The atmosphere of daily life in a great household such as Naworth during the Middle Ages is evoked with curious nostalgia by Thomas Shadwell, writing towards the end of the seventeenth century:

. . . 'Twas never good days but when great tables were kept in large halls, the buttery hatch always open; black jacks, and a good smell of meat and March beer; with dog's turds and marrow bones as ornaments in the hall. These were signs of good housekeeping. I hate to see Italian fine buildings with no meat or drink in'em. ('The Lancashire Witches', 1681)

The great hall was the heart of the castle, the scene of numerous dinners, dances, masques and musical entertainments of all kinds. Mummers and their like toured the country throughout the year, little bands of entertainers, complete with their own musicians and costumes, stopping for a night or even longer at each great house in turn. From Christmas Eve to Twelfth Night life was a continual feast, embracing the whole community. The Christmas plays put on by the family and guests became a sacrosanct tradition among the Howards which lasted until the twentieth century.

When Lord William and 'Bess' were in their seventies, a contemporary diary gives a glowing account of the writer's visit to Naworth Castle, where the couple continued to hold court in patriarchal splendour. In the end, Lord William's marriage, which had been arranged for such mercenary reasons and had been the cause of so many traumatic years, proved a triumphant success. They had been a prolific couple – ten children survived infancy – and Bess believed in the concept of the extended family. At one point it is said that she had over 100 direct descendants all living together under the Naworth roof – sons and daughters, their husbands and wives, children galore, unmarried sisters, cousins, uncles and aunts. She must have been a formidable lady. It would appear that she was also a happy one. The visitor, after extolling the generous hospitality found at the castle, says of the old couple: 'These noble twain [who] could not make above twenty-five years both together when first they married, that can now make above 140 years . . . are very hearty, well, and merry'.

Charles Howard, who was created 1st Earl of Carlisle in 1661, was a great-grandson of Lord William. He was a vivid, somewhat unscrupulous character, an adventurer and soldier of fortune, a skilful and ambitious opportunist with a truly remarkable talent for survival. In the course of his dramatic life he switched sides, from Royalist to Parliamentarian, and from Catholic to Protestant, whenever it seemed expedient, was imprisoned twice on charges of high treason, and, as a result, very nearly lost his estates and his fortune. Yet at one time or another both Cromwell and the King had trusted him with high office.

The historian Gilbert Burnet was not enamoured of the first Earl's double-dealing: 'He loved to be popular, and yet to keep up an interest at court; and so was apt to go forward and backward in public affairs.' Howard himself explains his volte-face over Catholicism: 'As monarchy had been so long interrupted by rebellion and faction, so had episcopacy by schism and heresy, and that no one that spoke against episcopacy offered anything better.'

He had begun his career as plain Captain Howard, a soldier in King Charles I's army. After an abortive trip to France in 1646, which ended in shipwreck, he was captured by the Parliamentary forces and imprisoned for the first time. He was released on payment of a crippling fine – £4,000: this was the price, at the time, of a castle, a ship, or the equivalent of a bishop's annual revenue. Howard was forced to retire from the political scene for a few years, but by 1650 he was back in evidence again, this time supporting Cromwell. He was given the job of dealing with a number of witches, whom he claimed to have discovered living in Cumberland, a task which must have been eminently suited to his devious character.

Howard was a brave man. At the Battle of Worcester he distinguished himself by exceptional gallantry, as a contemporary state paper attests: 'Captain Howard of Naworth, captain of the Life Guards to his excellency, has received divers sore wounds . . . but with hope of life . . . Captain Howard did interpose very happily at a place of much danger, where he gave the enemy (though with his personal smarts) a very seasonable check, when our foot, for want of horse, were hard put to it.' This episode consolidated his position with the Parliamentarians, and in 1653 he entered Parliament for the first time, as MP for Westmoreland. The following year he returned to military service in the forefront of Cromwell's army. He was made captain of the Lord Protector's personal bodyguard, and in 1655 was given his own regiment, elevated to the rank of Colonel and deputed to deal with the rebels and insurrections currently breaking out all over the north. Two years later he was rewarded by Cromwell with the title of Baron Gilsland and Viscount Howard of Morpeth.

Thus, by the time Charles II returned to England, Charles Howard had already proved his ability to survive. The new King needed such men, and the two, in effect, struck a deal: Howard supported the

Restoration, and in return was made, in quick succession, a privy councillor, Lord-Lieutenant of Cumberland and Westmoreland, a vice-admiral and joint-commissioner for the office of earl-marshal. In 1661, when he was still only thirty-two, Charles II created Howard 1st Earl of Carlisle.

In later years Burnet describes the Earl as having 'run into a course of vice'. There is a splendid example of Carlisle's extravagant way of living in a contemporary record of the meal referred to as an 'ante-supper':

... the manner of which was to have the table covered at the first entrance of the guests with dishes as high as a tall man could well reach, filled with the choycest and dearest viands sea or land could afford, and all this once seen, and having feasted the eyes of the invited, was in a manner throwne away, and fresh set on to the same height, having this advantage of the other that it was hot.★

In 1664 Charles II sent Carlisle as an ambassador-extraordinary to Russia, Sweden and Denmark. His mission was to restore the favourable trading conditions which had been granted to the Muscovy Company by the Tsar in the previous century, but which had been subsequently withdrawn. Carlisle, armed with costly gifts and accompanied by an impressive entourage which included the poet Andrew Marvell, was sent to negotiate a fresh contract. Around this time the 1st Earl was described as being:

... of comely and advantageous stature, a majestic mien, and not above 34 years of age ... he had a peculiar grace and vivacity in his discourse and in his actions great promptitude and diligence. In a word, he was adorned with all perfections that could render a man acceptable, and specially with those that were requisite for the discharge of so important an affair.

This assessment of Carlisle proved woefully inaccurate. He was far

★ There is some confusion as to whether, in fact, this particular description refers to the lifestyle of the 1st Earl of Carlisle: it may have been written about one of his ancestors.

too violent a character to make a successful diplomat, and in fact the embassy ended in farcical failure. Carlisle lost his temper, and his decibel count rose with shattering results. Guy Miège, another member of the party, records that on 17 February 1664:

My Lord Ambassador had another conference in the Palace, where his Commissioners read to him their answers to his two papers, but refused to give him yet a copy of it. In that answer all things were quite contrary to his expectations, so that he thought fit thereupon to speak somewhat hard to them. Then it happened that one great casement of the room, wherein they were assembled together, fell down with such a horrid noise, that the Lords Commissioners were quite astonished, and wished my Lord had spoken more gently. An Interpreter of theirs, who was an outlandish man, speaking afterwards to that purpose said, 'If two or three words of anger of My Lord Ambassador's do shake off the house, how would they tremble, if they heard King Charles thundering at their ears with just indignation?'

By the time he was in his fifties Carlisle was a spent force, worn out by the exigencies and dramas of his life. Two years before his death, in 1685, he was described by the Duke of Ormond as 'the decrepidest man that I ever saw out of bed'.

The 1st Earl died in 1685 and was succeeded by his eldest son, Edward, the first of the family to be known by the courtesy title of Viscount Morpeth – a title which has continued to be used by the heirs to the earldom of Carlisle ever since. Morpeth was a much more straightforward and sober character than his father. He sat in the House of Commons, as a Whig, for nineteen years and was the founder of the long tradition of dedicated allegiance to the Whig party, and its principles, which was to last among the Howards until the demise of the party itself. (And even after that, in the sense that most of them then went on to join its natural successor, the Liberal party.)

During his Parliamentary years Morpeth lived mainly in London at Carlisle House, a mansion which had been bought by the 1st Earl

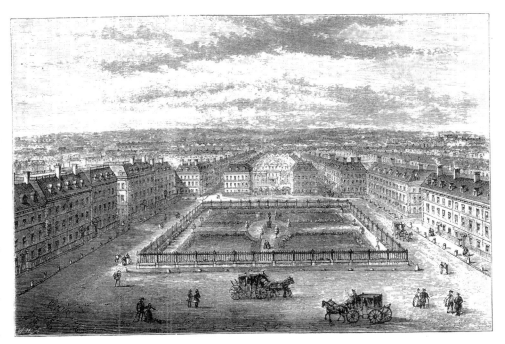

Carlisle House, the Howards' family residence in London, was in Soho Square, one of the most fashionable areas in town in the eighteenth century. The original building, designed by Sir Christopher Wren, was demolished by the 3rd Earl and replaced by a more ostentatious mansion.

during one of his more affluent periods. It was situated in Soho Square, at that time one of the smartest and most fashionable areas of the town. Built during the Restoration, it was an elegant, spacious square with a statue of Charles II in the centre and a number of tree-lined walks. This original Carlisle House is thought to have been designed by Sir Christopher Wren, but was demolished, unfortunately, at the end of the eighteenth century. The 3rd Earl, suffering from a bad attack of *folie de grandeur*, decided that the original building was too small and commissioned a larger and grander one, also known as Carlisle House, on the other side of the same square. Among the Howards' aristocratic neighbours, according to contemporary records, were the Earl of Fauconberg, the Lords Foley, Mansel, Gainsborough and 'many others of the first quality' (John Macky, 1714).

13

Edward Howard, 2nd Earl of Carlisle, died in 1692 at the age of fifty-six – and it was his eldest son, Charles, who built Castle Howard.

This, then, was the financial and cultural inheritance upon which Castle Howard was founded. The family fortunes continued to prosper; the outlook remained fair; and if the actual zenith of their power was yet to come, the bases of wealth and land upon which it would rely had been firmly established. In the course of the next century the Carlisle Howards would continue to rise until they became universally acknowledged as one of the greatest families in Britain: leaders in the worlds of politics and society, of agriculture and local government, of fashion, of the arts, and of architecture. They would build a great house, fill it with treasures, and, for several generations, lead lives of glittering splendour. The tide of their fortunes would falter from time to time, but the family's status would remain. It was not until the beginning of the twentieth century that the Howards, like most of the great aristocratic dynasties, began to find themselves in grave financial straits.

'A Sublime Elysium'

There are two known paintings of the 3rd Earl of Carlisle: the first, by Sir Godfrey Kneller, *c.* 1705, shows a rather smug young man, with arrogant eyes and a disdainful expression; it is a fleshy, sybaritic face, with a bulbous mouth, already showing signs of a double chin. A not particularly interesting, somewhat spoilt young nobleman, typical of his time, one would assume. It is a misleading portrait: there is no indication of the intelligence and aesthetic discrimination which was to create one of the loveliest houses in England. The second, painted more than twenty years later when the Earl was approaching his sixtieth birthday, is clearly intended to illustrate his consequence and to advertise the success he has made of his life. He is wearing his full Coronation regalia, holding an enormous coronet in one hand, and posing in front of a painting of his supreme achievement – Castle Howard. But this too is misleading, for the image of a rich and powerful man is betrayed by the Earl's expression. It has lost its arrogance, and the eyes are almost sad. The trappings are too heavy; the grandeur meaningless. In the first painting he is so sure that the world is his for the taking; in the second he has become aware that it is not.

Charles Howard, Viscount Morpeth, was born in 1669, the eldest son of Edward, 2nd Earl of Carlisle, and his wife, Elizabeth, daughter of Sir William Uvedale. He was only twenty-three when his father died in 1692 and he succeeded to the title as 3rd Earl of Carlisle. But he had begun to chafe at the restrictions of life at Naworth, implicit in the castle's geographical situation, long before that. From an early age Morpeth showed an exceptional interest in the arts, coupled with an alert and eager intelligence; appetites which the limited society on offer round Naworth was quite unable to satisfy. Moreover, he was already showing signs of blazing social ambition; Morpeth had no intention of settling for life as a wealthy northern nonentity. When his father arranged a marriage for him at the age of nineteen he was only too delighted, and saw it as the obvious means of escape.

The bride was Lady Anne Capel, who, from the political point of view, seems a surprisingly bold choice. The 2nd Earl was, of course, a staunch Whig, but, mindful of the family's previous problems, he had always steered clear of controversy and made a point of caution in his politics: Lady Anne, however, was the daughter of the 1st Earl of Essex – whose trial for treason had been one of the great dramas of recent years. Essex had been accused of participation in the supposed Rye House Plot in 1683, and sent to the Tower. He committed suicide in prison by cutting his throat – on the day of the trial of Lord William Russell for the same alleged offence. Russell, who was a friend and political ally of both Carlisle and Essex, had in fact been framed; but it was not until after he had been found guilty of treason and executed that his innocence was finally proved.

Whatever the political associations she brought with her, the immediate fact was that Lady Anne was only thirteen at the time of the marriage, and it was reported that 'through the greenness of their years, [they] do not co-habit together'. Since the couple were too young to live together, Morpeth left his wife at home and went happily off on a Grand Tour. At the end of the seventeenth century the practice among aristocratic families of sending their sons off to spend a year or two pottering around Europe was just coming into fashion. It was a form of higher education, a means by which the young men might study classical art and culture at first hand. At the same time the Tour served as an introduction to European society, from whom, it was hoped, they would acquire a certain sophistication and elegance of manner. Morpeth found the Tour an enthralling experience whose direct influence is reflected again and again in the design of Castle Howard.

★

A View of Rome in the eighteenth century. The 3rd Earl of Carlisle spent more than two years on the Grand Tour studying classical art and culture: the Italian influence is reflected again and again in the design and decoration of Castle Howard.

Morpeth was away for nearly two and a half years, from November 1688 to February 1691, and covered all the usual ground. The tour began in Flanders; from there he went to Holland, and on, via Germany, to Vienna, then over the Alps and down to the plain of Lombardy. From the delights of Venice and Vicenza he went on to Padua, where he signed the embassy visitors' book on 1 January 1690. But it was clearly the art and architecture of Rome, where he stayed for over a year, which made the strongest impression on Morpeth. The two small commonplace books which he wrote while he was in Rome provide the best evidence of the way in which his artistic taste was developing, and explanation of the direction it was later to take when he came to design Castle Howard. One of the books is headed 'Remarks out of several Books in Latin, French and English' and shows the extent of his interests, and that he took his studies seriously. The commonplace books show that he has been reading and making notes on the work of all the major artists: Leonardo da Vinci, Raphael, Holbein and Titian are among those mentioned. He has been sightseeing all over the city and the surrounding country, and at the same time he has been reading Cicero, Seneca and other classical authors. But he has also been finding out about contemporary Italian art. There is a note that 'Charles Maratti is counted ye most famous Painter now of Europe', and another that 'Gordian at Naples is also very much esteemed'. Another Neapolitan, 'the Cavalier Bernino', is mentioned as being 'very much esteemed for his works in painting, sculpture and Architecture'; the Chevalier Fontana 'is counted one of ye most famous sculptors at Rome'.* Many other names are noted for future reference, and, indeed, crop up years later in the Castle Howard accounts.

In the second notebook Morpeth lists the foremost Roman families of the day and indulges in the odd item of society gossip. It was in Rome, too, that he became seriously interested in the great contemporary passion for collecting. Whether collecting is regarded as a commendable hobby, or as a dangerous mania, there is no doubt that the English aristocracy's habit of relieving Europe of as many of its treasures as it could find formed the basis of most of the great collections on view today in their stately homes. Although there is unfortunately no record of the particular spoils brought back to England by Morpeth, there are plenty relating to his son's Grand Tour some twenty-five years later. And the future 3rd Earl himself emphasizes in his notes that he has made the acquaintance of one of the best-known collectors in Italian society, Gian Petro Bellori, who is 'a great vertuoso' and 'hath a very good closet' (i.e. room in the house used to store or display books and *objets d'art*).

Morpeth returned to England at last in the spring of 1691, and on the death of his father the following year succeeded to the title. The new

* The correct names of these four major Italian artists are, respectively, Carlo Maratta, Luca Giordano, Gianlorenzo Bernini and Carlo Fontana.

Earl and his wife – who was now seventeen, and therefore old enough to live with him – made their home at Naworth, where the first of their five children began to arrive. For a few years he appears to have been content with life in the country; he needed time to familiarize himself with the complexities of his vast inheritance, to meditate on the most lucrative approach to the estates – for Carlisle was already aware that he had expensive tastes. Besides, the young Earl, like the rest of his generation, was a dedicated sportsman and the Naworth estate offered plenty of scope. The shooting was excellent; there was fishing in the rivers and tarns; and hunting several times a week in season. He went racing regularly and even began to breed his own race-horses.

As a couple, the young Carlisles dominated local society. They entertained at Naworth and took part in all the traditional festivities. Northern hospitality was generous, jovial and boisterous – but it was not sophisticated. Once again the Earl began to hanker after more subtle pleasures. It was time to launch himself on London.

He had already made his début in Parliament, standing as the Whig member for Morpeth, one of three 'rotten boroughs' in the gift of the Howard family. On succeeding to the earldom he had been made Governor of Carlisle and, soon afterwards, Lord-Lieutenant of Cumberland and Westmoreland, both quasi-political posts; but the Earl wanted more than such parochial sinecures. He had already set his sights on serious power.

His first action of note, on arriving in London, was indicative both of his character and of the way his life was to develop. As has been mentioned in the previous chapter, he demolished Carlisle House, the existing family residence in London, deeming it far too humble for the kind of entertaining he had in mind. The original house did not even have a ballroom, an omission which made it quite unsuitable for a man of Carlisle's social ambition. He had been most impressed by the elegance and style of the salons in Paris and Rome, noted the premium placed on lavish display, and determined to emulate their example. Carlisle was already an advocate of the blatant status symbol.

He built a splendid new mansion in the same fashionable area, Soho

Square. In decorating and furnishing the new house, he was able to give full rein to his taste for extravagant display and, at the same time, to experiment with his ideas. Carlisle had enormous visual imagination – to which Castle Howard is, of course, the final testament. But even the records of the London house, which he decorated while still only in his early twenties, indicate the range of his interests. Many of the ideas he had absorbed in Italy were translated into tangible works of art for Soho Square. He commissioned painters, sculptors and cabinet-makers. Among the accounts extant at Castle Howard are records of £28 paid to Henry Cook, a painter who had trained in Italy, for decorating one of the ceilings; £14 15s. to Richard Osgood, a fashionable contemporary sculptor; £12 18s. to Louis Cheron, a French Huguenot who had settled in London, 'for two pictures'; and £66 to 'Mr Johnson ye Cabinettmaker', in 1698. (This was Geritt Jensen, a specialist in highly decorated furniture much patronized by the Royal family.) He bought ornaments, lamps, china and 'a rich Indian quilt', added to his collection of books, and commissioned a catalogue of the library – adding an order that five volumes bought for his wife should be 'covered with green vellum and gilt'. The house in Soho Square was the first upon which Carlisle was able to lavish his love of beautiful things, and he indulged himself to the hilt. It was a sumptuous house, even by the high standards of the 1700s, and it was the perfect background for the Earl in his bid for social and political recognition.

Carlisle's timing was right. It was the leaders of the Whig party who had largely engineered the Bloodless Revolution of 1688 and had been the prime movers in the subsequent invitation to William of Orange. When the Dutch King, who was a Protestant and a Parliamentarian, accepted the English throne, the rout of the Tories was complete. Carlisle, as head of one of the great Whig families, was well placed to aim for the highest political office. The Earl thought his future secure – somewhat naïvely, and quite wrongly, as it turned out a few years later. In the last decade of the century, however, his star was in the ascendant, and he was quickly accepted into the inner circle of the Whig aristocracy. The Earl was already a well-known figure at Court, and was soon on terms of personal friendship with the new King. The strength of Carlisle's position was confirmed in the summer of 1700, when King William made him a Gentleman of the Bedchamber. This post was one of the plum sinecures in the Royal gift, carrying a salary of £1,000 a year – no mean sum by contemporary values. He was then appointed, in quick succession, a privy councillor, deputy earl-marshal of England (during his cousin the Duke of Norfolk's minority), and a Commissioner for the Union with Scotland. In December 1702 he was made First Lord of the Treasury, a job which at that time wielded more power than any other. His political career was meteoric; it had taken less than five years to reach a position of indisputable authority. So perhaps it is not surprising that he overreached himself in one direction at least, and that a natural conceit turned into arrogance.

For while the Earl was concentrating on his successes at Court and in London, his constituents in the north were becoming increasingly irritated, both with his attitude and with his actual behaviour. At the beginning of the eighteenth century the line between acceptable canvassing and unwarranted interference in the Parliamentary elections was finely drawn. Basically, it was normal practice for a landlord to use whatever influence he could muster, on both the electorate and the selection committees. But he was expected to confine his energies to his own estates. Carlisle continually flouted this rule and interfered in electoral matters beyond his province. On several occasions he attempted to foist candidates of his own choosing on to the selection committees, and to sabotage others. In 1695 Carlisle wrote to one of the major landowners in the neighbouring county of Westmoreland:

Considering it may be of dangerous consequence ye admitting Mr Grahme to be a Parliament man every body being acquainted with his father's principalls, I do think it is absolutely necessary for every well wisher to this Government to keep him out, if they can, therefore I must take ye liberty to presse you heartyly to espouse Mr Lowther's interest.

Five years later Carlisle was still trying to get his friend adopted, rather than the local candidate, for the same seat in Westmoreland – a seat which had no connection with the Howards whatsoever. Mr Grahme senior, father of the sitting Member, complained that:

A letter is handed about in the name of the Earl of Carlisle in favour of Major Lowther. It is a new thing for any man who has no lands in a county to concern himself in elections there. The Earl's grandfather and father enjoyed the posts he has in these northern parts, yet never meddled with elections in Westmoreland.

In fact, Carlisle appears to have behaved in a thoroughly autocratic manner; the locals were outraged and the whole affair became something of a scandal. Matters came to a head in 1701 when the Earl's interference triggered a question in the House of Commons. James Lowther reported that many of the members objected strongly to:

Lds meddling at Elections & there was a Vote pas't Nem: Con: That for any Ld Lieutts or Peer of the Realm to concern themselves at any Elections of Commoners to serve in Parliament is a high infringement upon the Liberties & Priviledges of the Commons of England. This gave Occasion to Sr. Chr. Musg[rave] to take notice of my Ld Carl. writing Circular Letters for the Gentlemen to stay for his coming down to consult about a Knight of the Shire & of his calling the Justices together for that purpose when he came down.

The Lowthers were neighbours and long-standing friends of the Howard family, but eventually even they had had enough of Carlisle's intervention in the politics of their county. A year later James Lowther wrote that:

It is plainly to be perceiv'd that his [Carlisle's] aim is to bring all the elections of the 2 counties to his own nomination and I can see that he will do nothing to help any bodies interest in the county but his own.

Parliament's criticisms had fallen on deaf ears. Nevertheless the Earl realized at last how unpopular he had become and simply stopped going to the north, unless it was to deal with urgent business concerning the estate. Aware that he would be accused by the electorate of desertion, he pleaded ill health, in fact with an element of justification. Carlisle suffered from gout even as a young man, and by the end of his life was completely crippled by it. But the real truth of the matter was that he no longer had any desire to spend time at Naworth. The Earl was already committed heart and soul to a far more exciting project – the building of Castle Howard.

The euphoria consequent upon the Restoration led to a tremendous surge of building among the aristocracy. In the course of the last two decades of the seventeenth century the Duke of Kingston had built Thoresby, the Duke of Montagu Boughton House, the Duke of Somerset Petworth, and the Duke of Devonshire Chatsworth. Carlisle, though neither a duke nor as rich as some of these men, moved in the same circles and had stayed in their splendid new mansions. He had seen the increase in status which such grandeur conferred on their owners. Carlisle had attended the Whig Congress held at Petworth in 1693 and observed for himself the role which a great house could play in the affairs of state. Again, the King had recently been to stay at Althorp, and, after praising the magnificence with which he had been entertained by the Earl of Sunderland, he remarked that '. . . nothing made a Gentleman look like a Gentleman, but living like one'. It was not in the 3rd Earl's character to lag behind his peers. He wanted a power base of his own, a setting worthy of his ambition. Castle Howard would serve both as a symbol and a magnet. It would be a tangible expression of his position in the hierarchy of power.

Moreover, there were a number of practical reasons why Naworth was no longer suitable as the Earl's principal residence. It was too far from London. The journey often took ten days, even longer in really hazardous weather, hardly a feasible proposition for a serious politician. Again, Naworth was too small; by the beginning of the eighteenth century the 'dogs-and-straw' concept of communal living had given way to an emphasis on privacy and space. It was a time of financial prosperity, prosperity which not only allowed, but positively encouraged its beneficiaries to lavish money on art and splendour. Conspicuous display was a means of giving consequence to wealth. This kind of expenditure differed from others in that it served a whole dynasty, because it lasted – unlike, for example, a medieval banquet. As Lord Lonsdale, a neighbour of Carlisle's, who had just built Lowther Castle, explained:

... a Good hous is a Debt owing to a ffamilie ... that besides my own satisfaction and Eas I was apt to think it could not be done att a more reasonable time, nor with lesse Expence than I was capable of performing it; That some Expence was even Necessary more than I cared to be att in Magnificent living to redeem the ffamilie ffrom Envie and Objection; That this therefore was likelie to be a lasting advantage to my ffamilie. That I was willing that my Posteritie should participate in the advantage off the Expence, and that it might not be consumed in my own Luxurie.

A rather more specious argument, much used at the time by all builders of magnificent houses when charged with conspicuous extravagance, was that these buildings fulfilled a necessary function. They provided employment for the poor. This philanthropic motive was also cited by Lord Lonsdale:

Nothing could be a greater relief to the Poor in the Neighbourhood. Not even so much money given them would have done them so much good.

All these arguments could, and probably did, apply to the 3rd Earl of Carlisle. Nevertheless, the most cogent reason for his decision to build Castle Howard probably lay in his ambitious nature. When he decided to build it, Carlisle was on the crest of a wave. As Charles Saumarez Smith writes in *The Building of Castle Howard*:

The trajectory of the third Earl's brilliant, but brief, political career as a minister of William III indicates that the plans for Castle Howard were made at exactly the moment when he was looking for promotion at Court. Building a great house was a means of drawing attention to his capabilities, of demonstrating his potential usefulness as an ally of the king. The evidence suggests a man of strongly autocratic disposition, who used architecture as a means of social and political aggrandisement.

Finally, Carlisle, in company with many of his friends, was an active and willing patron of the arts. He was a highly educated, cultivated man, with a strongly developed aesthetic sense. He had studied architecture in Italy; he was a connoisseur of both contemporary and classical painting, of sculpture and of other *objets d'art*. He had discovered the delights of collecting when furnishing the London house. His new building would provide tremendous scope. It would be a continual challenge and excitement. He would create a glorious monument to his personal taste, a visual feast for the world to admire. And it would be a magnificent tribute to the name of Howard. The Earl dedicated Castle Howard to the founder of his line, Lord William Howard, in the inscription carved on the Pyramid in front of the house:

O THEE, O VENERABLE SHADE
WHO LONG HAST IN OBLIVION LAID,
THIS PILE I HERE ERECT:
A TRIBUTE SMALL FOR WHAT THOU'ST DONE,
DEIGN TO ACCEPT THIS MEAN RETURN,
PARDON THE LONG NEGLECT.

In 1714 the Earl built a great Obelisk, ostensibly to honour the Duke of Marlborough's recent victories but more realistically, considering the inscription, to signal his own achievements. For this too bears an inscription lauding the family name, and is addressed to his heirs:

IF TO PERFECTION THESE PLANTATIONS RISE
IF THEY AGREEABLY MY HEIRS SURPRISE
THIS FAITHFUL PILLAR WILL THEIR AGE DECLARE
AS LONG AS TIME THESE CHARACTERS SHALL SPARE
HERE THEN WITH KIND REMEMBRANCE READ HIS NAME
WHO FOR POSTERITY PERFORM'D THE SAME
CHARLES THE III EARL OF CARLISLE
OF THE FAMILY OF THE HOWARDS
ERECTED A CASTLE WHERE THE OLD CASTLE OF

HENDERSKELFE STOOD, AND CALL'D IT CASTLE-HOWARD
HE LIKEWISE MADE THE PLANTATIONS IN THIS PARK
AND ALL THE OUT-WORKS, MONUMENTS AND OTHER
PLANTATIONS BELONGING TO THE SAID SEAT
HE BEGAN THESE WORKS
IN THE YEAR MDCCII
ANNO D: MDCCXXXI

Such were the general considerations which, almost certainly, moved Charles Howard, 3rd Earl of Carlisle, to undertake his great building project. The precise moment at which they bore fruit was the summer of 1698. He had already chosen the site where he would raise his castle – Henderskelfe, in the North Riding of Yorkshire. And he had decided to call it Castle Howard.

The name 'Henderskelfe' means 'village of a hundred springs'. It was originally a small sixteenth-century parish, centred round the ruins of an ancient castle. Only a score of cottages remained, which the Earl demolished, re-housing the villagers elsewhere on the estate. Henderskelfe is a bleak, windy, barren part of the country, on the edge of the empty Yorkshire moors. It is an indication of Carlisle's enormous visual imagination that he could foresee the potential of such a seemingly inhospitable site. The complex of buildings, gardens and landscaped park he already had in mind would come to be acclaimed as one of the very loveliest landmarks in the English countryside. The environs of Castle Howard were described by Horace Walpole as 'the grandest scenes of rural magnificence' created in the eighteenth century. Walpole was staggered by Castle Howard. After his first sight of the estate he wrote:

... Nobody had informed me that at one view I should see a palace, a town, a fortified city, temples on high places, woods worthy of being each a metropolis of the Druids, the noblest lawn in the world fenced by half the horizon, and a mausoleum that would tempt one to be buried alive; in short, I have seen gigantic palaces before, but never a sublime one.

This eulogy, however, was written in 1772, long after the founder's death, when the castle and its grounds had had time to settle and mature. At the time of building, of course, there were all sorts of minor problems. The most serious were the result of unrealistic estimates. If it remains difficult today, with all the aid of modern technology, to get an accurate estimate from a builder, it was almost impossible in the eighteenth century when so many of the craftsmen, however skilled, were illiterate. And, in fact, the Earl ran into financial difficulties almost immediately, causing considerable delays in the programme. The finished product is a triumphant witness to the energy, enthusiasm and determination of three men, in almost equal proportion – Lord Carlisle, John Vanbrugh and Nicholas Hawksmoor. The really remarkable thing about the building of Castle Howard is that of these three men only one, Hawksmoor, had any previous experience of building. Carlisle had imagination and taste. He also knew what he wanted. Vanbrugh had an artistic flair amounting to genius but no architectural qualifications whatsoever. Castle Howard was the first house he had ever attempted to design – an incredible feat in the circumstances. And, although Hawksmoor had trained under Sir Christopher Wren, his function and building experience were those of a foreman, a clerk of the works, rather than of an architect on the grand scale.

Vanbrugh had not been Carlisle's original choice for the tremendous job the Earl had in mind. In 1698 he had asked William Talman, currently the most fashionable architect on the London scene, to submit ideas and plans for a suitable house and grounds. Talman went up to Yorkshire twice (at a fee of fifty guineas a visit, plus travelling expenses), but failed to secure the commission. He appears to have quarrelled with Carlisle about money, and, in any case, the Earl found his drawings of the proposed house boring and much too conventional. Carlisle expected superlatives. He wanted a house that was original, splendid, flamboyant, extravagant, possibly ostentatious, certainly sensational; a house which would rival Chatsworth and Petworth. Chatsworth had become the marvel of society in the 1690s, described by Bishop Kennett as looking '. . . too great for the design of a Private subject, it seems rather the Model of a Palace becoming the greatest Prince, and the effect of a Publick Fund'; and a contemporary account of Petworth states that 'This Palace is every way answerable to the Grandeur of its great Master'. That was the kind of comment Carlisle wanted to hear about *his* new house. He needed a man whose vision and flair would match his own, no pettifogging conventional contractor but an architect who could think on the grand scale. He found just such a character in John Vanbrugh, an ex-soldier turned dramatist, whose plays were currently taking the town by storm. Vanbrugh was taken up by the Whig nobility and elected to the Kit-Cat Club, their inner sanctum and nightly rendezvous. It was at this club that Vanbrugh met Carlisle; their subsequent partnership, which led to the creation of Castle Howard, is one of the very best examples of eighteenth-century artistic patronage. Since the Kit-Cat Club came to play the role of midwife during the birth of Castle Howard it is worth examining this curious institution in some detail.

The Kit-Cat Club was started during the Restoration by Jacob Tonson, a publisher and bookseller. It was named after Christopher Cat, a pastry-cook who specialized in mutton pies, the gastronomic feature of the club. The club's professed aim was to promote 'the Improvement of Learning, and keeping up [of] good Humour and Mirth', but in fact the tavern near Temple Bar quickly became the ex-officio headquarters of the Whig party. The members of the Kit-Cat Club, including Lord Carlisle and other like-minded liberals, formed themselves into a cabal, almost a mafia; and as such they had become a distinct and powerful force in the politics of the day. The club's stated policy was described in 1688 as being 'Opposed to the arbitrary measures of James II and conduced to bring about the Revolution'. Walpole, in retrospect, credits the club with securing the Hanoverian succession: 'The Kit-Cat Club, generally mentioned as a set of Wits, were in reality the Patriots that saved Britain.'

The club had an equally important role in contemporary society as a major literary and artistic centre. It was an essentially egalitarian gathering, a place where men who were not necessarily of the same social background could meet on neutral territory to discuss everything and anything without prejudice – from politics and poetry to sculpture and scandal. Thus although the membership included most of the Whig cabinet, no less than eight dukes and seven earls, it also included many of the country's most interesting and lively intellectuals, writers and artists from quite different backgrounds. Jacob Tonson was the foremost publisher in London for at least twenty-five years, and at one time or another had numbered Milton, Dryden and Swift among his authors. Congreve, Addison and Steele all became members of the Kit-Cat Club at the end of the seventeenth century, while the political lions included Sir Robert Walpole and the Dukes of Devonshire, Somerset and Marlborough. All forty-eight of the members had their portraits painted by the most esteemed artist of their generation, Sir Godfrey Kneller, who was himself a member.

The club had its frivolous side. The members appear to have drunk inordinately, in the approved eighteenth-century mode, and they certainly revelled in gossip and scandal. For example, one of the members complains that he has been 'cheated of a hundred guineas for a second-hand maidenhead'. Slightly more elegant evenings are indicated by the Kit-Cat custom of electing an annual 'Toast', or 'Belle of the Year'. This would be an unmarried girl of good family, often the daughter of one of the members, and sometimes no more than a potential beauty – at the time of her election Lady Mary Montagu, who was later to become a life-long friend of all the Howards, was only eight years old. Richard Steele, founder editor of the *Tatler* magazine, was a pivotal member of the club: writing in the magazine under the name of the gossip columnist Isaac Bickerstaff, he describes the ritual of the 'Toast':

. . . Though this institution had so trivial a beginning, it is now elevated into a formal order; and that happy virgin, who is received and drunk to at their meetings, has no more to do in this life but to judge and accept of the first good offer. The manner of her inauguration is much like that of a choice of a doge in Venice: it is performed by balloting; and when she is so chosen, she reigns indisputably for that ensuing year; but must be elected a-new to prolong her empire a moment beyond it. When she is regularly chosen, her name is written with a diamond on a drinking glass. The hieroglyphic of the diamond is to show her that her value is imaginary; and that of the glass to acquaint her that her condition is frail, and depends on the hand which holds her. This wise design admonishes her, neither to over-rate or deprecate her charms . . .

All in all, the members of the Kit-Cat Club were an amusing and interesting mix of men. A liberal philosophy, combined with a cultivated attitude to the arts, brought out the very best in the eighteenth-century aristocrat. The 3rd Earl and his friends lived at a time when aristocratic patronage was not only taken for granted, but regarded as a duty. It was one of the hereditary obligations concomitant upon wealth and privilege. The Kit-Cat Club provided an ideal breeding ground for such patronage; the perfect setting for the kind of introduction between nobleman and creative artist such as that which led to the tremendously successful partnership of Vanbrugh and Lord Carlisle.

By all accounts John Vanbrugh was an attractive character. Debonair, convivial, flamboyant, even slightly rakish, and with a distinctly bawdy sense of humour, he seems to have been almost universally popular. (The Archbishop of Canterbury was one of his few detractors; he was shocked by Vanbrugh's plays and succeeded in getting them banned from the Haymarket Theatre.) Alexander Pope called Vanbrugh one of 'the three most honest-hearted, real good men of the poetical members of the Kit-Cat Club'; Lord Chesterfield went even further and said that he 'knew no man who united conversational pleasantry and perfect good humour in so eminent a degree'. This was praise indeed, coming from two of the crabbiest figures in society.

Vanbrugh had an immense zest for new experiences and revelled in challenge. He was excited and delighted to be offered the chance of designing Castle Howard and, showing a magnificent nonchalance about his almost complete lack of either qualifications or experience in the field of architecture, accepted at once. Throwing his versatile mind into high gear, he began work on the first designs with all his customary energy, talent and zeal. Vanbrugh went up to Yorkshire for preliminary discussions on site with the Earl, and by Christmas 1699 was writing to his fellow members of the Kit-Cat Club about the proposed plans and canvassing their opinions:

I have been this Summer at my Ld Carlisle's and Seen most of the great houses in the North, as at Ld Nottings: Duke of Leeds, Chattesworth &c. I stayed at Chattesworth four or five days the Duke being there. I shew'd him all my Ld Carlisle's designs, which, he said was quite another thing, than what he imagin'd from the Character yr Lordship gave him on't; He absolutely approved the whole design, particularly the low Wings, which he said wou'd have an admirable effect without doors as well as within, being adorn'd with those Ornaments of Pillasters and Urns, which he never thought of, but concluded 'twas to be a plain low building like an orange house.

The Duke should have known better. Neither Vanbrugh nor Carlisle would have dreamt of being associated with a building to which the adjectives 'plain' and 'low' could be applied.

The design of a great new country house was always the subject of general speculation and discussion. When Vanbrugh came to build Blenheim some years later he wrote that:

The Duke of Marlborough, your Grace [the Duchess of Marlborough], my late Lord Godolphin, the Duke of Shrewsbury, the late Duke of Montagu, Sir Christopher Wren and several others were thoroughly consulted in the matter; and several meetings there were upon it, at Kensington, Montagu House &c, when the Modells were inspected, and that of Sir Christopher Wren, Stuck full of pins.

Even the King became involved; he certainly took a personal interest in the building of Castle Howard. In the summer of 1700 the

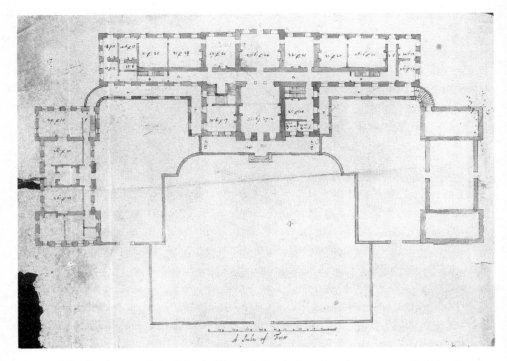

The first known plan of Castle Howard, dated 1699: there is, as yet, no thought of a dome.

3rd Earl took a wooden model of the proposed building to Hampton Court, for the King's approval. Building began in earnest the following spring.

The 3rd Earl of Carlisle was, as has been mentioned, *one* of the richest men in England. But he was nowhere near *the* richest. In comparison with a few of his peers, who were also building at the time, he could ill afford Castle Howard. His average income, during the first decade of the eighteenth century, was over £7,500 a year. This, of course, was an absolute fortune by the standards of 99.9 per cent of the British public, considering that the average family lived on less than £30 a year. But the Duke of Somerset's income, when he was

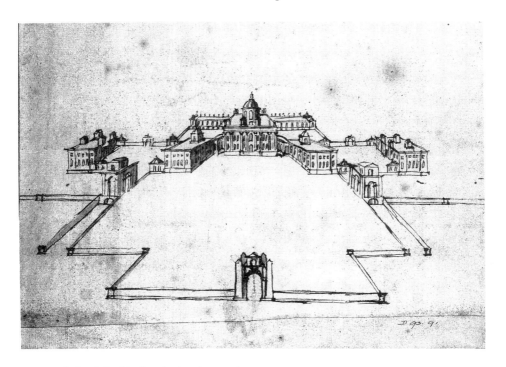

A sketch by Vanbrugh, dated 1718, showing the architect's intended vision of the completed house.

building Petworth, was more than double Carlisle's – between £15,000 and £16,000 a year. And several of his contemporaries were even richer than Somerset. Professor Geoffrey Holmes has said that: '. . . by 1710 three giants [of the peerage] were topping £30,000 a year, at least four other peers were amassing between £20,000 and £30,000: over £10,000 had become perfectly commonplace'. To put the cost of building Castle Howard further into perspective, Carlisle was spending at least one third of his income on building whereas Petworth cost the Duke less than 10 per cent of his. Again, when the Dukes of Devonshire and Leeds were building Chatsworth and Kiveton respectively, both had considerably greater funds at their disposal than Carlisle.

When the Earl decided to build Castle Howard he must have

known it was going to be tight financially. But at that time he held a lucrative job in the Government and had every expectation of continuing his career in politics. He was obviously banking on a certain amount of earned income to supplement the revenue from his estates. But his hopes had one weak strand – the life of the King, William III. When this unexpectedly came to an end in 1702 – the King was killed in a freak riding accident – the supremacy of the Whigs was over. Queen Anne favoured the Tories, and lost no time in dismissing Carlisle from his post. As it turned out, and to the Earl's great sadness, this was virtually the end of his political career. He was never again to hold high office.

If the cost of building Castle Howard did not actually cripple the Earl financially, it certainly caused immense problems. Time after time the money ran out, forcing him to stall the builders; again and again he juggled with his income, sold things, borrowed money and even resorted to gambling in order to be able to continue. In 1707 Vanbrugh wrote to a friend that 'My Lord Carlisle as been a good while in Towne, won Two thousand pounds of the Sharpers, and is gone downe again to lay it Out in his Building: but they are following him to Henderskelf to have their Revenge, And ten to One they get it.' In fact, Carlisle made an overall profit on his gambling, amounting to 7 per cent of his annual income. There are records that he has sold 500 trees for £1,000; that he has raided his grandmother's strong-box, sold jewellery and even tried to let his London house. He borrowed £1,000 from a moneylender, one Peter Walter, who was described by Swift with suitable acidity as: 'That rogue of genuine ministerial kind, Can half the peerage by his arts bewitch, Starve twenty lords to make one scoundrel rich.' It was a constant fight; and even the Earl, with all his lust for grandeur, must occasionally have wondered whether he had been mad to embark on such an expensive project.

All in all he had a harrowing time. That Carlisle refused to accept financial defeat is a testament not only to his passionate enthusiasm for the project, but also to his business acumen. He was an adroit and canny financier, meticulously checking every single account himself:

'this leaf is cast up too much by a shilling', is written in the margin of one of his account books.

Though he may have known the figures to the last shilling, the knowledge appears to have made no difference to his attitude – an attitude which remained, at bottom, extravagant. Far from turning miser, or even practising minimal economy, the Earl carried on merrily in his usual grandiose style. Admittedly the eighteenth-century peerage was notoriously extravagant. It was a glamorous, colourful age; a time when men gloried in their appearance and flaunted their latest acquisitions. Conspicuous spending was part of the aristocratic creed – and Lord Carlisle was only too happy to conform. The following is a small selection of the items he ordered from London during those years: 'good pickled herrings and smoaked salmon' . . . 'chocolate from Mr Bull's in Ludgate Hill' . . . 'green tea from Mr Contarelle's' (tea first appeared in England during the Restoration, and had become the fashionable drink) . . . 'a handsome summer druget for a coat, & a pritty fashionable dammask silk for waistcoat & britches' . . . 'six dozen of pints of ye best canary' and 'some extra-ordinary good rich Florence, or some very good Burgundy, of ye strongest or any other good rich wine' . . . He ordered shagreen and silk buttons, and pearls for the buttonholes; velvets and lace, silk and satin and damask, both for the family's wardrobe and the house furnishings; pictures and picture frames; silver dishes, table linen and a china teaset; orange-flower water and asses' milk for his wife – it was used as a skin lotion; grapes, figs, raisins, six pounds of chocolate and twelve dozen oranges and lemons; both Imperial and Bohea tea; and twelve quires of gilt writing paper, upon which, no doubt, he was looking forward to writing the magic words: 'Castle Howard'.

3

'. . . Magnificence, Delicacy and Splendour'

The aristocracy, in the eighteenth century, were hampered by none of the restraining disciplines implicit in the need to earn a living. Nevertheless there was nothing haphazard about the way they lived their lives. There was a definite pattern to the social year, dictated as much by the obligations of their position as by the pursuit of pleasure. Moreover, in this private and privileged world, leisure itself was regarded as a serious occupation. Activities which today would be classified as hobbies could take on the complexity of careers. Both ladies and gentlemen worked at their sports, their appearance, their social life, their amusements, and even their vices, often with the zeal of real professionals. In an age so devoted to colour, fashion was of the first importance, elevated, in fact, to a definite art; it was also extremely time-consuming – dressing for dinner could take several hours. Such emphasis on personal appearance seems unacceptable by today's standards, an indication of spurious vanity – and particularly so in the case of the men. But, at the time, dress was regarded as yet another means of demonstrating both status and taste, a necessary adjunct to the role of a gentleman. Elegant conversation was another art, to be studied and acquired. Eloquence was at a premium and wit a favoured accomplishment. The mistress of a great house regarded entertaining as an obligation, as much as a means of demonstrating her charms and her skills. Indeed, many of the eighteenth-century hostesses have acquired a legendary reputation. It is fashionable today to deride the accomplishments of aristocratic young ladies, but many were genuinely talented; their needlework and water-colours have come to be valued highly in the antique markets today.

Georgiana, 5th Duchess of Devonshire (centre) at a Court ball at Windsor Castle in 1777. Her daughter, another Georgiana, became the 6th Countess of Carlisle.

The 3rd Earl of Carlisle and his family were the first generation of Howards to live at Castle Howard. By the end of Queen Anne's reign a way of life, centred around the house, had been established which was to last, with only marginal deviations, for more than 200 years. The social year in the eighteenth century conformed to a definite pattern, and though Castle Howard remained the focus of their lives, the Howards and their peers were constantly on the move. In the spring they would go to London, for the 'season'. This was the time when débutante daughters were fired into society by conniving mothers in search of suitable husbands. 'Almack's' was the most select of the clubs, where the girls were displayed at weekly dances, like so many fillies for sale. The rules at Almack's were strict and inflexible: it was obligatory for men to wear white breeches – the Duke of Wellington himself was once refused entry because he was wearing trousers. Almack's was understandably nicknamed the 'marriage mart'.

In this respect, the 3rd Earl and his wife failed dismally with their three daughters, Elizabeth, Anne and Mary. Elizabeth married Lord Lechmere first, against her father's wishes. She became a notorious alcoholic and an inveterate gambler. In 1725 Lady Mary Wortley Montagu reported that:

The discreet and sober Lady Lechmere has lost such Furious summs at the Bath that 'tis question'd whether all the sweetness that the Waters can put into my Lord's blood can make him endure it, particularly £700 at one sitting, which is aggravated with many astonishing Circumstances. This is as odd to me as Lord Tenham's shooting himself, and another Demonstration of the latent Fire that lies under cold Countenances.

Both Lady Lechmere's husband and her father refused eventually to pay any more of her gambling debts. Ten years later alcoholism had driven her to despair. A tragic letter written by her second husband, Sir Thomas Robinson, to the Earl shows the state to which she had been reduced. It is a long letter, but it deserves quotation, both for the very precision with which it describes Lady Lechmere's condition, and as an example of one of the most prevalent evils of eighteenth-century life:

. . . If I longer concealed my thoughts from the only person, whose advice and authority can save my Lady Letchmere, in short, my Lord, the evil now complained of, has been, more or less, not only some years before, but also ever since I married her, but is now arrived to that pitch, as if not speedily stopt, must soon put an end to my cares and her own life, I will speak out, I mean her drinking both spirituous and other liquors, and so frequently to such an excess, and so very publickly that 'tis now too late to conceal its being universally known to everyone, who ever heard her name. I assure yr Lordship this appeal comes to you unwillingly, 'tis a shocking subject for me to trouble yr Lordship with in your beloved retirement at Castle Howard . . . I did not apply to others for their aid 'til I had done all that my own strength of reasoning suggested + of late following the sentiments and advice her family here have given me, tho none of them has cared to speak to her about it, nor is she willing I should talk to her on it in their prescence . . . as I have great obligations to Lady Letchmere, such as I can never forget, and have a character to maintain in life, I am on this occasion, both for her and my own sake, ready and willing to give up any favourite point, come into any scheme whatever, to stop this growing evil, which if not done, a reformation will come too late, all remedies will be applied in vain – twice indeed since my marriage the Baths have saved her from the fatal consequences of pursuing this passion, which of all others, surely is the most unnatural, and unaccountable in the female sex, and the most mischievous in its effects, since 'tis capable to destroy the best of understandings, change the most agreeable disposition + good nature, which are characteristics justly due to Lady Letchmere when free from this evil.

The Earl's second daughter, Anne, fared better in life, though her husband, Viscount Irwin, was described even by friends as a 'fop', and by his enemies as a 'rake' as well. The letter he wrote to his brother, just before the wedding, certainly indicates a thoroughly dissolute young man-about-town – even if his attitude to love and marriage is probably typical of the times. The letter is again sufficiently vivid to deserve quoting at length:

Possibly you may have heard of my intentions in entring into the holy state of Matrimony, all preliminaries are agreed to & in a little time I shall be turn'd of, but the day of execution is not yet fix'd . . . I come now to begg a favour of you that is to buy a ffan it must be a very good one being a present for my Doxy, the woman you know . . . The ladies of Castle Howard are all in town & your Brother Irwin: I believe I shall swive my little Nymph before his hore getts into possession of his mannor of Tufton and Cufton and they all goe into Yorkshire in about 20 days + a short time after follows consummation. Your brother Arthur is no changeling he drinks & fucks dans toutes les bourdelles de la ville, Charles designs to gett into the Gards & fucks as often as his mighty Member can be raised which wee hear his women cannot always prevail with to a stiff erection.

His wife appears to have risen above all this. Lady Irwin was the most amusing of the 3rd Earl's daughters, and something of an intellectual.

The youngest daughter, Mary, led a much quieter life, albeit against her will. She never married – the reason, it was rumoured, being that the Earl refused to give her a dowry, preferring to spend every available groat on Castle Howard.

In July, with the end of the London season, the aristocracy returned to their country estates. Social life revolved round a series of splendid house parties which often lasted for several weeks on end. Autumn was the season of serious sport, with hunting or shooting six days a week. All the Howards were passionate horsemen, but it was a costly business. In 1787 the 3rd Earl's grandson, the 5th Earl, kept his own pack of hounds at Castle Howard. But even he, arguably the most spendthrift of all the Carlisles, was forced to give it up after two years because he found it was costing over £800 a year to maintain.

During the cold weather the fashionable spas came into their own. Before the Prince Regent 'invented' Brighton, the two most popular resorts were Bath, in the south of England, and Harrogate, in the north. Both were patronized by the Earls of Carlisle and their families.

Stone-built mansions can be cheerless and draughty in winter. Castle Howard was no exception, despite Vanbrugh's enthusiastic assertion to the contrary. He had written in 1713 that:

... tho' we have now had as bitter storms as rain and wind can well compose, every room in the house is like an oven, and in corridors of 200ft. long there is not air enough in motion to stir the flame of a candle.

Lord Carlisle's original verdict on the comfort of the house seems to have agreed with his architect. Vanbrugh, comparing the relative comfort of Castle Howard and Blenheim, wrote:

I am much pleased here [Castle Howard] ... to find Lord Carlisle so thoroughly convinced of the Conveniencys of his new house, now he has had a year's tryall of it ... For my Lord Carlisle was pretty much under the same Apprehensions with her [the Duchess of Marlborough], about long Passages, High Rooms &. But he finds what I told him to be true. That those Passages woud be so far from gathering & drawing wind as he feared, that a Candle wou'd not flare in them of this he has lately had the proof, by bitter stormy nights in which not one Candle wanted to be put into a Lanthorn, not even in the Hall, which is as high (tho not indeed so big) as that at Blenheim. He likewise finds, that all his Rooms, with moderate fires Are Ovens, And that this Great House, do's not require above One pound of wax and two of Tallow Candles a night to light it, more than his house at London did Nor in Short, is he at any expence more . . . but three housemaids and one Man, to keep the whole house and Offices in perfect cleanliness, which is done to such a degree, that the Kitchen, and all the Offices and Passages under the Principall floor are as dry as the Drawing Room: And yet there is a great deal of Company, and very good housekeeping. So that upon the whole (except the keeping of the New Gardens) the expence of living in this Great fine house do's not amount to above a hundred pounds a year, more than was Spent in the Old one.

But in 1713 the Earl was in the first throes of his love affair with Castle Howard, and, besides, he was still a hale young man, impervious to the freezing cold of Yorkshire winters. As he grew older, however, and his health deteriorated, it became his custom to head south for the winter, where he found warm and comfortable lodgings in Bath. Moreover, the water from the Bath springs, however unpleasant and sulphurous it tasted, was widely acclaimed for its curative properties. 'Drinking the waters' seems to have been recommended by doctors as an almost universal panacea. Towards the end of the Earl's life, when he was almost completely crippled by gout, his youngest daughter, Lady Mary Howard, was still pinning her faith in their efficacy, and wrote urging her father to join her in Bath: '. . . I steadfastly think it would do your Lordship a great deal of good. The doctor has been with me this morning, and says he is mighty glad you have thoughts of coming; that he is confident you'll find these waters strengthen your blood and your limbs.' This letter was written on 27 December 1729, when the Earl was sixty – and he was in fact again in Bath for his health at the time of his death nine years later.

The various resorts and spas were well run and attractive, and they formed an integral part of eighteenth-century life. Each had its own peak 'season', and attracted its own regular visitors. Bath had a short winter season, starting after Christmas, and another longer one from July to September. Harrogate came into its own in August. The resorts had their own Assembly Rooms, Pump Rooms, promenades, and gambling clubs, and there was a constant round of private parties. The social potential was part of a resort's attraction. It was the ideal milieu for making new acquaintances, and for socializing on a slightly less formidable scale than that inherent in a London season. The Howard ladies, however, had no great opinion of the company to be found in Bath. Lady Irwin, writing to her father in 1729, complained that:

The company increases daily, but everybody complains that they are people that nobody knows; for my own part I think it is no great difference whether 'tis a crowd of quality or plebeians. Harrison's rooms are so full every night 'tis to me very disagreeable; if one had an inclination 'tis next to impossible to get a table to play, which I have only done once since I came. My sister Mary seems to relish the place as little as I do, and proposes staying only six weeks from the day we got here.

Lady Irwin added to this last letter that she intended going on to stay at Althorp, the Earl of Spencer's country house, but she was worried about the journey. The weather had been appalling, with continuous rain, and the roads were in a terrible state:

. . . At present this country is all in a sea and every little brook hardly passable . . . The road between Altrop and this place is so extremely bad that the coachman won't undertake it under four days, though it is but 64 miles. Everybody here tells me that I shall run great hazards in going by that road, but the coachman that drives me has provided me a very good set of horses, and will engage to carry me safe . . .

Eighteenth-century letters are full of complaints about the hazards of travelling. Apart from the obvious dangers caused by rough surfaces and bad weather, highway robbery was a very real threat. Lady Irwin twice came into contact with highwaymen; her stories make exciting reading. In 1730 she reported to her father that:

'. . . Magnificence, Delicacy and Splendour'

I've had a good journey [*en route* from London to Castle Howard], and am very well, but escaped being robbed upon Finchley Common most narrowly. The York coach, not forty yards before me, was stopped and robbed; I saw the rogues do it, and could expect nothing less myself, having no other guard but Tom Bulfin; but upon seeing him armed, they rid off with such violence, either on purpose or design they had near thrown Tom off his horse. Thus I fortunately escaped, but they took in another stagecoach about 100 yards behind me, and got a good booty – two watches, and above twenty pounds. People have seldom much money going from London, especially those that pay all their debts there; but I was charge with a commission to your Lordship which I should have been much concerned should have miscarried; I have in bank-bills and money near 160 pounds to pay you. I hope I am now safe from any attempt of this kind, or any other danger . . .

Two years later she had another lucky escape. Miss Elstob, a friend of the Howards, was attacked by highwaymen just outside London:

. . . I yesterday saw Miss Elstob: they had a sad conclusion to their journey, which I fancy your Lordship may have seen in the news. The account from her is this. About a mile of this side Baldock they were attacked by five highwaymen; three robbed and two watched. They were not content to take from 'em what they had about 'em, but pulled 'em all out of the coach, searched them narrowly, and upon being disappointed of what they expected, threatened to strip 'em. They were near an hour in the robbery; they took away their portmanteaus, Miss's two gold watches, all Mr Elstob's clothes, pocket-book and other things, to the value of a hundred pound . . . I met the same honest collectors; they rid with me over part of Finchley Common, crossed the coach several times, and I really thought would have stopped me. The coachman knew 'em to be noted highwaymen, but being but two, and I having two attendants, they let me escape . . . Had I been in the dusk, I think I should have paid the usual fine; for both the men and horses answered exactly to the description of those who robbed Mr Elstob . . .

★

The great houses of the aristocracy were designed for entertaining, and they made the ideal setting for the grand parties which were such a feature of eighteenth-century life. On occasion these large country house parties could be dauntingly formal affairs, in which the mood of the party was governed by rigorous protocol and etiquette. Night after night twenty or thirty guests would sit down to dinner – and the guests were expected to conform to a code of behaviour which must have been particularly intimidating for the uninitiated since it was never properly explained. To verbalize matters of etiquette was considered almost as bad manners as getting it wrong in the first place – guests were expected to know how to behave by osmosis, as it were. The level of ceremony depended, of course, on the house in question. The 6th Duke of Somerset, for instance, carried his obsession with formality to an absurd degree at Petworth. According to a contemporary writer, the Duke, who was an almost exact contemporary of the 3rd Earl's:

... always delighted to live in Magnificence, Delicacy and Splendor; constantly preserving that Respect and Dignity which was due to his Rank; and, like a Man of Birth and Fortune, ever moved in a Sphere above the Vulgar ... His House was always kept with that Grandeur and Decorum, as formerly was used by the English Kings and Men of Quality.

Moreover, it is said, this particular Duke was so enamoured of his own importance that he disinherited one of his daughters because she took the liberty of sitting down in his presence; that his servants were forbidden to speak to him and were obliged to communicate by means of signs; and that, when he travelled, the country roads 'were scoured by outriders, whose duty it was to protect him from the gaze of the vulgar'.

But life at Petworth was already considered an anachronism by the early years of the eighteenth century. The house parties at Castle Howard, and those to which the young Howards and their friends were usually invited, tended to be much jollier affairs. (In any case the atmosphere at Castle Howard itself was coloured by the Whig principles of its owner – liberalism and tolerance, as exemplified by the members of the Kit-Cat Club, who were frequent house guests.) As soon as the young men came of age, and the girls 'came out', they would be off on the country house circuit. From an early age the Howards got to know, and appreciate, such spectacular establishments as Blenheim, Cliveden, Euston and Lowther Castle, all of whose owners were friends of the Earls of Carlisle. Long before the 6th Earl of Carlisle married a daughter of the 5th Duke of Devonshire, the Howards and the Cavendishes had been friends: generations of Howards stayed regularly at Chatsworth and generations of Cavendishes came to Castle Howard in return. Country house visiting became almost a way of life in the case of certain bachelors, who would move from one establishment to another, often staying for months on end – which saved the expense of running their own.

'High society' was a closed shop: a clearly defined, close-knit, tight little circle, confined to the very upper class, whose members all knew each other, and knew everything there was to know about each other. Moreover they were very often related, if not by blood, then by marriage. Rules about what constitutes incest – marriage within prohibited degrees of kinship – have varied in different countries and societies, but the eighteenth-century Whig aristocracy certainly took full advantage of the relatively free rules then operating in the Church of England, which allowed marriage between first cousins. As a result, house parties often turned into family reunions; the means of visiting a married daughter, or of catching up with a favourite cousin.

One of the most frequent visitors to Castle Howard was Lady Mary Wortley Montagu, a Yorkshire neighbour and life-long friend of the whole Howard family. She describes the desolate atmosphere on the occasion when propriety forbade the daughters of the house to entertain any gentlemen. (The death of Queen Anne, in 1714, had led to political uncertainty about the succession; the spectre of a Jacobite revival was once again in the air, a possibility which caused panic in the Whig party. The 3rd Earl abandoned his family and rushed off to join in the political fray.) Lady Mary writes that:

. . . The poor Ladys at Castle Howard are as much afraid as I am, being left all alone, without any hope of seeing their father again (tho things should prove well) this 8 or 9 months. They have sent to desire me very earnestly to come to them an bring my Boy. 'Tis the same thing as pensioning in a Nunnery, for no mortal man ever enters the doors in the absence of their father, who is gone post.

Lady Mary was one of the liveliest and most interesting members of the Earl's circle. Regarded as one of the great female 'wits' of her day, she was an astringent conversationalist and prolific correspondent, who must have added a most refreshing element to the staid Yorkshire society. She revelled in scandal, although often the subject of it herself (her own morals were notoriously lax), and could be thoroughly malicious, even libellous, at times. But she appears to have spared the Howards. At any rate, Lady Irwin, though somewhat ambivalent about Lady Mary's character, certainly appreciated her company:

She [Lady Mary] is here often and contributes not a little to the enlivening conversation: her principles are as corrupt as her wit is entertaining, and I never heard a woman, let her practice be never so scandalous, maintain such arguments. She was here two nights ago; the conversation turned upon constancy; Lady Mary immediately attacked me for a practice so inconsistent with reason and nature . . . I had the better of the argument, but not having her wit to support it my answer will appear flat . . .

Lady Mary's views were often ahead of her time, but they were exactly the kind of novel doctrines which appealed to the Whigs and were likely to have been discussed at Castle Howard. And, as such, her letters are worth quoting in some detail. She was an ardent and active Whig, but one who had a thoroughly pragmatic approach to politics. In a letter to her husband, Mr Wortley, she summed up the liberal credo:

. . . I should be pleased to share so glorious a poverty with you; but as the world is, and will be, *'tis a sort of duty to be rich*, that it may be in one's power to do good; riches being another word for power.

This was an attitude with which the ambitious 3rd Earl would have fully concurred. At the time when Carlisle was First Lord of the Treasury, Lady Mary hoped that he might be induced to give Mr Wortley some post in the Government. She wrote to her husband urging him to put himself forward and assert himself; her advice on the matter is an excellent example of contemporary attitudes (but would be equally pertinent today).

. . . The first qualification is impudence, and the second is impudence, and the third still, impudence. No modest man ever did or ever will make his fortune . . . The Ministry is like a play at Court; there's a little door to get in, and a great crowd without, shoving and thrusting who shall be foremost; people who knock others with their elbows, disregard a little kick of the shins, and still thrust heartily forwards, are sure of a good place. Your modest man stands behind in the crowd, is shoved about by everybody, his cloaths tore, almost squeezed to death, and sees a thousand get in before him that don't make so good a figure as himself . . .

In one respect Lady Mary was a real exception to the majority of women of her generation. She was a passionate believer in the education of women, a cause with which the 3rd Earl was in complete agreement. He had taken immense pains over his own daughters' education, and Lady Irwin, at least, grew up to be recognized as something of a literary figure in her own right. The usual attitude taken by society towards feminine learning drove Lady Mary to despair: 'My sex is usually forbid studies of this nature, and folly reckoned so much our proper sphere we are sooner pardoned any excess of that than the least pretensions to reading or good sense.' And again: 'There is hardly a character in the world more despicable, or more liable to universal ridicule, than that of a learned woman.'

In fact Lady Mary, though denied the benefit of such an enlightened parent as Carlisle, became a noted classical scholar, almost entirely self-taught. But such was the atmosphere in which she was reared that it was necessary to disguise her interest and study in secret:

47

I was a great admirer of Ovid's Metamorphoses, and that was one of the chief reasons that set me upon the thoughts of stealing the Latin language . . . I used to study five or six hours a day for two years in my father's library, and so got the language whilst everyone else thought I was reading nothing but novels and romances.

The library at Castle Howard, which already contained several thousand volumes, and a number of rare incunabula, must have been a delight to Lady Mary.

An estate the size of Castle Howard is never really 'finished', in the sense that there is no more that is either needed or desirable to be done to improve it. The buildings, and even more so the surrounding gardens and parkland, evolve over centuries. Fashion and taste change with successive generations; each owner, each wife, and each heir-apparent will have their own, and often wildly disparate views, on the priority of the moment. Similarly one cannot be didactic about the use to which various rooms were put, as different families have different needs. Moreover, as Dame Christian Howard, who was born in 1916 and has lived all her life either at Castle Howard or on the estate, once pointed out: 'Even in my lifetime we used all sorts of different rooms at different times. It was a question of moving from one part of the castle to another, often to economize, by shutting up whole sections of the building. Anyway one family can only inhabit a limited number of rooms at a time.'

Broadly speaking, it is acknowledged that the 3rd Earl built Castle Howard, the 4th Earl furnished it, and the 5th Earl consolidated the land.

The 3rd Earl was surrounded by builders, joiners, painters, and other craftsmen for the whole of his lifetime. When he first moved in he took up residence in a set of rooms in the 'rustic', or semi-basement – a far cry from the splendid apartments he later took over on the principal floor. Despite Vanbrugh's aforementioned claims to the contrary, it must have been cold and uncomfortable in the early years. Certainly the Earl of Oxford thought so, as late as 1725, by which time the family had at least moved upstairs:

The east wing is taken up with the useful part and in which the family live, though it seems to be not so convenient as might have been wisht in that place where so much expense has been made. The House is extremely damp.

Nevertheless, the 3rd Earl's tremendous enthusiasm never faltered. He was a perfectionist, but he was also a man who disliked delegating responsibility, and, in fact, he personally oversaw every single bit of work carried out on the estate. He chose all the interior decoration himself, commissioned furniture, tapestries and fabrics from all over Europe and selected the classical themes for Pellegrini's marvellous painted frescos of the dome, the High Saloon and the great staircase walls. (Many of these were destroyed in the catastrophic fire of 1940.)

By 1706, four years after building had begun, the only rooms ready to be furnished were the ones on the south front which the Earl intended to use as his private apartments. From the record of the materials he ordered it is obvious that his passion for grandeur was in full spate. The enormous four-poster bed was festooned with silk damask, the most luxurious and expensive material obtainable at the time. The fabric was described as having a pattern of crimson flowers on a silver tissue background, and was repeated in elaborate drapes all round the windows. The walls of this room were hung with four tapestries, specially commissioned from John Vanderbank, 'His Majesty's chief arras maker', and were described by a contemporary visitor as being 'a very beautiful mixture of colours, Chinese men & women in variety of postures all sorts of birds, beasts & fish . . .' The Earl's bedroom must have been a glorious sight, but the State bedroom, decorated a few years later, was even costlier because gold thread was used in the material rather than silver and the bed was decorated with red and white ostrich feathers.

By the 1720s the Earl was concentrating his ambition and creative talent on the garden and its buildings,* at the expense of the house

* The schedule of building in the grounds was as follows: 1719, the Pyramid Gate; 1720–25, the bastion wall which surrounded the park; 1724–28, the Temple of the

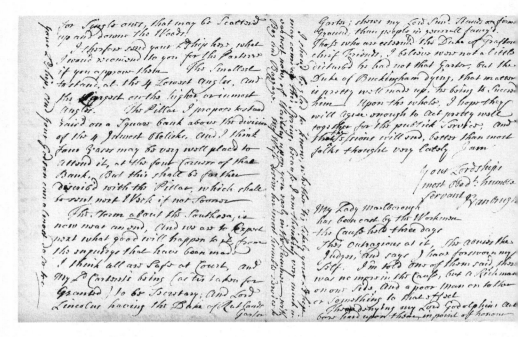

A letter from Vanbrugh to Carlisle, dated 20 February 1720. He writes with ideas for garden sculpture, the South Sea Bubble and Court gossip.

itself. By this time the main block and the East Wing had been built and furnished, but not the West Wing. It was originally intended by Vanbrugh and the Earl that the two wings should be symmetrical, so as to present a uniform façade. However, since what money there was was all going on elaborate buildings and beautification of the park, the Earl decided to leave it to his heirs to finish the actual house. Unfortunately, after his death, his son-in-law, Sir Thomas Robinson,

---

Four Winds, which derives from Palladio's Villa Rotonda and is one of Vanbrugh's most elegant creations: 1728, the Howard Pyramid, commemorating Lord William Howard. During the same decade Ray Wood was landscaped and decorated with statuary, fountains and a summerhouse. The garden itself is described in detail in a later chapter.

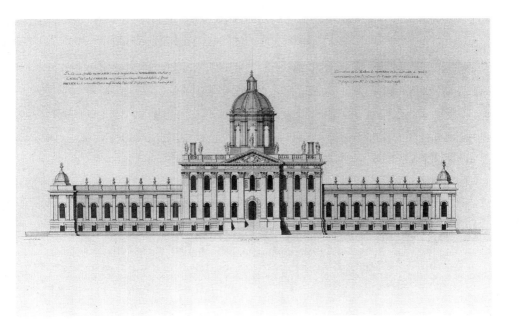

South elevation of Castle Howard in Colen Campbell's Vitruvius Britannicus
of 1715.

who fancied himself as an amateur architect, took over the job.
Robinson elected to scrap the plans and design a completely different
West Wing – which accounts for the uneven aspect of the house
today.

Since the 3rd Earl's fall from political grace in 1702 he had
eschewed London and the Court, except for the occasional visit, and
lived all the year round at his beloved Castle Howard. Nevertheless,
Lord Carlisle continued to keep in touch with the world he had
forsaken, and for many years, despite his self-imposed 'exile' to
Yorkshire, was regarded as an *éminence grise* by the Opposition. Even
as late as 1727, when the Earl had been out of politics for more than
twenty years, his old friend and colleague, the Duke of Newcastle,
wrote that 'The King was very glad to hear your Lordship had

thoughts of coming soon to town, where your presence must always be of service to his Majesty's affairs ...' And his daughter, Lady Irwin, constantly confirms that her father is still a remembered and respected figure in the minds of the Court. When George II came to the throne she wrote from London to say that she had been twice at Court and that:

the King and Queen both made particular enquiry after your Lordship. I believe you would like the Prince; there's a frankness and affability in his way very different from his rank, and very engaging ... Tonight I am going to Sir John's Provoked Husband [a play by Vanbrugh], where I am sure I shall be well entertained.

The 3rd Earl continued to take an immense, albeit vicarious, pleasure in hearing about Court life. Lady Irwin was both an excellent correspondent and a mine of gossip, and her letters must have been a delight to the Earl, isolated at Castle Howard during the long winters. In January 1729 she wrote that:

... There was deep play at Court last night, but I have not heard who was successful. The Dowager Duchess of Marlborough and the Duke of Norfolk were two who entertained the King. Prince Frederick and the Princess Royal also played ...

But she also bothers to tell her father that an express has just come with news that the galleons recently dispatched to Spain have arrived safely, and the letter finishes with news of the current speculation over the King's possible choice among the various candidates for the latest vacancy in the Royal gift – the Deanery of Windsor, an extremely lucrative sinecure. And when John Gay produced the *Beggar's Opera* the following month, Lady Irwin reported on a rival attraction, presented in its wake:

... The Village Opera is at present the fashionable diversion; I go this week ... 'tis an imitation of the Beggar's Opera. The town does not seem quite so mad of it as they was of the other performance. The very name of it will secure it from too great a party, the country being thought incapable of entertaining, and beggars of some kind or other being the only proper inhabitants of this place . . .

Not a view of life in the country to which the Howards and their friends would have subscribed. Nevertheless, Lady Irwin would risk a good deal to get to London, as the following letter indicates:

. . . Your Lordship may conclude we had a very bad journey by the length of time we were performing it, though thank God no real accident; numberless frights, breaking our axle-tree, horses plunging into holes, and sticking fast, was our daily exercise. I never saw the roads so bad in my life . . . I am resolved never to be engaged in the like difficulties, and would rather never see London again than pay so dear for the sight of it. I have got a great cold by being obliged to get so often out of the coach, and getting wet of my feet . . .

Needless to say, the resolution did not last.

By the 1730s the Earl's health had deteriorated to such an extent that he was a virtual cripple, confined to a wheelchair, unable to entertain, and living alone at Castle Howard. His children suggested all sorts of unlikely cures, including the current panacea for all ills, the notorious 'Mr Ward's Drops'. In the summer of 1731 his son-in-law, Sir Thomas Robinson, had written him a long screed from Paris urging their efficacy, which the Earl had clearly ignored. Nothing daunted, the egregious Robinson wrote again:

I am fully convinced Mr Ward's drops would have been of great service to you both as to the gout or any other complaints your Lordship may have; and though I am very sensible how difficult it is to persuade anyone to take a new remedy, the ingredients of it not being known, yet could I have told your Lordship some particulars of these drops by word of mouth, I am sure you would make no hesitation in trusting yourself to them. Mr Ward has met with vast opposition here from the whole body of physicians, apothecaries, and surgeons, though he has cured these three last years above 2,000 people of all ranks and conditions, and there is no one instance of their ever having done harm . . .

Lord Carlisle was allergic to quacks and it is highly unlikely that he took the slightest notice of either Robinson or Mr Ward.

While his son-in-law fussed over the old man's health, his daughter Elizabeth, Robinson's wife, sought to divert the Earl with long chatty letters about the gay life they were leading in Paris. After the usual gossip one of her letters ends with a pompous piece of moralizing which she obviously thought would impress her father:

The Duke of Wharton has at last finished a despicable, extravagant life. His estate and character died before him, and his name will not long survive him. I believe no person in the time ever made so effectual a dispatch of both, and it will be difficult for any genius that comes after him to imitate him through all the circles of his short course of life . . .

Lord Carlisle may have become an invalid but he was in full possession of his faculties. This kind of hypocrisy, coming from the daughter whose reputation as an alcoholic and gambler was already legendary, can only have annoyed him. Lady Irwin's amusing correspondence would surely have been much more to his taste. In a letter written in March of 1736 she wrote that she was soon to be given an official appointment at Court, as lady-in-waiting to the young German Princess Augusta, who was betrothed to the King's eldest son, Prince Frederick. Lady Irwin reported to her father that both the King and Queen had received her very graciously, and 'made many enquiries after your Lordship; the King talked to me a good deal about the mausoleum [at Castle Howard], the fame of which I find has reached this place'. The arrangements for the Royal wedding are mentioned and then Lady Irwin goes on to give a devastating account of the notion society has of the poor Princess – before they have even met her:

. . . Report does not so much as flatter her with beauty; she is said to be low, fat, and marked with the smallpox, not above 17, too young to have any character but a good disposition, which has been carefully preserved by a strict retirement, her mother, with whom she lived, having secluded herself from the world for some years, being a widow. She neither speaks French nor English, but what she has learnt since this match was in treaty, and therefore she will I suppose for some months remain in a state of being dumb; but women, your Lordship knows, will always find a tongue in one language or other . . .

The 3rd Earl of Carlisle died on 1 May 1738. One of his last acts was to calculate the total amount of money that he had spent on Castle Howard. All his life he had kept meticulous accounts, in a series of closely written volumes titled the 'Book of my Disbursements relating to my Building'. The final reckoning shows that, from its conception in 1701 until Midsummer 1737, he had spent £78,240 2s. 10d. 'on my buildings, gardens, plantations + outworks'. It is not, of course, possible to equate such a sum with modern prices;★ suffice it to say that even by contemporary eighteenth-century standards it was a huge amount – but, nevertheless, a minute investment considering the magnificent return.

★ In 1700 an agricultural labourer was paid at the rate of 14 pence per ten-hour day, i.e. about £17 10s. a year; and a craftsman approximately 20 pence for the same working day – i.e. about £25 a year (C. Cipolla, *Before the Industrial Revolution*, Methuen, London, 1981, p. 217).

4

'A Summer and Winter Servants' Hall'

Primogeniture is sometimes a mistake. The 3rd Earl of Carlisle would almost certainly have preferred his second son, Charles, to succeed to the title and inherit Castle Howard, rather than his first-born, Henry, the legal heir. Of all the Earl's children Charles Howard was the only one who made a success of his life in his own right. A man of charm, intelligence and energy, Charles was both a popular courtier and a distinguished soldier. He represented the family interests in the political arena as the Whig member for Carlisle for forty years and was knighted in 1749. Moreover, he was devoted to Castle Howard and in tune with all his father's ambitions.

Henry Morpeth, the heir, was a very different character, an aesthete who had spent much of his early life abroad. He seems to have disliked England, preferring the life he had made for himself in Rome, where he bought a house. He took no more than a token interest in English politics, and it can only have been from a sense of filial obligation that he returned occasionally during the 1720s and 1730s to take his seat in the House of Commons, as the member for Morpeth. When he did attend Parliament his performance was perfunctory, and there is no indication that he ever aspired to Government office.

The 3rd Earl's heir had, however, inherited one vital element of his father's character which was to prove of immense benefit to Castle Howard – he was a dedicated and discriminating collector. By the age of forty-four, when he succeeded to the title, he had already acquired a considerable reputation as a connoisseur of the arts. During the first half of the eighteenth century the English aristocracy's penchant for buying up the treasures of Europe was at its peak, and the concept of moral principles had yet to be involved in the matter. The 4th Earl was in his element. During the years he lived in Italy he travelled all over the Continent, amassing a fortune in booty wherever he went. This treasure trove was shipped back to Yorkshire and formed the foundation of Castle Howard's fabulous collection of antiquities. Many of the 4th Earl's spoils are still on display in the house (although even more, including some of the very best items, were disposed of in one way or another by subsequent generations). Nearly all the extant sculptures at Castle Howard were brought back from Europe by the 4th Earl, as well as much of the French and Italian furniture.

His heir's long absences abroad, and his apparent lack of concern for the estates he would eventually inherit, must have been a major disappointment to the 3rd Earl. Morpeth's letters can have been of little comfort either: he was a confirmed valetudinarian, if not a hypochondriac, and wrote almost exclusively about nothing more interesting than the state of his health, or the latest fashionable 'cure'. In fairness to Morpeth, there was some justification for this obsession with medical matters. His private life was, for many years, dominated by tragedy.

His first marriage was to Frances Spencer, the lovely daughter of an old friend of his father's, the Earl of Sunderland. The young couple produced five children, three sons and two daughters; one after the other four of the children died, leaving only a single daughter. Then Frances herself died, when she was still a comparatively young woman. His brother Charles remained unmarried, and it seemed as though there would be no direct heir to the title. Although already in his fifties, the 4th Earl – as he had become in 1738, when his father died – married again. His new wife, much younger than himself, was Isabella Byron, a daughter of the 4th Lord Byron. (The poet was her great-nephew.) She gave birth to two more children, of whom the daughter also died in infancy, but the son, Frederick, who was born only ten years before the 4th Earl's own death, survived. He became the 5th Earl of Carlisle.

Isabella, while married to the 4th Earl, seems to have been a model wife. (Her career after his death in 1758, however, became a constant source of embarrassment to the Carlisle family: she left her second husband, Sir William Musgrave, soon after the marriage and eloped with a thoroughly bogus French nobleman. Even after that affair foundered she carried on creating scandals for years. Still more disastrously, Isabella ran up serious debts, which harried the next generation until her own death in 1795.)

Isabella was in many ways an ideal consort for the 4th Earl, and, during his lifetime, an exemplary chatelaine of Castle Howard. She shared the same aesthetic tastes as Carlisle, and was a considerable artist in her own right. She was particularly well known for her etchings.

As Countess of Carlisle, Isabella wrote a 'Receipt Book', which is also a homeopathic manual. The recipes are most unlikely to appeal to the modern cook, considering the impracticality and expense of reproducing them, let alone the nature of some of the ingredients, but they give a vivid picture of life in an eighteenth-century kitchen. There is a recipe for viper broth, in which a stock is made from 'one chopped viper and a lean chicken' – the resultant brew is highly recommended 'For an ague'. Another starts off 'take a gallon and a half of brandy and three pints of the best salad oil', and goes on to include 'half a bushel of poppies, half a handful of rue and half a handful of wormwood', plus a whole cornucopia of herbs – sage, balm, hyssop, mint, sweet marjoram . . . etc. This powerful concoction is intended to cure 'A surfeit of water'. The kitchen must have smelled like a slaughterhouse on the days they made the countess's black pudding. The recipe begins with the daunting command to 'take the Blood of a whole Hog and about 8lbs of the kidney fat . . .' It is followed by another recipe, for a sweet, known by the unappetizing name of 'white hog's pudding'. This one is made from pounding the marrow bones of the hog with almonds and innumerable spices; the mixture is then liberally laced with various wines. Her recipe for mince pies sounds equally nauseating:

Take hearts Tongue, boil it and mince it very fine Then take an equal Quantity of Apple and Suet: minced severally as you can guess by your eye, with the Tongue then mince them together with salt and some Pounded Mace and nutmeg, put to this 4 Pounds of Currants and one Pound of Stoned Raisins, preserved Orange and Citron minced small, and some Plain Orange Peel and put in, a Pint of Sherry.

Isabella was a meticulous housekeeper. From the household account books kept during her reign at Castle Howard it is possible to get an idea of the relative values of money in the latter half of the eighteenth century. It would be otiose to try to translate eighteenth-century prices into exact modern equivalents; the emphases of expenditure were quite different from those of today. Nevertheless certain commodities are a constant factor, and it is interesting to note the comparative costs. For example, the Castle Howard accounts, for one week in October 1748, were itemized as follows:

Wines	£4	0s.	6d.
Groceries	£5	15s.	7d.
Butcher's meat	£7	9s.	5d.
Bread and drink	£7	11s.	6d.
Fire and candles	£5	17s.	2d.
Kitchen provisions	£9	10s.	9½d.

Another week the entire household expenses came to no more than £36 0s. 7½d. but, unfortunately, there is no record in the account book of the number of people in residence at the various times. The evidence of other entries indicates that the family must have been alone. The expenses for the month of September 1754, for example, are much higher – it was the height of the shooting season and the 4th Earl was probably entertaining a large house party. £67 18s. 6½d. was spent in a single week, including £14 7s. 3d. on wines and £16 16s. 6d. on meat. The total for the whole month comes to £212 2s. 6d.; whereas the expenditure the previous August had only amounted to £164 9s. 6d. As the cost of catering for the staff was a constant factor (except when the family moved to London, when they took the senior servants with them, leaving a skeleton staff on board wages at Castle Howard), the large fluctuations in household expenses are a clear indication of frequent entertaining on a grand scale.

Candles are always one of the major items in an eighteenth-century budget. Beeswax not only cost three times as much as tallow but, in 1710, Queen Anne had imposed a tax on it, of 4d. in the pound. Most great households made their own candles, from the estate produce, but the best wax was imported, from Holland and Portugal, or even from as far away as the Americas. The Duke of Chandos, for example, imported vast quantities of myrtlewax and scented green wax from Carolina, New England and Barbados. The myrtlewax cost 7d. a pound, but in 1739 the Duke was prepared to pay as much as 10d. a pound for New England wax. The number of candles which could be produced from one pound of wax obviously depended on their size. The lighting for a grand ball demanded candles that would last eleven hours, and, of these, no more than four could be made from a single pound of wax; shorter candles, at six to the pound, which lasted for six hours, were used for more mundane evenings.

Lighting, therefore, could be very expensive, which led to definite social distinctions. A tutor or governess, for example, might well stipulate the right to the use of beeswax, rather than tallow, candles in their terms of employment. The dog-ends of the beeswax candles became one of the recognized perks of the upper servants – the Duchess of Marlborough was castigated for her meanness when she stopped her lady's maid from selling them to a tallow chandler.

The number and quality of the candles in a house varied enormously; as a conspicuous manifestation of wealth it was an obvious subject of gossip. Sir Thomas Robinson, for example, shows a distinct note of envy in his description of the lighting provided by Sir Robert Walpole at Houghton, where he was staying for a bachelor hunting party:

We were generally between 20 and 30 at two tables, and as much cheerfulness and good nature as I ever saw . . . Young Lady Walpole and Mrs Hammond

[Walpole's sister] were the only ladies . . . They hunted six days in the week, three times with Lord Walpole's fox-hounds and thrice with Sir R[obert]'s harriers and indeed 'tis a very fine open country for sport. During the Duke of Lorraine's being there the consumption both from the larder and the cellar was prodigious. They dined in the hall, which was lighted by 130 wax candles, and the saloon with 50; the whole expense in that article being computed at £15 a night.

In 1732, John Tracey Atkyns, a London barrister on a walking tour, visited the estate. After waxing lyrical about the approach to Castle Howard, the building and furnishings, he inspected the staff quarters and wrote:

The offices are in ev'ry respect the most convenient that I ever saw the kitchen & answerable to so noble a house, a summer & winter servants' hall, cellars in great numbers, in the wine cellar 20 hogsheads of Port Claret & Burgundy: fourscore hogsheads of strong beer in another cellar, the house-keeper's room very commodious, and sweetmeats it's proper furniture in great quantity, my assurance fail'd me (a wonder too you'll say) or I would have ask'd the venerable matron who presided over these delicious viands to have gratify'd my mouth with one dry'd apricot, twenty rooms for better sort of servants, very excellent places to lie in. There was a very convenient building appropriate to poultry of all kinds, a female by way of guardian who keeps watch and ward and has a little lodging room, that she may have 'em always in her eye and defend 'em from all harm, a basin of water in the middle of a green court, and ranges of apartments, for the several uses of feeding roosting and breeding and in short ev'ry thing that a hen hussy can desire . . .

After the 4th Earl's death in 1758, an inventory was made of the complete contents of Castle Howard. From the pages concerned with the domestic offices it is easy to understand the complexity of life below stairs, and to visualize the frantic activity which must have continued virtually round the clock. The great kitchen in the basement had deep ovens built into its walls, and an enormous open fire, furnished with '4 pot hooks + a Spit Back + Guide'. There were two vast tables, a walnut spice cupboard and a twenty-four-hour clock. A large number of firearms were kept in the kitchen – apart from the danger of robbers, always prevalent in the wilds of Yorkshire, it was only a few years since the Rebellion of 1745. The weapons listed on permanent stand-by included '6 musketts, 6 bayonets, a blunderbus'; 2 'broad swords + basket hilts'; and 'a pair of servants horse pistols', alongside which entry the writer has added, in brackets, a laconic comment – 'useful'.

Copper, and to a lesser extent brass, were the usual materials used in cooking – both equally time-consuming to clean and potentially dangerous from the point of view of hygiene. There was an immense *batterie de cuisine*, evocative of a formidable amount of work in the scullery. Around 150 copper pans are mentioned in one list alone and there are several different lists, including one 'for the servant's use'. They include, apart from all the obvious pans, a carp boiler, chocolate pots, ice moulds, and other such indications of *haute cuisine* – the Carlisles employed a French chef. There is a reference to one tea kettle 'with a lock', and one without. (At the beginning of the eighteenth century a pound of Imperial Tea cost £2, and Bohea, the cheaper brand, not much less. It was still considered an expensive luxury fifty years later, although, by Isabella's time, the custom of the after-dinner tea-tray had become widespread.) There was a special 'turbot pan and cover and plate' and another special utensil for poaching salmon, a pan for boiling ham and a mushroom pan – separate coppers were, in fact, kept for each individual ingredient. Other items mentioned include '2 little boiler or broth pans + a very large stewpan'; '18 graded stewpans', '7 lesser ditto with covers' and a further '5 small ditto with covers'; '2 poupatoneau and cover for stewing herbs + roots'; graded soup pots; numerous brass pattypans; twenty-three brass candlesticks and five coal-scuttles; a tin pepper box, a salt tub and marble mortars.

The 'Scullery', scene of so much prodigious scrubbing, housed the servants' plates – '19 deal double trenchers + 10 round ditto'. Presumably the differentiation between wooden platters and china plates is yet another indication of hierarchical snobbery in the servants' hall – only the upper servants being allowed to eat off china. The 'Wet Lairder' was next door to the scullery, and housed the lead pickling cisterns and a salting tub. Salted herring have always been a traditional mainstay of the northern diet, but the use of lead must have been a serious health hazard.

Young girls in service were as strictly chaperoned as the débutantes they worked for. The maids were hardly allowed to converse with the male servants, let alone go out with them, and any breach of the rules was liable to mean dismissal. The reason that working in the laundry was so popular with the girls was that it provided unique opportunities for fraternizing with the opposite sex. To minimize the effect of the heat and smell of washing, the laundry was always situated on the outside edge of the complex – often next to the stableyard, with all its obvious attractions. Many a clandestine flirtation must have been carried on between the laundry maids and the stable boys, sneaking in and out of the courtyards.

The 'Landry' [*sic*] at Castle Howard, according to the Inventory, contained '14 flat irons and 2 long ironing side tables'; a 'large range' and a small stove; an iron plate for 'heaters' and irons; clothes-horses, pulleys and a mangle. The 'Wash House' is listed separately, with 'one large + one small copper with a Furnace + Barrs to each'; two large water tubs; a 'rinsing tub' and a 'bathing tub', presumably for the servants' baths; fourteen wash tubs of different sizes; seven forms and five stools. It indicates a remarkable amount of washing in an age hardly remarkable for its cleanliness.

The 'preserving room', the 'store room', and the 'still room' each had their individual identities and attendant acolytes. The outbuildings were equally complex in their management and included a 'Bakehouse', a 'Swineherd's Room', a 'venison house' with '2 cleavers' and a separate 'Slaughter House'. The 'menagerie' was housed in yet another separate building, which had five small rooms, including a parlour and a 'tea room'. Beer, rather than water, was the staple drink of the servants as well as of their masters, and enormous quantities were made on the premises. The inventory mentions four separate rooms devoted to the manufacture of ale, again including separate sitting-rooms for the men who worked there. There was a 'Brewhouse' and a 'Brewers Room', a 'Coopers Rm', and a 'Malthouse and Chamber'. This plethora of separate rooms for separate functions emphasizes both the hierarchy of the domestic staff and the policy of segregating the sexes.

It always seems, looking at contemporary accounts, as though servants were appallingly badly paid. The earliest records of wages at Castle Howard show that the highest-paid member of the household was the cook, at £36 a year; the Clerk of the Kitchen came next, with £30 a year; but the butler received only £10 a year, while the groom, the footmen and the under-butler earned no more than £6 a year – and all of these were deemed 'upper' servants, with related status. The skivvies' salaries were so low that the contemporary accountant has not bothered to record them. These rates of pay continued, with no more than proportionate increases, right up to the twentieth century; as late as 1910 a local maid was earning only £10 a year.

But these figures are misleading. All the upper servants came into daily contact with the Castle guests and would thereby have earned a great deal more than their salaries in tips – or 'vails', as they were called at the time. Anyone who came to stay in a house such as Castle Howard automatically tipped the butler, the coachman, the head-keeper and probably the chef as well. Valets and ladies' maids usually travelled with their employers, but might well be called upon to assist the resident staff during a large party, and would be rewarded accordingly. The most trifling service or errand could earn a footman or groom an extra guinea, and even the lesser servants could expect the occasional tips. The size of the tips naturally varied, according to the temperament as well as the purse of the donor, but it was not unusual for a senior servant to receive as much as £5 at the end of even a relatively short visit. When Queen Victoria came to Castle Howard in the summer of 1850 she left £100 to be distributed among the staff after a visit of only two nights.

Moreover, although the actual wages were so meagre, all expenses were paid, including clothes; in fact a servant's clothes often cost his employer more than his salary, particularly in the case of livery. The Castle Howard staff wore a yellow and blue livery, which had been designed by the 3rd Earl and was one of his expensive status symbols. One of the nineteenth-century account books gives the cost of the coachmen's livery as £16 0s. 6d. each, the postillions' as £9 19s. 0d. and the first footman's £11 15s. 0d.

Those servants who did not qualify for a uniform or livery were compensated by a special allowance for clothes. The butcher's wages, for instance, were specified in the 1726 accounts as £10 a year plus '£10 12s. 0d. clothes' and the same principle was applied to the brewer, at '£20 12s. 0d. inc clothes'. Even peripheral retainers' salaries were genuinely comprehensive: the gamekeeper £12 a year plus £17 2s. 0d. 'allow'd in Cloaths, Candles, Whips, etc', and the resident 'plumber and glazier £12 4s. 0d. + clothes, aprons + candles £10 11s. 0d.' And, in the same account, there is another entry to the effect that Isaac Elliot, the gamekeeper, needed: '1 green coat + jacket; Fustian shooting jacket; Fustian overall; 2 pairs cord breeches; 2 waistcoats; 1 top coat'.

Finally, it must be remembered that the servants, particularly the more important ones, lived extremely well. In a letter dated 10 September 1770 the butler wrote that he had ordered 'good red port for the steward's room'; to give substance to this quote there is the record which shows that *eight dozen* bottles of port were consumed in the steward's room in a single month during the nineteenth century. The furnishings of this room evoke a comfortable gentlemen's club: leather chairs, a walnut chest, a 4½ by 5½ ft oval dining-table, a walnut basin stand, two carved gilt wall sconces, forty-nine prints on the walls and a couch with a checked linen cover. The housekeeper lived in equal splendour with her own suite of rooms – sitting-room, bedroom, and private 'closet'. Her four-poster bed was hung with blue serge curtains and the closet with '2 pieces of Green Lindsey Hangings' and 'a large chest of drawers'. The list of contents of the maids' quarters is considerably less inviting, confined to various terse references such as 'boarded bedstead', 'Old Table' and '1 Old Chair'. The junior servants slept in dormitories but at least they had an adequate allowance of coverings, with '3 blankets, a rug, and a bolster' to each bed.

Nor was domestic life invariably confined to routine chores; the more educated servants often developed alternative interests. Betty Radcliffe, for example, lady's maid at the end of the eighteenth century to a friend of the Carlisles, was a highly talented copy-artist and seamstress. Her reputation spread in society, and her water-colours, embroidery pictures and silk flowers became greatly sought after as works of art. Others decorated furniture, made cushions or painted screens – many of the artefacts so treasured by antique dealers today were made by the maid rather than the mistress.

A career in service meant security, freedom from want, and a comfortable old age with a guaranteed pension. Betty Radcliffe, for example, was so greatly valued by her employers that when she retired they gave her an annuity of £100, and her case was by no means unique. Service, in fact, could be reasonably profitable, relative to the economic plight of the working classes in the outside world. Living free made it possible to save, and there are many instances of servants who retired with enough money to lease their own small-holding, go into trade or open an inn. One contemporary record shows that the housekeeper left £1,300 in her will, a considerable fortune for a woman who had started her life in service without a penny of her own.

It was not until 1745, seven years after his death, that the great mausoleum which had meant so much to the 3rd Earl was finished and able to receive his body. As it stands today the mausoleum is certainly the most impressive building on the Castle Howard estate – and is generally acknowledged to be one of the finest masterpieces of eighteenth-century architecture.

The idea of a commemorative building as a burial place for the Carlisles, rather than an ordinary graveyard, was first mooted in 1720 by Vanbrugh, in conjunction with the 3rd Earl himself. The concept of an enormous private tomb was thoroughly in keeping with his character, and besides, like many Whigs, Carlisle had no particular

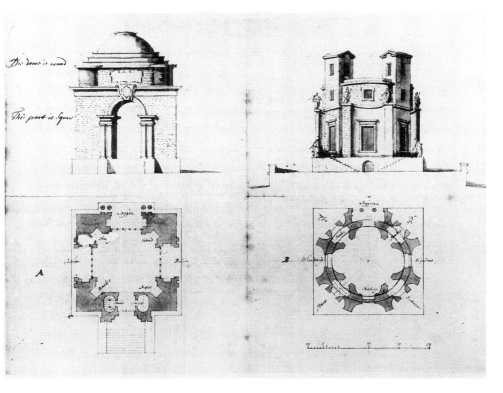

*Nicholas Hawksmoor's plans for the magnificent mausoleum at Castle Howard –
Horace Walpole wrote that it 'would tempt one to be buried alive'.*

liking for the accepted ritual of the Church. Finally, the mausoleum
would be a magnificent opportunity to set the seal on his architectural ambition. Carlisle's intentions were specified in his will,
written while Vanbrugh was still alive, and many years before his
own death:

I do design to build a burial place near my seat of Castle Howard, where I
desire to be lay'd, My Funeral to be very private, I would have no body
invited, desireing only to be attended to my grave by such of my Children
as shall happen to be with me at ye time of my death, & my Servants my
Chaplain to preach sermon exhorting to repentance & a good life, for I take

67

it yt upon such occasions & at such times people are generally better dispos'd to receive good impressions . . . but in case this burial place which I propose to build should not be finish'd at ye time of my death, I then desire yt my Body may be deposited in Bulmer Church, to remain there till such time as my Son shall build a Burial place & when such Burial place is finished then my Body to be remov'd & lay'd therein & in case this Burial place for ye family is not finished by me, I recommend it to my Son to be performed by him as a thing very proper nay absolutely necessary . . . I recommend to my Son & desire that he will consult & take ye opinion of Sir John Vanbrugh, & Mr Hawksmore, with who's performances I am very well satisfied & I believe they are very skillfull & knowing in ye science of Architecture. I think this Burial place should be built in ye form of a little chapple to hold about 40 or 50 people with a Cupola or Tower upon it . . . I would have no other inscription upon ye stone under which my Body shall be lay'd than this, here lyes Charles ye 3rd Earl of Carlisle of ye Family of ye Howards who built this house called Castle Howard & made ye plantations yt belong thereunto.

Simplicity and moralizing were all very well for a transitory funeral service but the founder of Castle Howard wanted to be remembered. This colossal mausoleum, the largest private tomb in England, would be the 3rd Earl's final statement to posterity, a reiteration of his persona to all who came to Castle Howard in the future. And so it is.

The 3rd Earl did indeed die before the mausoleum was anything like finished, but even more unfortunately, so did Vanbrugh. Hawksmoor took over but, lacking the social stature and authority of Vanbrugh, he was prevented from carrying on with the original plans. The 4th Earl allowed his brother-in-law, Sir Thomas Robinson, to intervene; Robinson, who thought himself every whit as good an architect as Vanbrugh, let alone Hawksmoor, spent the next few years sabotaging one design after another. Then, in 1732, cracks began to appear in the foundations: Hawksmoor was told of 'some failings in ye walls of ye inward part of ye Vault of the Mausoleum'. The whole thing became a nightmare for Hawksmoor, under constant criticism from Robinson, from the 4th Earl, and eventually from Lord Burlington as well. In the end, however, the mausoleum was completed much as the original plans had specified. The idea of a vast circular drum, copied from the tomb of Cecilia Metella in Rome, which had caught the 3rd Earl's imagination in his youth, was retained; so was the colonnade with its thirty-six Doric columns. But the concept of a free-standing building, dominating the landscape in glorious isolation, was abandoned. In an attempt to soften its impact, the mausoleum was enclosed by a surrounding wall and a series of steps, copied from Lord Burlington's villa at Chiswick, were added to the approach. Nowadays architectural opinion regards these additions as superfluous and irrelevant, a case of gilding the lily quite unnecessarily. Nevertheless the mausoleum remains, in essence, a formidable, almost a personal, monument to Nicholas Hawksmoor; it is the supreme example of his skill as a builder and architect, and has rightly been called 'The noblest invention of them all'.

At the time when the mausoleum was under construction, Richard Boyle, 3rd Earl of Burlington, was the leading amateur architect in the country. He had, in fact, taken an interest in the development of Castle Howard virtually since its conception. Born in 1694, he was an exact contemporary of the 4th Earl of Carlisle, and their families were old friends as well as Yorkshire neighbours. Burlington's principal residence and estates were at Londesborough, in the East Riding of Yorkshire, some thirty miles from Castle Howard. As children, they must both have been aware of the local excitement when the old Earl of Carlisle began building. They would have watched the massive house taking shape as they themselves grew up, heard the various plans being discussed and, very probably, offered their own ideas on the subject to anyone who would listen. As a young man, too, Burlington was elected a member of the Kit-Cat Club, where he would have met the founder of Castle Howard on equal terms, as well as all the other virtuosi of the day. Within a remarkably short time Burlington had been accepted by his contemporaries as the ultimate arbiter on all questions of cultural taste. He had an enormous influence on English architecture, which survived long after his death and lasted well into the next century.

Burlington was a charismatic figure. He was the archetypal eighteenth-century Whig nobleman, patrician to the core but egalitarian in his dealings with the world at large; a serious scholar with an immensely cultivated mind; enormously rich and a considerable philanthropist. He became a great patron of the arts, his interest and financial aid extending far beyond his own specialized field of architecture. Horace Walpole summed him up when he wrote:

Never was protection and great wealth more generously and more judiciously diffused than by this great person, who had every quality of a genius and artist, except envy.

The Earl's London residence, Burlington House, in Arlington Street, became the artistic centre and mecca of the virtuosi. Several of his protégés actually moved in, and lived at the Earl's expense on a more or less permanent basis. William Kent, the brilliant interior decorator who designed much of the furniture at Castle Howard, was one of the first artists to be 'adopted' by Burlington; he was installed at Burlington House and given his own set of rooms, which he kept until his death some thirty years later.

The very real, and lasting, friendship between Kent and Burlington is a classic example of the Whig aristocracy's ability to transcend class. (Within the confines of their own chosen élite, that is to say.) Kent came of working-class stock and had originally been apprenticed to a coach-maker; 'discovered' by Burlington and brought under his patronage, Kent's artistic talents bloomed. He became the darling of society, badgered on all sides to paint ceilings, execute murals and design everything from furniture to gardens and even, on a special occasion, ball dresses. Walpole noted that:

. . . so impetuous was fashion, that two great ladies prevailed on him to make designs for their birthday gowns. The one dressed in a petticoat decorated with columns of the five orders; the other like a bronze in a copper-coloured satin with ornaments of gold.

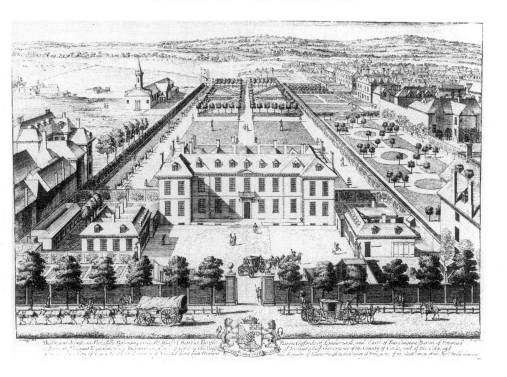

An early eighteenth-century engraving of Burlington House in Piccadilly.

The two men not only came from completely different backgrounds but were also polar opposites in character, and in their respective outlooks on life. While Burlington was an austere ascetic, rigorously formal in manner, Kent was happy-go-lucky, indolent and a sybarite, happy to take full advantage of his rich host – but in the nicest possible way. When Burlington went away, leaving no drink in the house, Kent rectified the situation immediately and, quite unabashed, wrote to inform the Earl that he had:

... bought ... some excellent claritt and Scotch sack & Cyprus esquisito, I have had but one feast in my room since you went, but I can assure you, was drank fourteen bottles of wine in one setting and neather I nor company was sick or sorry for the next day.

Kent's greedy habits provoked the following letter from Alexander Pope, a mutual friend of theirs and Carlisle's, who was well known for his Puritan attitude to life:

If His Majesty's Principal Painter (for so I read in my paper, the Gazeteer) would follow my example here for as many months (for so many at least it will take), to cleanse his pencil, and purify his pallat, from all that greasy mixture and fatt oyle they have contracted, he would paint like a Raphael, and look like an Angelo: whereas if he proceeds in his carnality and carnivoracity, he must expect not to imitate Raphael in any thing but his untimely end.

Kent and Burlington developed an enormous admiration for each other's work; in a letter written in 1732, after many years of working together, Kent's verdict on their partnership was that whereas the French considered the contemporary English a hundred years behind them in civilization, Burlington and he were a hundred years ahead of the average Englishman. Burlington was an amateur architect, but only in the sense that he was not paid for his services. On the contrary, he frequently subsidized public buildings out of his personal fortune; he repaired St Paul's church in Covent Garden at his own expense. Vertue considered that Burlington's technical knowledge and skill put him 'in the first rank' of architects and that, as such, he should be classed as a true professional. He was a rigid classicist who came to be recognized as the founder of English Palladianism. This passion found its ultimate expression in the villa he built at Chiswick, an almost exact replica of Palladio's Rotonda, near Vicenza; it became a favourite rendezvous for the glitterati and virtuosi, with Swift and Pope among the regular guests. Pope rightly described Burlington as 'a positive man', for, in matters of style, Burlington was totally inflexible, uncompromising in his attitude and authoritarian, even didactic, in his opinions. But, however rigid the form of a building, he was equally adamant that it should be utilitarian. Burlington agreed with Pope that:

Something there is more needful than expense,
And something previous even to taste, 'tis sense.

Many of the great new houses built during the first half of the eighteenth century came under the direct influence of Burlington: Holkham, for instance, the gigantic palace built by Thomas Coke, Earl of Leicester, owes as much to the amateur aristocrat as to the paid architect concerned. And Sir Thomas Robinson reported of Wentworth Woodhouse, under construction during the 1740s, that 'the whole finishing will be entirely submitted to Lord Burlington'. Burlington's friends asked his advice, submitted to his decrees and relied on his opinion. In fact, anyone who could claim the slightest acquaintance with the Earl was liable to try to enlist his interest in their plans; many went so far as to send unsolicited drawings of proposed buildings before they had even commissioned the work. Burlington's verdicts, quoted in innumerable letters, were usually accepted without question. It was therefore almost inevitable that, when the design of the Castle Howard mausoleum was being decided, Robinson should subjugate his personal arrogance, for once, and defer to Burlington.

Lord Burlington married Lady Dorothy Savile, a daughter of the Marquess of Halifax, another member of the Carlisles' set, in 1721. He gave his bride a fortune in jewellery, including a number of fabulous diamonds, one of which alone was worth £1,575. This kind of figure, taken in conjunction with the amount of cash deemed necessary to pay for his honeymoon, puts the cost of living into perspective. Records show that on his wedding day Burlington was given thirty pieces of gold, worth £10 each, to cover his expenses. And this was clearly considered lavish.

The Countess was an amateur artist who achieved a certain celebrity in her own right, particularly for her caricatures of their friends. She became a great hostess who not only accepted quite calmly that her house had become a cross between a free hotel and an artists' commune, but played an active part in encouraging her husband's protégés. The Burlingtons collected virtuosi from all over the Continent as well as Britain, the Countess in particular favouring those connected with music or the stage. Among the incumbents of Burlington House, at one time or another, were such luminaries as

Lord Burlington's house at Chiswick. Burlington, who was an exact contemporary of the 4th Earl of Carlisle, took an active interest in the development of Castle Howard from its conception.

the playwright John Gay, the composer Handel, and 'Violetti', a Viennese dancer, who became the rage of society and was a particular friend of the Carlisles. Walpole called her 'the finest and most admired dancer in the world', and she completed her triumph by marrying the great actor David Garrick. On her marriage the Burlingtons behaved with typical generosity and gave Violetti a dowry of £6,000. According to a contemporary society column, 'Violette [*sic*] is constantly at Lady Carlisle's suppers'; and, after her marriage, both she and her husband often stayed at Castle Howard.

During the summer months the whole glittering caravanserai moved north, and York, then at the height of its popularity, became the centre of social activity. This was the season when Castle Howard really came into its own, as the principal house of the neighbourhood. Although one of the Earls of Carlisle recorded angrily that it had taken him three *days* to get from York to Castle Howard, thanks to continuous blizzards, the distance, in fact, is only twelve miles – an

74

easy hour and a half's ride under ordinary conditions. York was the Howards' local town, the place where they shopped, and went racing or dancing, and where they were duly recognized as the leading grandees of the district. The 4th Earl and Isabella naturally entertained the local gentry throughout the year, but when the York season arrived, attracting members of the *haut monde* from all over England, Castle Howard excelled itself with a series of splendid parties. Lord Burlington, Lord Rockingham and the other aristocratic neighbours brought their own guests over to dine at Castle Howard, and the Carlisles themselves held continuous house parties. The highlight of the season was undeniably Race Week in August, which combined the excitement of racing with the most glamorous ball of the northern year, held in the newly built Assembly Rooms. It was during Race Week that the dichotomy of York – its dark side, represented by the violence of the race track at Knavesmire, versus the superlative elegance displayed in the Assembly Rooms – was at its most obvious.

York, in the middle of the eighteenth century, was an exhilarating city. It had become the focal point of cultural life in the north, and a whole circle of literati and connoisseurs had made it their headquarters. Moreover, many of the nobility, attracted by the social life, built their own houses in the town, or nearby, so that they would not have to rely upon lodgings during the season. As a result of this influx of new wealth York developed into a major centre of the luxury trades, a magnet to skilled craftsmen from all over the country. Contemporary descriptions of the new buildings glowed with superlatives. Duncombe, for instance, which is attributed to William Wakefield, a disciple of Vanbrugh, was referred to as 'quite a Palace . . . The outside is in very grand Doric taste, rather heavy. The Hall is prodigious Grand, and in my opinion unexceptionably the finest Room that I ever saw.' Around the same time Colen Campbell built Ebberston, a miniature Palladian gem, which was designed as a '*garçonnière*' for one of the local MPs, William Thompson. But these buildings belonged in the domain of the rich. The true character of the city was a far cry from such gracious living.

York had little in common with Bath, that epitome of somnolent gentility, or with the other 'seasonal' towns; nor was the life of the city forced to revolve around Royal favour and political intrigue, as was so often the case in London. The rumbustious flavour of York originated from Knavesmire, the legendary racecourse with the additional attraction of a gallows, which could accommodate twenty criminals at a single session.

York had earned a reputation for violent revenge and ghoulish excess in the Middle Ages. The head of Richard, Duke of York, had been exhibited on the battlements of Micklegate Bar in 1460 – 'So that York may look upon the city of York'; and after the battle of Culloden, in 1746, the heads of prisoners who had supported the abortive Stuart rising were similarly impaled and left to rot in full view of the public.

The site of Knavesmire, on the edge of the town, was first used as a racecourse in 1751. The main meeting was scheduled for August – thus synchronizing neatly with the summer Assizes, and their inevitable crop of executions. It may be offensive to think of today, but it is a fact that until comparatively recently hangings were a popular spectacle. Execution day at York, in the eighteenth century, took on the tenor of a fiesta, attracting all the lowest and most vicious elements of the population. The hangings of 'Swift Nick' Nevison and Dick Turpin, two of the most infamous highwaymen of their day, drew enormous crowds at the time. Nevison was something of a local hero, debonair, handsome, almost a 'gentleman', whose daring and bravery captured the imagination of the people, and even earned a temporary reprieve from Charles II. Turpin, on the other hand, was a brutal man who tortured and raped his victims. A contemporary account describes him as being 'About five feet nine inches high, very much with the small-pox, his cheeks broad, his visage short'. All the same, thousands of spectators turned out to watch his execution. Dick Turpin played to the crowd at his hanging, determined to make the most of the occasion and go out in style. He bribed the warders to

John Jackson's portrait of Caroline, 5th Countess of Carlisle (1753–1824) with two of her grandchildren, Georgiana and Frederick

Portrait of Georgiana, 6th Countess of Carlisle (1783–1858), with two of her daughters, Caroline, later Lady Lascelles, and Harriet, later Duchess of Sutherland, by John Jackson

The 5th Earl of Carlisle with members of his family and household in Phoenix Park, Dublin, in 1781, by Francis Wheatley

Engraving showing the interior of the Grand Assembly Rooms in York, designed by Lord Burlington

Entertainment at York Races, an anonymous eighteenth-century watercolour

Thomas Gainsborough's portrait of Isabella Byron, second wife of the 4th Earl of Carlisle and great-aunt of the poet Byron

Nineteenth-century view of Castle Howard from the North Lake,
by Henry Barlow Carter

Nicholas Hawksmoor's initial drawings for the Mausoleum, showing alternative proposals for colonnade or arcade, c. 1729

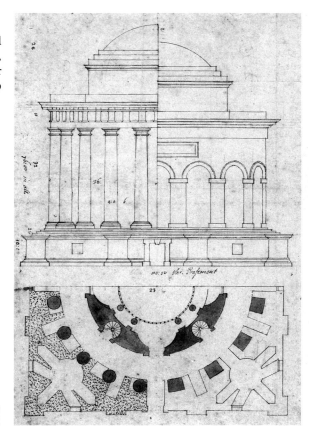

View of the Mausoleum in the grounds of Castle Howard

Charles Howard, 3rd Earl of Carlisle
(1669–1738), by William Aikman. Charles
Howard began work on the building of
Castle Howard in 1699

The three Howard sisters, daughters of the
3rd Earl, Ladies Elizabeth, Anne and Mary,
by Giovanni Antonio Pellegrini

South front view of Castle Howard, by William Marlow

Charles Howard, 1st Earl of Carlisle
(1629–85), by Sir Godfrey Kneller

Aerial view of Naworth Castle in Cumberland
– the original home of the Howards

The 5th Earl of Carlisle, with his youngest son Henry Howard, viewing a picture in the Long Gallery, by John Jackson

The 5th Earl of Carlisle with his lifelong friend George Selwyn, by Sir Joshua Reynolds

Lady Mary Howard (1823–92), youngest daughter of the 6th Earl of Carlisle, later Lady Taunton, by John Jackson

allow his friends to smuggle into the prison all the paraphernalia of conventional mourning – white caps, black ribbons, nosegays and oranges; paid five professional mourners ten shillings each to follow the cart on its way to Knavesmire; wore a brand new set of clothes on the day; and gave all his friends the traditional mourning presents – hat bands, gloves, and even a mourning ring, suitably inscribed. Turpin's courage carried this horrible charade through to the end; he waved and bowed to the crowd lining the route to the gallows, and chatted to the hangman while he adjusted the noose. The audience responded with 'a steady buzz of admiration'.

Cock-fighting, one of the nastiest sports ever invented, provided further opportunities for violence and gambling. John Stevens envisages the loathsome scene at these contests in his recent book *Knavesmire*:

... Cockpits, reeking of ale and resonating to the yells and curses of the blood-thirsty, were the scene of another sport. For York races drew some of the best 'stags' in the land – birds which hacked at their opponents in blind fury, spurs of silver or steel ripping into feather and flesh until nothing remained but the crow of triumph.

Bookmaking had not yet become an established trade, which meant that all betting, whether between noblemen or commoners, took place either on location or in the taverns. The York Tavern was the most popular venue, much frequented by the younger Howards and their friends. It was a rowdy place; when Lord Fitzwilliam spent a night there during Race Week with a party of friends their bill came to thirty-two pounds and fifteen shillings. They had drunk, between them, hock, gin, lemon and sugar, malt liquor, madeira, lemonade, Bristol water, brandy, claret, sherry, port, seltzer water, tea and coffee. An impressive list, and not untypical of a certain section of society. Stevens condenses the general atmosphere at Knavesmire as one of: 'Racing and hangings; gambling and hangings; cock-fighting and hangings – this was race week at York in the eighteenth century . . .'

It was to minimize the impact of this unsavoury crowd that the stewards, led by the Marquess of Rockingham, commissioned John Carr to build the first grandstand at Knavesmire in 1754. Before this the aristocracy had watched the races from carriages, perambulating around the middle of the arena in the wake of the action, and within easy hailing distance of the *hoi polloi*. Rockingham at the time was the undisputed 'King of the Turf' and a powerful factor in local politics. His principal estate marched with the boundaries of Castle Howard, and he belonged to the same Whig circle as Carlisle and Burlington. (Rockingham became one of the great Whig statesmen of the age, and was twice Prime Minister, in 1766 and again in 1782.) He was also a member of the virtuosi – and fanatical about racing. Rockingham bred his own racehorses, many of them legendary winners; the exploits of one of his horses, Gimcrack, inspired the foundation of one of the oldest racing clubs in the world, known as 'Ye Ancient Fraternitie of Ye Gimcracks'.

Rockingham's attempt to elevate the tone of Knavesmire was only partially successful. Although the new grandstand provided the desired segregation of the classes, nothing had yet been done about the view of the gallows. Executions were still being carried out next to the racecourse, accompanied by the usual audience of ghouls: not only did the victims often take several hours to die, in agony, but their ghastly corpses were left hanging from the gibbet for days, as a warning to potential malefactors. And all this went on in full view of the race-goers. It should also be remembered that at this period justice was an arbitrary business, and many of the condemned died protesting their innocence. A man of seventy-seven, for example, one George Fawcett, was executed for stealing four sheep from a common. His own story was – and there is no evidence to suggest that it was not the truth – that he had been asked by his adult sons to drive them off the land, and that he had no idea he was doing anything illegal. The whole gruesome scene at Knavesmire must have been enough, one would have thought, to throw any delicately nurtured young lady into a swoon. The bottle of sal volatile must have been as necessary an adjunct to racing at Knavesmire as binoculars. Anyway, by 1756, aristocratic sensibilities prevailed, and the mass hangings, at least, were

postponed until the day after the race meeting finished. According to
Stevens:

The final day of the 1756 race meeting at York was reported having been 'a
day offering excellent sport'. Entertainment continued the following day,
with Elijah Oaks dying 'very penitently' on Knavesmire for burglary.
Alongside him were David Evans, condemned for highway robbery and
horse-stealing, Richard Varley, another highway robber and John
Holsworth, who had broken into a house.

So much for the black side of York: on another level the city was
just as conspicuous for its brilliance. In 1730 the burghers of the town
decided that the success of the York season, and the wealth of the
customers which it attracted, deserved better facilities for entertainment than that which was already on offer. They asked Lord
Burlington to design a magnificent new set of Assembly Rooms, and
raised the necessary funds by public subscription. The 3rd Earl of
Carlisle was among the first to respond, albeit with the minimum
stake of £25, and a later guest list includes the 4th Earl, with all his
sisters and their husbands – Lady Lechmere and Sir Thomas Robinson,
Lord and Lady Irwin and Lady Mary Howard – Lord Burlington and
all his family, Sir Robert Walpole, the Coventrys and Fitzwilliams,
and Mr Lascelles, who later became the Earl of Harewood – in other
words, all the local celebrities. The foundation stone of the Assembly
Rooms was laid with suitable pomp and ceremony the following
spring, and the building was finished in time for the August Race
Week of 1732. It was a triumphant success, both architecturally and
socially, and remains one of the glories of York. According to the
Monthly Intelligencer, '... The Earl of Burlington gave a magnificent
Centre Lustre which, with twelve others, is to illuminate the Great
Room'; he also contributed a handsome fireplace. The whole of
society, including the Howards, turned out to christen the building
with an inaugural ball. The Countess of Stafford's description of the
event again reads like a contemporary Court Circular:

There was a vast deal of company this year at the races. Lord Burlington received great applause for the opening of the great room and I think really with justice, for 'tis certainly very fine performance. My Lady was also extremely liked for her easy civilities to every body. They brought all their plate and kept a constant table and indeed a very good one. The principal people at York besides the above-mentioned were, Duke of Rutland, Lord and Lady Faulkonbridge, Lord and Lady Widdrington, Lord Carlisle and all his daughters, Lord Malpas, Lord Lonsdale, Lord Mountcastle, Lord Irwin, all Lady Ramsden and Winn's family, General Churchell, Mr Conoly, Mr Bows and a vast many more fine men I have forgot . . .

The Assembly Rooms became the heart and focus of social life in York, a centre of the utmost elegance and decorum, but at the same time, in accordance with Burlington's creed, they were thoroughly functional. Rooms were set aside for gambling and dining, and every Monday night there was music and dancing. These Monday balls were again by subscription and were presided over by an elected 'Queen of the Assemblies'. The local aristocratic matrons took it in turns to perform this function and whoever was chosen held the power of veto over the guest list, thus ensuring that no undesirable elements crept in. *Georgian York*, which was written by a historian of York, R. Grundy Heape, in the 1930s, contains a fictional description of one of the balls, in which the author has imagined that he is himself one of the guests. If the prose is a shade flamboyant the atmosphere is authentic, and it certainly evokes an easy nostalgia for the glamour of the Assembly Rooms, and of that vanished world inhabited by the early Howards:

The dancers and gamblers are arriving, carriages are rolling up. Sedan chairs, escorted by servants bearing flambeaux, rapidly deposit their occupants within the pillared portico . . . The Round Room on the right is the gaming room. Here for hazard, quadrille, basset, faro or whist, assemble the sporting subscribers of the Assembly Rooms. No more fitting medium than the card-table existed for the display of lace cuffs and jewelled hands above the piles of gold.

Opposite the Round Room is the Refreshment Room, where tea and chocolate are served, and where, in the intervals of dancing with inimitable grace, the beaux hand glasses of Arrack, Mountain Wine and French Claret, Hearte cakes, and plates of Orange chips to fair ladies.

There is laughter and merry talking. The band is playing as I move back to the Great Hall where some of the young people make bold and dance the minuet. Above the Ball Room are windows through which people are looking down into this gaily lighted place, with the beautifully coloured figures dancing to the music below.

Among the throng of distinguished men and women are the Duke and Duchess of Ancaster and their Graces of Hamilton, near by the Marquis and Marchioness of Rockingham, the Countess of Northumberland and many other famous beauties . . .

What splendour! These are some of the four or five hundred subscribers whose costumes made a pageant of gorgeous colour, and whose voices and laughter mingled with the bird-like music of the flute, haut-bois and the viol de gamba, as they danced and gambled in the Assembly Rooms in Georgian York . . .

Later, the author goes on to imagine the guests' departure:

The lily-fingered ladies in their rich brocades and damask dresses, trimmed with gold and silver lace and coloured silks, are seating themselves, their jewels scattering strange fires in the light of the torches. The bearers are picking up their straps, and the gentlemen of the party walk on either side as they go out into the night . . .

The eighteenth century was certainly a time for extravagant dressing. At a ball given in the Assembly Rooms in honour of the Queen's birthday, for example, the Duchess of Leeds wore '. . . a crepe petticoat, richly embroidered with lilac and silver spangles, drawn up in festoons, with bunches of China-asters and white lilacs, green foil leaves, trimmed with silver fringe and tassels. The train was light green and silver gauze.' The same contemporary account continues: 'Lady Jane Long's dress was a white body and crepe train petticoat, adorned with bouquets of emery; a drapery of the same plant, interspersed with India weed, and silver crescents fastened with silver twist and gland [*sic*], a parterre of Indian weed round the bottom, with sprouts of emery, silver fringe and tassels.'

This was also the Age of the Dancing Master. When the Assembly Rooms first opened Edward Allen taught dancing at the the Sycamore Tree Inn. All the Howard girls went to his classes, where they were taught, in addition to the ubiquitous minuet and the gavotte, a number of marginally less stately country dances. In 1773 some of the favourites were 'The General', 'The Russian Dance', 'The Spaw Stage Chase', 'The Nabob', 'The News from Denmark' and 'Tristram Shandy', in deference to the novel, which had just been published and was an enormous popular success. Others were named after real people, such as 'Slingsby's Reel', 'Mrs Cartwright's Delight', 'Tringham's Fancy' and 'Count Struensee's Whim'.

The 4th Earl was made a Knight of the Garter in 1756 and died two years later. The young man who had seemed so indifferent to his inheritance in the early years of the century had, by the end of his life, proved one of Castle Howard's greatest benefactors. He had fulfilled every one of his father's ambitions: the mausoleum was finished and the West Wing nearly so; the garden had become one of the great delights of the estate; the house was furnished, and functioning in as splendid and extravagant a style as even the founder could have wished.

Castle Howard had become yet another symbol of aristocratic splendour, on a parity with Blenheim and Chatsworth as compulsory viewing on the cultural tour. The Countess of Oxford's description of Castle Howard, written in 1745, gives an idea of the way the rooms were arranged at the time – and a very vivid impression of their beauty:

. . . There is in the House 13 state rooms on the first floor, besides the Hall. The Hall is a fine room over which is a lofty Dome: that and the Saloon are both paved with freestone and black marble: there are two grand staircases on each side [of] the Hall, in which are several antique statues and bustos collected by the present Lord. The first room on the right hand of the Saloon is furnish'd with crimson damask and tapestry, and in the corners are antique marble bustos on terms of oriental agat. The Drawing Room is blue flower'd velvet; in this room is a very fine Cabinet highly ornamented with precious stones. The Bedchamber and Dressing Room beyond are furnish'd with yellow damask. The next room is at the end of the house on that side, and has a bow-window and 2 Cupolos. In this room is a fine octagon Table of Egyptian Granate with an inlaid border. There is a picture of his Lordship's 3 sisters. In the first room on the left hand of the Saloon the furniture is crimson, and in the Drawing room ... are several views of Venice by Canalitti lately put up there. There is also a Jewel Box of her Ladyship's richly inlaid and ornamented with stones. The Bedroom beyond is Green Damask and Tapestry of Chinese figures which is extremely pritty. The Dressing room and the room beyond it are both furnish'd with green. In every room on this floor there is some Tables of the finest Marble, Granate or Porphyry, and also very much ornamented with antique statues and bustos, particularly in the left hand blue velvet Drawing-room is a most beautifull statue of Minerva about 2 feet high, the head, feet and hands of jett and the drapery of transparent agat.

Up one pair of stairs over the Saloon is a large Anti-room in which are two very fine Tables of the black and white Arabian Granate, and 2 others of the yellow marble veined with red. There are four apartments on this floor consisting of a bedchamber and dressing room. Lord and Lady's own apartment is in the wing and newly fitted up ... Below stairs are a great quantity of Statues, Bustos, Table[s] & that are not yet disposed on. Din'd at the Inn by the House and in the afternoon return'd to York.

A rather more prosaic description of Castle Howard in the middle of the eighteenth century was written by Mrs Lybbe Powys, an indefatigable sightseer who kept a meticulous, and often critical, record of her impressions wherever she went. Mrs Powys visited Castle Howard in 1757, and, though she carps about the size of the original rooms, she is as enthusiastic as Lady Oxford about their contents:

... The House is of vast extent (340 ft) and makes a fine appearance at the distance, but I think the rooms in general too small, though in the wing now building there seems by the plan some fine apartments to be intended [she refers to the West Wing, designed by Sir Thomas Robinson, which was finished a year later] ... the furniture is magnificent, and there are many curiosities that my Lord brought over with him fifteen years since from Italy and other countries, such as pictures, busts, figures of oriental alabaster, and above thirty different sorts of Egyptian marbles, with other things too numerous to mention, as valuable as ornamental ...

The 4th Earl had inherited much of his father's business acumen: under his astute management a precarious hand-to-mouth balance sheet had been replaced by a steady increase of wealth, and the income from the estate had risen to approximately £20,000 a year. Unfortunately, however, he not only failed to settle the outstanding debts but incurred a great many new ones. By the time he died the estate was in debt to the tune of £60,000 – a situation which was to haunt the next generation for years to come.

Nevertheless, in the course of his tenure of Castle Howard, the 4th Earl had managed not only to gild and glorify the interior of the house, but to enlarge the estate by buying more land. During the 1750s he bought the villages of Terrington, Slingsby, and Bulmer. By the end of the nineteenth century the Carlisles had become one of the largest landowners in England, with some 80,000 acres, divided between Cumberland, Northumberland and Yorkshire.

In the course of only two generations, and little more than fifty years, the founder's dream had become a powerful and magnificent reality. By 1758, when the 4th Earl of Carlisle died, Castle Howard had become recognized as one of the most important buildings in private hands in the country. It has retained that status ever since.

5

'A Wide and Too Gay World'

Frederick Howard, 5th Earl of Carlisle, was probably the most glamorous of all the owners of Castle Howard – in his early years: in later life he was one of the most unpleasant. Frederick succeeded to the title, with its concomitant fortune, when he was only ten years old. It was a stupendous inheritance – and it went to his head. The 5th Earl launched himself upon a career of spectacular profligacy while still in his teens; by the time he came of age he had already become notorious throughout society as a libertine and a gambler, with extremely expensive tastes. By that time, too, he had already acquired a mountain of debts on his own account, over and above those he inherited from his father.

Many years later, when he was an old man in his seventies, he looked back on his dissolute youth, in his diary: 'It was my lot, not my good fortune, to be launched into a wide + too gay World at the Early age of 17 . . .' The diary goes on to remember the immorality of that world with the typical outrage of a reformed rake:

After the peace of 1763 France was opened to all our travelling youth, with all its refinements of elegant profligacy + no wonder these were very quickly imported + planted in this country . . . When I came into the World I found no Lady who might be said to move with any splendour in it, or to lead it, but had an avowed Lover, + no Husband cared what paths his Wife trod, provided he was unmolested in following his own . . . I can enumerate from memory, + limited to a period of a few years, 37 Ladies who presided over the Town who wd all have been affronted had you supposed there had been a grain of conjugal fidelity among them . . .

It is safe to assume that Carlisle was speaking from considerable personal experience.

The experience had begun at Eton, where the young Carlisle had become friends with Charles James Fox: it was a friendship which, though it lasted for the rest of their lives, was to have grave consequences and a devastating effect on the Howard fortunes. In 1767 the two young men set off on the Grand Tour, which they rapidly turned into a glorious spree, flirting, drinking and, above all, gambling their way through the capitals of Europe. Carlisle and Fox were an attractive pair, rich, grand, intelligent and charming – the epitome of privilege. Glowing with that special breed of arrogant confidence which is the hallmark of gilded youth, they were fêted wherever they went. The 5th Earl was elected a Knight of the Thistle and invested with the insignia of the Order of Turin by the King of Sardinia, both remarkable honours to be bestowed on a youth who had not even attained his majority. Over fifty years later Carlisle – by then a distinctly querulous patriarch – was thoroughly scathing in his reminiscences of all Grand Tours, and their effect on contemporary youth. On the subject of the young men's return from Italy, he wrote that:

. . . they affected languor + weak constitutions . . . they drank lemonade and ate macaroons, in short were perfect fops, only they were Italian fops. It was very laughable to see the clumsy copies of these in many – full of health, beef and ale . . . To these succeeded another race, equally perhaps conceited, but quite of a different character. The former affected to be able to do nothing, the latter everything. These danced well, rode well, were always in action . . . fox-hunted, were shooters, skaters, kept race horses, dressed with the most ruinous expense . . . This, I am sorry to confess, was not the reign of matrimonial felicity.

But these strictures are unfair, the jaundiced view of an old man regretting the wasted opportunities of his youth. And while it may have been true that some of the young noblemen learnt no more from the Grand Tour than how to show off, the majority found it an immensely rewarding experience. As for Fox and Carlisle, although they clearly embarked on the Grand Tour in a pretty frivolous spirit, and although their daily routine may appear to have been one long glittering party, both young men were far too intelligent to waste their time completely. Besides, they had both been brought up in households which put a high premium on education in general and the arts and politics in particular. For Carlisle the Grand Tour was a marvellous opportunity to explore European art and to clarify his own aesthetic values – as it had been for his father and grandfather before him. Again following the example of his forebears, Carlisle spent a comparative fortune on paintings and other *objets d'art* while he was in Europe, buying mainly Italian old masters, and shipped them back to Castle Howard.

The prices he paid for some of the paintings he bought seem unbelievably low by any standards, even contemporary ones. In Venice he bought a Titian, at auction, for one guinea – *A Mastiff Dog with Cats*. (Although both this painting, and another Titian which Carlisle bought subsequently from his friend Lord Cawdor, for £145, have been authenticated, it must be said that the young English noblemen doing the Grand Tour were regarded as fair game by Italian dealers, and were often sold fakes.) The accounts at Castle Howard include a bill for £175 15s., dated Rome 1768, which represents the purchase of, among other items, Giovanni Bellini's *Head of a Lady at her Toilet*, which is still on view at Castle Howard, and at least six other Italian old masters. Another receipt accounts for 229 'Sequins', spent on more 'pictures and statuary from Florence'. (Sequins, the local currency at the time, were gold coins, originally Venetian; 300 sequins had an approximate value of £135.) In Venice Carlisle bought Salvator Rosa's *Archita with a Mechanical Dove*, which today hangs in the Octagon at Castle Howard; in Rome two paintings after Guido Reni and Domenichino; and in Naples the *Portrait of a Lady*, after Parmigiano, which is also still in the Howard collection.

★

The 5th Earl returned to England in the summer of 1769, in time to celebrate his twenty-first birthday. The party was held at Naworth, a reminder that this medieval castle in Cumberland, the founthead of the Howard fortunes, could still take precedence over Castle Howard as the favourite venue for major occasions. 'A List of Gentlemen entertained at Naworth' for that week in June shows that it was a bachelor party with fifty-four male guests, accompanied by fifty-four servants. If it had been held at Castle Howard a hostess would have been required to chaperone Carlisle's sisters, local obligation would have demanded a far larger party and the whole affair would have become far too staid for the young Earl's liking.

The following year the 5th Earl moved to London and took his seat in the House of Lords, though it is clear that, at this time, his interest in politics was minimal. Carlisle and Fox, still inseparable and hell-bent on pleasure in all its forms, soon became famous for their wild behaviour – which, in fact, was not so very different, or very much worse, than that of innumerable rich young men on the town since time immemorial. There were constant parties, dangerous gambling, and plenty of casual love affairs, both with *demi-mondaines* and with girls of their own class – the Earl was considered to be particularly eligible since he was already in possession of his great inheritance, but both were in equal demand with ambitious mothers.

Carlisle and Fox became known as the two best-dressed men in town – and that was in an age which made a religion of fashion, when the mere business of getting dressed in the morning could take three hours. Men spent a fortune on their clothes, covered themselves with jewels, even on their shoes, wore amazingly elaborate wigs and changed the entire lot several times a day. Carlisle and Fox affected the style known as the Macaroni, quite the most ridiculous and extravagant of all eighteenth-century fashions. It was also the most exigeant, since three-inch-high heels and wigs a yard high made for dangerously precarious balance. This kind of outrageous dressing was, in fact, an eighteenth-century equivalent of punks or Teddy boys, probably no more than a statement of rebellion, motivated by a desire to shock their elders as much as to attract the opposite sex. And, of

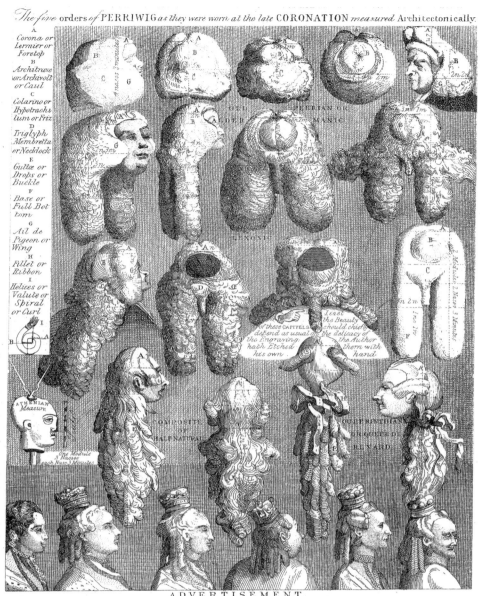

An advertisement showing a variety of wigs fashionable around 1760. In their youth the 5th Earl of Carlisle and Charles James Fox were nominated by the Gentleman's Magazine as 'the best dressed men of their times'.

course, the more their elders objected the worse they became. The *Gentleman's Magazine* described this period of the 5th Earl's life many years later in its obituary of him:

Carlisle . . . became one of the gayest noblemen of the capital. Possessing a small but elegant figure, in which symmetry was happily blended with agility and strength, he shone one of the meteors of fashion. Elegant in his dress and manners, with his green ribband across his vest, and a brilliant star sparkling at his side, he was considered one of the chief ornaments of the Court. At this period, his Lordship and Mr C Fox, though it will scarcely be believed, were considered as two of the best dressed men of their times.

The Carlisles' family house in Soho Square had been sold during the 5th Earl's minority to Theresa Cornelys, a former opera singer and courtesan, who turned it into an élitist house of entertainment. Fanny Burney, at the age of eighteen, was overwhelmed by '. . . the magnificence of the rooms, splendour of the illuminations and embellishments, and the brilliant appearance of the company'. And Horace Walpole wrote about her activities as a hostess:

This is a singular dame . . . Of late years she has presided over our diversions. Her taste and invention in pleasures and decorations are singular. She took Carlisle House in Soho Square, enlarged it and established assemblies and balls by subscription. At first they scandalized, but soon drew in both righteous and ungodly. She went on building and made her house a fairy palace, for balls, concerts and masquerades.

On 26 February 1770 the 5th Earl borrowed, or rented, the house back from Mrs Cornelys and gave a fabulous fancy dress ball.

The *Gentleman's Magazine*, not usually much given to reporting social trivia, devoted two whole columns to the event. The article gives an excellent – if somewhat sycophantic – impression of eighteenth-century entertaining at the grandest and most extravagant level:

. . . the house was illuminated in the most splendid and picturesque masquerade manner imaginable with between three and four *thousand* wax lights. About one hundred musicians were dispersed in various parts . . .

There were approximately 800 guests and the report lists 'the principal masques'. The Duke of Buccleuch began the evening 'in the figure of Nobody . . . and after some time in that character withdrew and appeared in a most elegant dress of a Hungarian Hussar. The figure of Somebody; his companion, Colonel Fitzroy also afterwards appeared in another character – Cherokee Chief.' The Dukes of Grafton and Bedford, Lords Camden and Beaulieu, and 'most of the foreign ministers', who were clearly averse to fancy dress, contented themselves with wearing Dominos. These were hooded cloaks, worn with masks, much in fashion at the time, and usually made of some brightly coloured and expensive material. They would be pressed into service not only at private parties, but as flirtatious disguise, used by both men and women in such public places as the Opera and Vauxhall Gardens.

As always, the two great passions of the Whig aristocracy, politics and gambling, received their due representation among the costumes. One guest came as 'a Political Bedlamite, run mad for Wilkes and Liberty; – he was covered with an tattered blanket, with No 45 on his shoulder, a wisp of straw in his hand, and his continual cry was "Wilkes and Liberty"'. The *Gentleman's Magazine* adds that 'this masque occasioned much mirth'. Captain Coxe was the 'Gamester, with cards sewed all over his cloath, and a pack of cards in his hands, which he was continually shuffling, and offering to the company to play with him'. Among the ladies one is reported as 'almost sinking under the weight of pearls and beads', and others as 'uncommonly rich in diamonds' . . . Mr Garrick came as a Druid; the Duchess of Bolton as a Quaker – 'a very diverting figure, and divertingly sustained'; Lady Augusta Stewart as a vestal virgin; Miss Monckton as an Indian sultana, 'lovely in spite of her colour' and Lady Pomfret as a Greek sultana – with no qualifying crack about her complexion.

One gentleman caused a scandal at the ball by appearing as Adam: '. . . the unavoidable indelicacy of the dress (flesh coloured silk with an apron of fig leaves worked in it, fitting the body with the utmost nicety) rendered it the contempt of the company; the masque was universally shunned, and the party bore it all with great composure'.

A distinctly hypocritical, and almost certainly untrue, comment considering the bawdiness of the period. However, it appears that he was 'said to be a nobleman of great consequence, and that he did it for a wager', which, of course, made such behaviour quite understandable, even in the eyes of the magazine's gossip writer.

The host himself, Lord Carlisle, came as 'A Running Footman; the prettiest imagined dress at the ball; and showed the universal opinion of the wearer's superior taste of any kind has its foundation in truth'.

It was at this ball that Frederick proposed to Lady Margaret Caroline Leveson-Gower, daughter of the first Marquess of Stafford, and the following month they were married. Once again it was an alliance between two great Whig families, but it also appears that his taste for philandering was over, and that it was a marriage of love as much as convenience. A year after they were married, when she was pregnant with their first child, he wrote to his wife from Paris:

A thousand thanks, my dearest Caroline, for your two delightful letters. As you know I love you, you will know how happy I must be to hear you grow better every day + that you take care of yourself. My absence from you tells me how terrible it is to live without you + every woman that I see how much more charming, modest + beautiful you are than the whole nation of these painted devils. So you see a little travelling does me no harm.

The couple went on to have six more children, in all four sons and three daughters; and the marriage seems to have remained one of the more harmonious unions of that faithless age.

In spite of his marriage, however, the Earl continued his Rake's Progress round the gaming tables of London for the next few years. He was ably assisted in this particular vice not only by Fox, but by George Selwyn, a much more complicated character. Selwyn, though nearly thirty years older than the Earl, became one of his greatest friends and a very frequent guest at Castle Howard. One of the famous 'wits', a favourite at Court, and firmly entrenched as a leader of society, Selwyn was a scintillating companion for the young Earl –

but a dangerous one. He was a clever and cultivated man, but he was also a rake with a distinctly dubious reputation. For a start, Selwyn was an active member of the legendary Hellfire Club.

This institution had been founded by another mutual friend, Sir Francis Dashwood, in the 1750s, and it became a national scandal. The membership was composed of a group of aristocrats who delighted in every conceivable kind of depravity and held secret sexual orgies, laced with Satanic rituals. The meetings were held at Medmenham Abbey, some five miles from Dashwood's estate at West Wycombe, and an easy drive from London. It is thought that a number of man-made caverns within the boundaries of Dashwood's property itself were also, on occasion, pressed into the devil's service – they have been known locally as the 'Hellfire Caves' since the relevant period and remain a tourist attraction to this day.

There is absolutely no evidence that the Earl of Carlisle ever associated with Selwyn on this level, or that he was ever a member of the Hellfire Club. Such an institution would not have appealed to the fastidious side of his character. Carlisle, unlike Selwyn, was at heart a man of principle and religious conviction; even the wildest escapades of his salad days were conducted with honour and style. Thus, although Selwyn was so much older than the Earl, and a most persuasive and dominant personality, Carlisle was never in danger of succumbing to his particular brand of hedonism; in fact the reverse became true as their friendship progressed. Selwyn himself attests to the Earl's moral rectitude and, as the years went by, tried in vain to emulate the younger man.

Selwyn's letters to Carlisle span three decades and show that he was devoted to the whole Howard family:

. . . Lady Carlisle's rheumatism concerned me, but Lady G[ower] assures me it was a trifle. Gilbert calls the children in his letter rosy, which is an epithet I like for them; it is a sure indication of their health. I was pleased also with another expression which I met with the other day. Lord Northington brought me home two nights in his coach, and in one of them the conversation turned upon you. He said there was '. . . *nobody had a better idea of what a gentleman should be than Carlisle*; that you was so throughout'. There is a singularity and frankness in some people's manner of delivering their sentiments, by which they receive great advantage. You remember Sir R Payne's way of describing you, which was still more odd; he said that *if anybody looked through the keyhole at any time to see how you behaved when you were alone, that he was sure there would be no more impropriety in it than if you had a hundred eyes upon you.* I don't like commending you myself, but I like to hear others do so, and especially when they speak about what they think, and when what they think has the air of *vérité* in it . . .

This letter was written to Carlisle at Castle Howard in 1775, when the Earl was in the early throes of happily married life, and well on the road to reform; it is easy to detect a note of envy in the old reprobate's voice.

Selwyn's letters to Carlisle illuminate their mutual world, its glamour and its power, with all the authority of inside knowledge. They are a fund of gossip, both political and social, as well as a testament to contemporary values. They are one of the best original sources of the period and as such are worth quoting at length.

Although Selwyn at this time (1775) was approaching sixty he was still a dedicated socialite, tottering on from one party to another even when feeling exhausted. All the people mentioned in the following letter are, of course, not only friends of Carlisle's but leading members of the Whig party:

Lord Stanley's balls and suppers are constant . . . I dine today at Harry St John's and tomorrow at Eden's; and on Monday all the St John's in the world, old and young, dine here . . . Mrs Daamer had a supper last night . . . Lady Betty and Lady Julia stayed supper at Lady Sefton's, and I should have been the fourth, but I wanted to go home and get into bed. I was *fort abatu*, to tell you the truth.

Nevertheless, the following week the pace is the same:

Last night and the night before I supped at Lady Betty Stanley's. Their suppers are magnificent, but their hours are abominably late; however, they do not discourage my Lord of Worcester from staying them out. We are

very merry, all of us, and I think Mrs North the merriest of us all. At 2 this
morning, the Bishop and I were almost left alone; the rest of the company
were in their domino's and going to the Masquerade ... I have been with
Mie Mie [his daughter] at Gainsborough's, to finish her picture ... Lady
Holland has been really very ill. Her fever is gone, but she has a cough, and a
hectic look, which I do not like.

In another letter there is a bizarre glimpse of the mourning customs
appropriate to gambling:

The place of Nickster, which is in the Devil's gift, and vacated by John Scott
is not disposed of ... We go into mourning on Thursday. The waiters are to
have *crèpes* around their arms, and the dice are to be black and the spots
white during the time of wearing weepers, and the dice-box muffled.

Proposed changes within the Government were discussed openly at
dinner parties, and, indeed, virtually decided in the course of general
conversation at table:

Sir G[eorge] has been telling me today, that Lord Stormont is coming from
France, and is to have Lord March's place ... This must produce in all
probability other removes.

In another letter Selwyn describes the previous evening's session in
the House – 'there was rather too much flummery about Lord North
and that was all', and continues with news of the most recent Cabinet
appointments:

Lord Chewton goes with Lord Cornwallis to America and I believe they set
out this week ... Lord G Sackville seems in very great spirits – is quite
persuaded that all this will end after the first campaign, and that he himself,
as I take for granted, shall establish his reputation as a Minister by it.

The great scandal of the winter of 1775 was the Duchess of
Kingston's trial for bigamy. The case became a popular charade,
reported in detail by the daily press and attracting crowds from all
over the country. In fact the whole disgraceful business was a splendid
example of eighteenth-century hypocrisy, since even adultery was still
technically a criminal offence. (The law was said to be needed as a

safeguard against the potential consequences of adultery – for example, questions of dynastic precedence and disputed inheritance. Before the Married Women's Act of 1882, women, whether married or single, had little or no control over their own wealth.) Nevertheless, if the lady had been content to remain an accredited mistress the case would never have been brought to court: infidelity was rampant throughout society at the time, and adultery an accepted fact of married life – as Carlisle himself attested in the diary previously quoted. However, a modicum of decent pretence was considered the basic principle of survival in society – the Duchess had not only flouted convention for years by the blatant conduct of her numerous affairs, but appears to have thought she could even get away with bigamy.

Selwyn, who seems to be almost gloating over the Duchess's fall, described the excitement the case was causing in a series of letters to Carlisle. The interesting point about these letters is that Selwyn takes it for granted that Carlisle wants to hear every detail, and will want to journey down from Yorkshire just to attend the trial:

... I wish that you would send me some doe venison for Woodcock and Forsyth, and reserve a couple of tickets for people of that sort for the Duchess of Kingston's trial . . . There is hardly a crime upon earth for which she may not be tried; and when this abyss of guilt comes to be plumbed, what they will find nobody can say. There is forgery and perjuries without end; and a more complete rogue, fool, and bitch I take for granted cannot be found in history than are represented by the three *dramatis personae*.

The following week Selwyn writes again to Carlisle, saying that the Duchess is malingering, in an attempt to postpone the trial. He thinks that the villains of the piece, the Perreaus, will be hanged and goes on to sum up the scandal:

The D[uchess] of K[ingston] will afford conversation for two months, a great show for two days, and a trial for the astonishment of many years . . . You will be here for the Trial, I take for granted. It will be altogether the most extraordinary one that ever happened in this or I believe any other country. It is a cursed, foul pool which they are going to stir up, and how many rats, cats and dogs, with other nuisances, will be seen floating at the top, nobody can tell. It will be as much a trial of the E[arl] of B[ristol] as of her, and in point of infamy, the issue of it will be the same, and the poor defunct Duke stand upon record as the completest *coglione* of his time . . .

Gambling, among the 5th Earl's generation, was endemic. As Selwyn's letters show, huge sums were involved, often with disastrous consequences: '. . . Lady Harriot and Foley & arrived yesterday. Old Foley pays another £70,000 of debt . . . Lady C Edwin is dying, and her house near Putney will in all probability be disposed of . . .' (presumably because of her gambling debts). And again, in 1775: '. . . It is now near 5 o'clock, I must go to dress for Lord Edward [Bentinck]'s dinner . . . the Duke of Portland pays his debts, to the last *obole*, as Lord E[dward] has told me, and they amount to £27,000; and what is as extraordinary he pays his own, which amount, I suppose, to an enormous sum.'

Faro was the preferred game for really serious gambling, but whist, loo, and piquette were all popular. One or two addicts started their own faro bank at home, notably the Duchess of Devonshire, whose daughter Georgiana – pronounced 'Georg*ay*na' in those circles – was to marry Carlisle's heir. The Duchess, incidentally, was one of the most legendary gamblers of her day, even by the standards of her friends; her whole life was haunted by vast, unpaid gaming debts, which the Duke cavilled at settling. In another letter to Carlisle, also written in 1775, Selwyn reported a new gambling craze:

. . . the game of Commerce. Lady Betty has taken to this game, and she makes all the world, *bon gré, mal gré*, play at it till five o'clock in the morning. I live there almost; what with Balls . . . Tessier, commerce, Supper and Quinze, I am never out of the house. They have invited me to go to the Oaks, this Christmas, but if Castle Howard is too far, the Oaks, I assure you will be much further . . .

Gambling debts acquired a spurious quality of sanctity in the eighteenth century. They were regarded as debts of honour upon which no gentleman could possibly renege: tradesmen's bills, on the other hand, were often left unpaid for years, and even the servants' wages were paid many months in arrears. Credit was a strictly aristocratic privilege. Moreover, society's whole attitude to money was quite different from that which applies today. The aristocracy were so immensely rich that they took their wealth for granted and simply did not bother about money for most of the time. Their estates were so large, and their incomes so secure, that it was easy to believe the supply was everlasting. And if there was a financial hiccup – *tant pis*, there was plenty to sell. For that tiny percentage of the population the concept of poverty did not exist. It was this attitude, too – that money would always be available, if not today, certainly tomorrow – which enabled the aristocracy to borrow so freely from each other without any of the guilt and embarrassment which would be felt about a similar transaction today. The 5th Earl of Carlisle, for example, when he came of age, lent huge sums to his friends, almost without a second thought. His most serious act of misguided loyalty was to stand surety for Charles James Fox's gambling debts. It was this general approach to money, taken in conjunction with his own outstanding debts, which precipitated a serious financial crisis for the Howards in 1775.

In that year Carlisle's total debts stood at approximately £300,000 – an impressive achievement even for such a spendthrift as the 5th Earl. To understand just how he managed to accumulate such debts it is necessary to take into account several different factors, none of which would have mattered too much on their own, but which added together proved more than the estate could bear.

In the first place, the outstanding debts of his father, already referred to and amounting to £60,000, still hung over the estate. Unfortunately – but typically – the new Earl made no attempt to pay these off, but simply ignored their existence for years. As a result of compound interest, plus a number of previously hidden bills which came to light only after the 4th Earl's death, the figure for inherited debts alone had risen to £100,000 by 1775.

Moreover, the young Earl, exhilarated by the size of his inheritance, immediately began to celebrate it – in mammoth style. He embarked on a spectacular and continuous spending spree, and if not all the money was wasted a great deal of it was: on the credit side he instigated a number of improvements at Castle Howard and added to the art collection, but far larger sums of money were frittered away on gambling, racing, parties and loans to friends which would never be repaid. Carlisle was as renowned for his generosity as he was for his extravagant and lavish lifestyle. The result of this insouciant attitude to money was, of course, that he galloped further and further into debt, almost without noticing. By 1775 the Earl's personal debts alone had reached the devastating total of £200,000 and even he saw the gravity of the situation. Realizing that he was constitutionally incapable of economy if left to himself, the Earl showed great determination and character: with no further attempt to procrastinate he voluntarily relinquished control of the estate and put the whole of his property in trust. The three trustees, chosen from among his friends and relations, retained absolute control of the income for an unspecified length of time. Carlisle himself was rusticated to Castle Howard for a couple of years, and allotted an allowance of £4,000 a year by the trustees – a fraction of his previous annual expenditure. Spending at Castle Howard was cut back dramatically (they sacked the French cook, for example), and all improvements to the estate were cut back or stopped entirely, with one important exception – the beautiful new stable block. These buildings, designed by John Carr, had been started the previous year, and were deemed essential to complete since the old stables were no longer safe. The trustees applied the residue of income from the estate towards paying off the enormous debts.

The trust lasted for eleven years, until 1786. By the time it was wound up the majority, at least, of the debts had been paid, either out of income or by the highly regrettable sale of land. But even more to the point, the 5th Earl had given up gambling. In the course of his thirties he had begun to take a more serious view of life, and had learnt to accept responsibility for his inheritance. He was married to a pious and gentle lady, and was the father of a growing family. It was time to settle down.

As early as 1777 Carlisle had realized that, thanks to the constraint on his income imposed by the trust, he needed a job. The 1770s were an exciting time in politics, above all because they were the years of the American War of Independence – though at that time it was dignified by no such name. After some months of lobbying Carlisle was appointed treasurer of the Royal Household and a member of the Privy Council, and the following year Lord North sent him to America, at the head of a commission whose mandate was to negotiate peace terms with the rebels. The mission was doomed to failure from the start, since the rebels refused even to begin negotiations unless the Crown first recognized their Independence – a concept which was simply not on the Commissioner's agenda, and, indeed, seemed quite out of the question at the time. During the initial stages General Lafayette – the future hero of the French Revolution – took such offence at the phrasing of one of the Commission's proclamations that he challenged Carlisle, as its leader, to a duel. The Earl demonstrated his new-found sobriety by declining to fight; he quite properly informed Lafayette that his words on Government policy were not a matter to be questioned by an individual, and that he considered himself responsible for his views and conduct to his King and his country alone. Thanks to his restraint on this occasion, and to the general good sense and ability which he displayed in America, Carlisle came out of the whole débâcle rather well – certainly better than his reputation as a fop and hedonist had led anyone to expect. (Horace Walpole, who, like the rest of the Government, had foreseen that the Commission would be abortive, had snidely remarked that Carlisle was 'very fit to make a treaty that will not be made'.)

Carlisle had proved his worth to the Prime Minister, Lord North, and over the next few years was given a number of minor posts, including the traditional Howard sinecure of Lord-Lieutenant of the East Riding of Yorkshire. Three years after the American fiasco Carlisle was given another daunting assignment, the job of governing Ireland. By Christmas 1780 the Earl and his family were installed in Dublin, and Carlisle, as Lord-Lieutenant, had begun to realize the extent of the Irish problem.

Carlisle was convinced right away that it was impossible to maintain the existing political regime. In 1782 he wrote:

It is beyond doubt that the practicability of governing Ireland by English laws is become utterly visionary. It is with me equally beyond a doubt that Ireland may be well and happily governed by its own laws.

Already the seeds of the movement towards Home Rule for Ireland were in the air, that issue which was to cause such dissension in the next century, and which was to play such an important part in the destiny of the Carlisle family.

Despite the inherent difficulties of the situation, Carlisle was a success in Ireland and popular with the Irish people. When he was dismissed from office two years later, owing to a change in government, the Irish House of Commons passed a hearty vote of thanks to him 'for the wisdom and prudence of his administration, and for his uniform and unremitted attention to promote the welfare of this kingdom'. The 5th Earl was, after all, a man of great charm.

Carlisle's political career, however, like his grandfather's before him, was cut off in its prime. In the spring of 1783 he was made Lord Privy Seal in the newly formed Coalition ministry, but this proved to be his last major appointment. By the end of the same year William Pitt had succeeded to power, and the long reign of the Whigs was over. Nevertheless Carlisle had no intention of allowing himself to sink into obscurity, and became an active and articulate member of the Opposition. When George III first began to be suspected of madness, the 5th Earl played an important part in the discussions over the Regency, coming out strongly against the restrictions imposed on the heir apparent – 'when it came before the House of Peers, on December 23rd, 1788, his Lordship in a brief but elegant speech, asserted the claims of the Prince of Wales'. Carlisle, in company with most of his friends and the Whig party as a whole, had opted for the Prince's camp from the start of the trouble between the heir to the throne and the King. The Prince, in fact, became a personal friend of Carlisle's, and spent a summer weekend at Castle Howard in 1789. Pitt and his party, on the other hand, thoroughly disapproved of the

Prince, and were equally outspoken in their support of the King. The Prime Minister believed that George III's spasmodic madness was, at least at the start of his illness, grossly exaggerated by the Prince's party, from motives of spite and expedience. Popular opinion at the time was inclined to agree with Pitt – and so does posterity.

At this juncture it is relevant to glance at the general position of British politics during the eighteenth century, and to emphasize the difference between a contemporary politician and his modern counterpart. Political policy at the time still hinged on the shifting balance of power between Crown and Parliament. The Whigs, brilliantly championed by Charles James Fox, accepted the principle of the royal prerogative but had increasingly leaned towards a liberal interpretation of the law; the Tory party, on the other hand, including the young William Pitt, favoured retaining a considerable role in government for the Crown. This clash of ideologies was brought to a head in 1783, by George III.

The King had been brought up to mistrust and dislike the Whigs and all they stood for. He had resented their domination of Parliament since the death of Queen Anne and, in 1783, he decided to act. At that time, there was, and had been for many years, an elected Whig majority in the House of Commons; nevertheless, that December, the King exercised his royal prerogative and dismissed *all* the incumbent ministers. (A parallel, today, would be if the Queen presumed to make the leader of the Labour Party Prime Minister during an elected Conservative Government – although, in 1783, the political parties were the other way round.) Naturally enough under these circumstances none of the senior statesmen of either party were prepared to form a new Government – and William Pitt slipped into the vacuum. (Pitt thus achieved the incredible feat of becoming Prime Minister at the age of only twenty-four more or less by default – no one else wanted the job.)

Pitt erupted on to the political scene bursting with all the energy and zeal of his youth. His enthusiasm for work, his whole attitude, in fact, towards Parliament and the duties of a politician, was alien to his Whig predecessors. And, politics aside, it caused a mini-revolution in

A view of the House of Commons in 1742. The Howards were one of the leading Whig families throughout the eighteenth century.

a most unexpected quarter – London society. The hours he kept in the House wreaked havoc on dinner parties and Pitt became the absolute bane of political hostesses, Whig and Tory alike. The lengthy sessions the Prime Minister imposed upon the members meant that they were always late for dinner.

Politics, before Pitt arrived, had always been regarded as a leisurely sideline by the majority of Members, at least as far as the rank and file were concerned. A seat in the House was certainly not regarded as a full-time profession, nor as a way of life in itself. Attendance in both the Commons and the Lords was a duty, concomitant with a certain social status and only one of the many obligations incumbent upon all great landlords. Politics, prior to Pitt, had taken up no more than a fraction of the Members' day; they were accustomed to spend the rest of their time in the pursuit of pleasure and culture, or on the management of their private affairs.

For generations the House of Commons had sat for no more than two hours a day, from ten until twelve in the morning, and politicians were accustomed to go straight home afterwards. This meant that the highlight of the day, an elaborate dinner, lasting three or four hours with innumerable courses, could be served at two, or at the latest three, o'clock. (Lunch, as we know it today, would therefore have been irrelevant; it did not, in fact, exist until the nineteenth century, when it was called a 'nuncheon' and consisted of a light collation of cold meats and fruit.) Many of the great political hostesses kept open house in London while Parliament was in session; Lady Holland, at Holland House in Kensington, for example, often had no idea who would be coming to dinner, or how many guests to expect, until they actually arrived. Catering must have been a nightmare, and the waste of food, even allowing for the servants' consumption of the left-overs, appalling. At one period, the entire Whig Cabinet made a practice of dining daily at Holland House. They walked across from the Commons as soon as the session ended and continued their political discussions at table – which meant that the ladies were able to enter the argument. Proposed changes in the Cabinet, and even the most critical Government decisions, were discussed quite openly at

The new Vauxhall pleasure gardens were a popular summer attraction at the end of the eighteenth century. Dances, many of them masquerades, were held in the open air.

dinner parties. Eighteenth-century women may not have had the vote but, nevertheless, they could, and did, exert a formidable influence on contemporary politics.

These great dinner parties were one of the most splendid features of eighteenth-century life and it was intolerable that Parliamentary business should interfere with them. Moreover, after dinner the party might want to go on to the theatre, or the new Italian opera which was having such a success, and which started at 7.00 – impossible if people were still at table. There was often a ball or a masquerade to attend later in the evening; during the summer it had become fashionable to cross the river and listen to the band in the new pleasure gardens at Vauxhall, where people danced in the open air under flickering lights hanging from the trees. And, finally, at some time in the evening there would be a late supper, often as copious and elegant as the earlier dinner. All these pleasures were put in jeopardy by Pitt's outrageous hours. And while, of course, many of the men spent their evenings a great deal less graciously in their clubs, gambling and drinking, the point was that, however politicians chose to spend their time, there was plenty of it to spare from physical attendance in the House.

Not even Pitt could seriously impair eighteenth-century frivolity, but he could, and did, change the eating patterns of the upper classes for all time. The House, under his leadership, carried on sitting well into the afternoon – thus forcing the dinner hour back to 5.00, or 6.00, and eventually, even later. All through the late 1780s and 1790s irritated wives waited impatiently for Pitt to finish his speech and liberate their men so that the real business of the day could begin. In effect, the whole structure of the social schedule was thrown out of sync by Pitt's passion for work; dinner began to finish so late in the evening that there was hardly any time left for extra-political pursuits. Politics threatened to become a full-time career, the serious commitment that they should be, and that they are today. All the same, the precedent set by Pitt is partly responsible for the terrible hours demanded of politicians in the twentieth century.

The 5th Earl, like his grandfather, dabbled in writing all his life. Though most of his work was privately printed, it was widely circulated and achieved a considerable reputation among the cognoscenti. *The Father's Revenge*, a tragedy in verse, written when Carlisle was in his thirties, was highly praised by both Johnson and Walpole. Johnson wrote that: 'of the sentiments I remember not one that I wished omitted . . . with the characters, either as conceived or preserved, I have no fault to find'. And Walpole, writing about the same play to the Countess of Ossory in 1783, said: 'it has great merit; the language and imagery are beautiful, and the two capital scenes are very fine'. Others were equally fulsome in their praise. Anna Seward, the authoress, said of Carlisle's play *The Stepmother*: 'It gratifies me to see this Tragedy written in the Shakespearean school, as to style, and in the intermixture of wit and humour in the dialogue, and of the grotesque with the elevated, as to character . . .'

The full flavour of these plays, one of high melodrama and extravagant emotion, is encapsulated in the following extract from Carlisle's obituary in the *Gentleman's Magazine*:

In 1783 appeared 'The Father's Revenge, a Tragedy, and other Poems' . . . This tragedy is founded on an incident so interwoven with our passions, and followed by a punishment so disproportionate to the offence, that human nature shudders at the catastrophe. The scenery, consisting of palaces, gothic chapels, & with a view of Mount Vesuvius in the back ground, is grand, suitable to the occasion, and calculated to inspire awe; while the dramatic characters are formed to keep up the interest and prepare the mind for some important event.

The Stepfather, another tragedy in five acts, appeared in 1800, and, like the rest of Carlisle's work, was privately printed, bound in a handsome edition, and 'circulated by the noble author among his friends'. Comparing the two plays, the magazine said that:

The plot of this [*The Stepfather*] is less involved than that of the former [*The Father's Revenge*]; but the catastrophe is equally shocking. In the one we behold a parent presenting the fresh torn heart from the bosom of her lover to the agonized sight of a distracted daughter. In the other we find a father and son, instigated by a cruel and revengeful woman, inflicting mutual death. In both cases the scene, perhaps, is too afflicting for representation.

The final tribute to the 5th Earl's literary achievement could also serve as his epitaph. Sydney Smith wrote to Carlisle in 1819, when the Earl was already in his seventies:

The Pursuits of an English Nobleman should be Politics, Elegant Literature and Agriculture, and your three volumes are surely a proof of time wisely and gracefully employed – and time, to men whom Fortune has raised above the necessity of occupying themselves, is often the greatest of human evils. I read several of your smaller poems last night – and was extremely pleased with that written upon a Sick Bed which I think fine and affecting . . .

6

'The Halcyon Years – 1794 to 1825'

Baulked of political advancement by the defeat of his party, the 5th Earl turned his attention once again to Castle Howard. When the trust came to an end, in 1786, Carlisle was still only thirty-eight, at the height of his intellectual and physical power. Thanks to the diligence of the trustees and the years of economy, the financial situation was under control once more – or at least the 5th Earl considered it was. Financial prosperity was an attitude of mind, not fact, to all the Earls of Carlisle in the eighteenth century. The estate accounts never bore much relation to reality, and expenditure always exceeded income. Accounting was a balancing act, a matter of juggling according to the size and relative urgency of the debts. And, as has already been said, the 5th Earl was notoriously feckless about money, even by the standards of his wealthy contemporaries. Despite the fact that his income *trebled* during his lifetime, the outstanding charges on the estate at the time of his death came to more than £230,000, and he left personal debts of £156,000. As a young man the 5th Earl had proved his talent for expensive living, and in later life he saw no reason to modify his standards. In the 1790s Carlisle felt free, once again, to embark on a glorious spending spree – but this time round his extravagance was almost justifiable, and certainly constructive. The Earl had in mind a number of exciting new projects, almost all of which turned out well. These were the halcyon years for Castle Howard, busy, creative and prosperous.

Between 1794 and 1825 an enormous amount of work was carried out, encompassing every aspect of the estate. Carlisle's improvements included converting the dining-room into the present chapel, completing the Long Gallery, laying the foundations of the North Lake, building a brand new 'model farm', and installing new hothouses in the gardens. He revolutionized the efficiency of the estate by a policy of enclosures and agricultural reform; he inaugurated a massive planting programme in the park; and he launched the botanical tradition which was to bring such renown to the Castle Howard gardeners.

Whenever he had had any spare cash, the 5th Earl had continued to build up the family art collection. The 1790s were a particularly profitable period: in 1798 he bought five superb oil paintings at Christie's in London, for a grand total of £203 14s. The relevant account, dated 15 May 1796, lists the pictures – one Hogarth, £21; two Zoffanys at £38 each; and two Van Dyck portraits, one of Lord Herbert and the other of the Elector Palatine, which together cost £105. Thanks to the recent Revolution many of the French aristocracy were in serious financial trouble, a factor which enabled the 5th Earl, in 1798, to make the best investment in art that any member of the family has ever made: he joined forces with the Duke of Bridgewater and Lord Stafford to purchase part of the Duke of Orléans's fabulous collection. This deal made the Carlisles' own collection one of the most important in England. Among the paintings purchased by the 5th Earl which still hang in the house are Bassano's *Portrait of an Old Woman*, probably the artist's mother; a delightful self-portrait by Carracci; and a painting titled *The Dukes of Ferrara*, which was bought by Carlisle as a Tintoretto, re-ascribed as a Parmigiano, and is now thought to be by Bedoli. (Eighteenth-century collectors were far from infallible art critics.) At the same time as buying all these paintings, and many other *objets d'art*, Carlisle redecorated many of the rooms at Castle Howard and modernized the domestic offices. Much of the lovely furniture in the house was also bought by the 5th Earl, often specially commissioned for a particular room or gallery.

At various times during this period, too, Castle Howard boasted its own pack of hounds, the 'Castle Howard Hunt'; its own military force, the 'Castle Howard Riflemen'; and its own charitable insurance scheme, the 'Castle Howard Friendly Society'. The 6th Earl of

Carlisle said of his father's regime at Castle Howard that though it was 'not perhaps conducted in the most oeconomical manner, it tended to the employment and satisfaction of a considerable number of persons'. This was an understatement – on both counts. Opulence and philanthropy mixed happily in the 5th Earl's day.

In 1796 the 5th Earl founded the first Friendly Society at Castle Howard. 'Its sole object' according to the printed rules, was 'The relief of the poor, [those] labouring under the affliction of poverty, or any other family misfortune'. It must be said, however, that the Friendly Societies, though essentially motivated by philanthropy, were almost equally useful to the landed classes. Of course motives are notoriously hard to judge, and often mixed, but the fact remains that the Friendly Societies could also be used as a discreet means of bribing tenants and labourers, both to vote in the required direction and to abstain from lawless behaviour. During the troubled war years of the 1790s and 1800s crime had been on the increase all over the countryside and a criminal conviction meant automatic disqualification from the Friendly Society – which proved to be quite a deterrent at Castle Howard.

In any case, the Friendly Societies were, as it turned out, of immense benefit to the community as a whole, and to the poorest strata of society in particular. They amounted to an early form of social security, based on the concept of self-help and paid for by regular contributions. And they provided a safety net in times of trouble which was, at last, no longer dependent on the whims of charity but accepted as a legal right. The cost of membership was not exorbitant for those in work, one shilling per month per family, and the benefits paid were substantial by contemporary economic standards: the Castle Howard society paid eight shillings per week sick pay, funeral expenses and minimal old age pensions. Membership was confined to those who lived on the Castle Howard estates and there was both a minimum and a maximum age limit for joining – fifteen and fifty respectively, though the latter maximum age limit was lowered to thirty-five after a few years, presumably in an attempt to control numbers.

The Castle Howard society was an instantaneous success. Membership rose from an inaugural seventy-five, in 1796, to 583 in 1813, and 688 in 1823. By 1805 over £2,000 had been paid in to the society treasury and £892 paid out, in the form of relief. The balance was invested in 3 per cent consols, and later lent to members at 5 per cent interest. As the society became richer they also invested in property, intended for the use of indigent members. Lord Carlisle appointed a committee of twelve to run the Friendly Society, drawn from the ranks of the local hierarchy of tenants and domestics – for example the local clergymen and schoolmasters, Carlisle's huntsman, Isaac Grainger, his head gardener, Mr Abel, sundry farmers and other senior servants. Full committee meetings were held every quarter, and another house servant was appointed secretary to the society, at a salary of five guineas per year.

The estate agent, John Forth, managed the Castle Howard Friendly Society for its first twenty years, and was responsible for setting the moral tone of the enterprise. Although an ardent philanthropist, he was hardly in tune with the idea of democratic entitlement. A contemporary essay on the brotherhood of man, printed in 1805, was probably written by Forth and shows clearly that he still equated benevolence with charity, and both with an attendant moral obligation on the part of the recipient. If the style of this eulogy is any indication of Mr Forth's character, one cannot help wondering how popular he was with anyone other than his 'Noble Patron'.

Man is formed a social being. The sovereign ruler of the world has been pleased to place us in this life as dependants upon each other, and in continual need of mutual assistance and support; and has interwoven in our constitutions those humane and sympathetic affections which we always feel at the distress of any of our fellow creatures. How greatly is a beneficent and generous spirit rewarded in contributing to relieve that distress! Of all the delights which human nature is capable of enjoying, the most lively and transporting are those which flow from sympathy and social passion; as they are not only the most pleasing in their immediate exercise, but also in contemplation and reflection. Every benevolent mind therefore, which sincerely delights in the good of others, will not fail to improve every opportunity to promote the happiness and comfort of those (in particular) who are affected with sickness, lameness, blindness, or any other calamity, by which they are deprived of the means and power of supporting not only themselves, but perhaps a numerous family. That this is the true and laudable intention of this society ... where every disorder with which any of its members may be afflicted is, (as far as is consistent with the general good of the whole society) so relieved as at least to prevent want from coming within his doors. Such being the original intention of this institution, which has for its sole object the mutual benefit and advantage of every member thereof, it is sincerely to be hoped that no person thereunto belonging will ever be insensible of the obligations he lies under to the Noble Patron and the respective supporters of such a praise-worthy society ... Under this impression of gratitude, and the uniform good conduct of the respective members, and under the blessing of Providence, 'The Castle Howard Friendly Society' may justly be considered as promising to become capable of diffusing more general comfort and assistance through its component branches, than any institution of the sort ever established in England.

The mood and style of daily life at Castle Howard around the turn of the century is admirably caught by William Fowler, in the letters he wrote from there during the winter of 1804. Fowler was an antiquarian and engraver who was introduced to the 5th Earl by John Forth, and was immediately invited to stay. It is obvious from his writing that he was as much impressed by the courtesy shown him by the Earl, and by the flattering interest Carlisle showed in his work, as he was overwhelmed by the luxury of his surroundings. On arrival at Castle Howard Fowler wrote to his wife that he had:

... got a very pleasant introduction into this great family by Mr Forth. He has presented my works to the Lord of Carlisle, and his Lordship was very much pleased, and I have delivered him one of the portfolios for which I've received twelve guineas. His Lordship has likewise express'd a desire for me to make drawings from some of his Mosaics, etc., at the Castle, and has offered me a handsome room to myself and bed and fire and every convenience my work requires, and my board in the steward's room.

In a later letter, written to his brother, Fowler goes into elaborate detail about his daily routine at the Castle. He is clearly delighted with his comfortable situation — an indication, perhaps, that such generous treatment was not the usual lot of an itinerant artist. His reception at Castle Howard is typical of the thoughtful concern Carlisle always showed for the welfare of his guests, whatever their social background. After a long eulogy about the house and grounds, Fowler returns to the personal. He has been allotted:

... two servants, one who makes my fire, which is kept in night and day when I choose, and supplies me regularly with coals and water and towels, and makes my bed in the evening; another maid servant furnishes my table with a pair of candles and snuffers, etc., that are wanted for the evening, many of which things just mentioned are more than I even once thought of.

And it is indeed unlikely that this impecunious young man had ever been able to afford such luxury. He goes on to describe the food, again a matter of delighted comment. Incredibly sumptuous meals seem to have been served every few hours — and these banquets were eaten by the servants, in the steward's room, remember, not by the family upstairs. An eighteenth-century aristocratic household must have been a glutton's paradise. 'Add to this,' the letter continues,

I have my breakfast every morning with the first domestics of the family regularly at 9 o'clock, fine light cakes and tea etc.; at one o'clock our lunch in the steward's room, in the general five or six hot dishes of finest meat, exclusive of cold, and sauces to do. At 6 o'clock we dine about 20 and sometimes 22 of us in number. The moment I first entered the dining room I was struck with a sort of surprize. A very large table surrounded with chairs placed at a proper distance to sit down upon, six large lighted candles in a straight line down the centre of the table, and upwards of 18 or 19 different dishes with costly sauces. Ale and beer and two waiters to attend. After dinner the dessert and wine, after this tea and coffee, then at eleven o'clock a hot supper in the same room. Shall I add to this my privilege of gratifying my curiosity when I please in viewing all the beautiful architecture that surrounds and adorns these buildings and the magnificent rooms and galleries so well furnished with the most costly paintings and adorned with the richest marbles. Upon cool reflection my situation certainly calls loudly for thankfulness, and, my dear brother, I am thankful and very grateful for these kind favours.

All the Howards were passionate about hunting, but it was an expensive business. In the early 1780s the 5th Earl limited his financial contribution towards the upkeep of the local hunt to £300 a year. In all, the hunt cost more than £800 a year to maintain, and the cost was at first divided among a syndicate of landowners. However, after a few years, the other backers dropped out. Carlisle, who was feeling rich at the time – he had, at last, been able to break the entail on the estate, and was thus in a position to realize some of his assets – agreed to carry on alone, and to pay all the expenses himself. He had, in any case, been the acting M.F.H. for a number of years. In 1794 the official Castle Howard Hunt was established, with kennels at Castle Howard itself, and a pack of forty-two hounds in the care of the legendary huntsman Isaac Grainger, whom he inherited from a previous Master. As fox-hunting increased in popularity new packs of hounds were formed all over Yorkshire, which led to a series of territorial disputes. The 5th Earl, when he took over the hunt, laid claim to exclusive possession of more than 600 square miles of sporting rights, containing most of the best covers in the East Riding. He then discovered that a number of claims to certain sections of his territory had been outstanding against the previous M.F.H. for more than fifteen years, and had become definitely acrimonious. It is typical of Carlisle that he first tried to justify his territorial rights by claiming historical precedence, and then, when that failed, settled for a compromise – rather than fight the case and allow bad feeling to fester among his neighbours. The 5th Earl was far more popular with the county than his father or grandfather had been before him.

The Castle Howard Hunt was, in fact, short-lived, lasting only six years. By 1798 it was costing nearly £1,000 a year to maintain and the Earl was getting worried about his debts again. Besides, the war with France had already lasted five years, and Carlisle was having an attack of patriotic fervour. He announced that it was time 'to contract the stable [which included the foxhounds'] expenses into the smallest compass possible, for these are not times to *spend much money or time upon mere amusements*'. The 5th Earl really was a prime example of the maxim that there is no Puritan like the reformed rake: in middle age he had developed a conveniently short memory and a distinctly pompous streak. Later still he became so censorious of his children's behaviour that they were terrified of him and hardly dared speak in his presence. The charming young wastrel had turned into a querulous martinet.

In fact the hunt carried on for a further two seasons, and was finally disbanded in 1800. Isaac Grainger the huntsman lived on at Castle Howard until his death in 1811, by which time he had become such a respected figure in the county that he merited an obituary in the *Gentleman's Magazine*:

In his 81st year, [died] Isaac Grainger, long known in the Castle Howard country as the first huntsman of his day, having hunted it for many years under different establishments; but on the Earl of Carlisle giving up keeping the fox-hounds, his Lordship was pleased to withdraw him from that life, by retaining him in his stable department, where he had for many years enjoyed, under a long pressure of infirmities, every comfort and attention.

Another testament to the 5th Earl's consideration for his employees.

Most of the Castle hunters were sold at York, during race week in August 1802 – an event which would have caused even greater sadness among the Howards had they not been preoccupied at the time with the 5th Earl's latest venture, the formation of the Castle Howard Riflemen.

★

In 1793, when war was declared against France, the Government feared an invasion from the Continent. Volunteer forces were recruited throughout the country, to assist in national defence should the occasion arise. Lord Morpeth was one of the first to join and was soon made captain of a troop of yeoman cavalry. Five years later the Government launched another appeal for recruits, which galvanized the 5th Earl into raising his own troop of infantry. He wrote to the War Office in London offering:

To raise at my expense a company of riflemen consisting of sixty, to serve anywhere within the northern district in which the men so raised shall reside. The clothing to be furnished by me, also carriage and horses for quick conveyance in cases that require immediate exertion. Government to supply arms viz a rifle & bayonet for each man.

To be allowed from government a sergt. to instruct the men. I conceive it not unusual to request to have the nomination of two officers under me subject to the approbation of the lord lieutenant.

The Castle Howard Company of Riflemen was launched in 1798 and lasted for ten years. (It was disbanded at the same time as all the other volunteer movements, in 1808.) The corps was a parochial affair, with the men recruited from the estate and surrounding districts, and the officers from within the Howard family. The Earl made himself the captain of the troops, and his second son William an ensign. Lord Morpeth joined them as lieutenant as soon as the cavalry troop with which he had been serving was disbanded. By July 1801 the corps consisted of sixty-five men: one captain, two lieutenants (one being William Howard, whom the Earl had promoted from ensign), four sergeants, two drummers or trumpeters, and fifty-six rank and file. This force was almost doubled within the next few years. There was never any shortage of volunteers; on the contrary, Carlisle averred that he could easily have raised at least three times the number of men actually recruited if the Government had been more forthcoming with weapons. The estate agent, John Forth, was given the job of selecting the men, having been told by Carlisle 'to choose only those who would be most regular in attendance, of the best appearance and over whom we shall have the most influence'. The Earl added a rider to the effect that they must also be men who could be trusted to look after their expensive new uniforms, and only wear them when on duty. These uniforms were dark green, worn with regimental hats, black silk handkerchiefs and cockades. They must have been a splendid sight at Castle Howard, marching against the backdrop of Vanbrugh's great façade. It is not surprising that the men were so eager to join, in view of the deal on offer – extra pay, new clothes, and all the fun of playing soldiers with the Howards. Besides, the war with France was popular at the start, and patriotism ran high throughout the country.

It was an efficient outfit, run with military discipline by the drill sergeant provided by the Government. Drilling took place once a fortnight, in villages on the estate, or at Castle Howard itself, where the guns and ammunition were stored. The corps may even have had its own regimental march; a copy in the British Library of 'The Earl of Carlisle's March', by Freeman, is dated 1780 and was probably composed about then. Relatively speaking, a 'private army' was not that expensive to maintain: the cost of the Castle Howard Riflemen came to no more than £100 a year. In all, the Earl spent, over a period of ten years, less than £1,000 – whereas his hunt had been costing that amount in one year alone. The estate accounts show that the Earl bought his soldiers, besides the uniforms, 100 blankets, haversacks, black barcelona handkerchiefs, canteens, breast plates, cartridge boxes, powder horns, hats, pistols and ammunition.

By the end of the eighteenth century the emphasis of aristocratic life had moved away from the country. Whereas in 1700 it was customary for the great landowners and their families to spend nine months of the year on their estates, by 1800 it was often no more than three. London was too strong a magnet. The season in town got longer and longer, and produced more and more exciting attractions. Thus, as society increased in sophistication, it became necessary to find ways of making life in the country interesting, to structure the days and weeks, in order to avoid acute boredom – the traditional enemy of the leisured classes. Months of rustication on the family estates could be made tolerable, of course, if sufficiently amusing company was imported – which meant that the country hostesses vied desperately with each other to tempt their guests with spectacular attractions. Theatricals and charades were performed in the evenings and could be extremely elaborate productions. These entertainments were often controversial in content, written and acted by the most brilliant brains of the day, and provided country life with an intellectual outlet.

Another popular interest at the time was that of 'civilizing' the landscape, by means of a succession of pantheons, grottos and follies, all full of classical allusions, particularly in the sculptures. Arcadianism was equally rife. Like Marie Antoinette with her Petit Trianon, the English aristocratic wives played at country living. At Chatsworth there was a cow which was perfumed every morning, and at Castle Howard the Countess of Carlisle had her own dairy. But, in her case, this was no passing aristocratic whim, but a solid commercial proposition. For example, butter sold during the family's absence one season fetched £45. Lady Carlisle's dairy, built in 1811 at a cost of £467, was an offshoot of her husband's enlightened agricultural policy.

The agricultural revolution had begun to crystallize by the end of the eighteenth century. Ever since the first enclosures, at the end of the seventeenth century, interest in the actual science of agriculture had been on the increase: by the 1790s new methods of farming were being tried out all over the country, and the first Board of Agriculture had been formed. The two outstanding agriculturalists of their day were Sir Thomas Coke of Norfolk, operating at Holkham Hall, and the Duke of Bedford at Woburn, both of whom dedicated their estates to research and experiment, using their own home farms, and encouraging their tenants to adopt the new ideas. Most of the great landlords, including Carlisle, who was a great admirer of Coke's, followed suit, and in 1796 the Earl built a new model farm on the estate at Castle Howard. It was a commercial venture, with a strict accounting system and weekly progress reports, but it also served as a working model for the tenants and other interested farmers. Carlisle exercised his usual parochial instincts in naming all the fields after members of the family, or places associated with the Howards – for example, 'Lady Gertrude's field', after one of his daughters, and 'Naworth field', after Naworth Castle. It was a mixed farm, covering 260 acres, and as time went by and the farm continued to show a handsome profit, Carlisle began to install the very latest models of the new machinery. He bought, first, a threshing machine and grinding mill, and then, later, a bone mill, malt kiln and malt rollers. After only one year the Earl reported gleefully that 'The farm is in good order, and the profits beyond calculation, the cows and pigs the admiration of the Northern World.' Indeed they were: Lady Harriet Cavendish, Lady Morpeth's sister, was so impressed by the quality of life enjoyed by the Castle Howard pigs that she wrote, after a visit in 1804:

... My next expedition was to the farm, which is near a mile from the house. I cannot describe to you anything like the neatness and comfort of the whole thing, and the very pigs have an air of cleanliness and consequence about them. To be sure, if the farm was like any other farm, or the pigs like any other pigs, all the noble blood of the Howards could not walk over every part of it as they do, and it is no common sight to see so much dignity in a pigstye.

Castle Howard was virtually self-sufficient in the eighteenth and nineteenth centuries; the household lived off the fat of their own land. It must have been pleasant for the 5th Earl, sitting down to those elaborate dinners, to think that the game he ate came from his own woods, the meat from his own farm, the butter and cream from his own dairy, the vegetables from his vast kitchen gardens, and that exotic cornucopia of fruit on the table from his own new hothouses. The gardens, like the Earl's other agricultural enterprises, were run on commercial lines and produced an enormous quantity of every kind of fruit and vegetable, including a number of rare and exotic species. After catering for the household the surplus would be sold, making quite a profitable sideline. There is a note in the accounts, for example, dated 1768, that the Duke of Portland's head gardener at

Welbeck Abbey has ordered £30 worth of pineapple suckers and plants. Artichokes, broccoli and other delicacies also found a market among the neighbouring estates, or made original presents for friends and family.

The new greenhouses may have gratified Carlisle's taste for luxury, but they must have cost a fortune to run. During the long dark Yorkshire winters, when the wind battered against the delicate glass and the snow piled up against the walls, fires had to be kept going night and day. Nevertheless, the kitchen gardens continued to produce their tropical fruit and rare vegetables, and by the end of the eighteenth century had achieved a considerable reputation in the horticultural world. In August 1783 the *York Chronicle* reported that a 'Black Rock Cantaloupe Melon' weighing 14lb 9oz, and measuring 2 feet 10 inches in circumference, was cut in the gardens at Castle Howard. In 1771 Sir John Cullum, a horticulturist from Suffolk, made a special journey to see the kitchen gardens and wrote:

The Kitchen Garden is a remarkably good one. It is an Area of twelve Acres, inclosed and Intersected with lofty Walls. The Gardener's House stands in the middle of it: here live two young Men, who are studying Botany, and have brought into the Garden a considerable Number of curious Plants, which grow wild in these Parts, and are rarely to be met with elsewhere. Scarcely any where perhaps in the whole Kingdom is Horticulture carried on with greater Spirit. The Hot houses, Hot Walls & are without Number. No less than 26 Fires were last Winter burning here at the same Time. In this, and the Pleasure Grounds 33 Persons are employed. The Pine Apples are cultivated to a Degree of Luxuriance almost beyond Belief. Some of their Leaves were much above 6 Feet high; and the Fruit, I was told, frequently weighted between 4 and 5 pounds. Thus much Art may do, but the Climate is very unfriendly.

The Rev W. MacRitchie, touring Yorkshire some twenty-five years later, is equally impressed by the tropical quality of the produce, but he is also interested in one of the Earl's most successful innovations:

Here is the finest pinery I ever saw, and upon the whole the best kept hothouses. The vines most luxuriant; and here is what I never saw before, almond trees, peaches, nectarines etc., trained upon spars placed not as usual in a perpendicular but in a horizontal position, about two feet from the ground, and bearing an abundance of fruit.

Castle Howard was fortunate during this period in that the head gardeners were the legendary Robert Teesdales, father and son. The *York Chronicle*, in its obituary of Teesdale senior, in July 1773, described him as a man who was 'well known for his eminent abilities in that profession'. The head gardener, a position of importance in the estate hierarchy, was handsomely housed and received a salary of £50 per quarter, whereas the men under him were paid only 1s. per day, and the women only 6d. – a classic example of the respective status of the sexes at the time.

Robert Teesdale the younger was probably one of the young men studying botany whom Sir John Cullum noticed on his visit. Teesdale certainly pioneered the tradition of scientific and practical botany which persists to this day at Castle Howard. He was a founder member of the Linnean Society (still the foremost botanical society in Britain) and acknowledged his apprenticeship on the estate in the preface to a paper he delivered to the Society in 1792:

During the time I resided at Castle Howard some of my leisure hours were employed in herborizing. My business not admitting of long excursions, it enabled me to take the more pains in the collecting of the plants of my own neighbourhood. The woods about Castle Howard are extensive and the bogs near Terrington produce many valuable acquisitions to the curious investigator.

The botanical tradition was carried on into the nineteenth century, by Henry Ibbotson, who published, in 1851, the first serious guidebook to Castle Howard (quoted in detail later), and Richard Spruce, who went on to become a world-famous botanist and explorer. Spruce was born on the Castle Howard estate in 1817, the son of the local schoolmaster, and was fascinated by the science and theory of botany from the beginning. He spent fifteen years exploring and collecting plants in South America and, on his retirement, returned to Yorkshire. He lived on the estate until his death in 1893 and is commemorated in a plaque on the house.

The parkland and grounds at Castle Howard came in for the same lavish treatment as the gardens. In one year alone, 1810, the 5th Earl planted no fewer than 87,000 trees – including chestnut, sycamore, larch, oaks, ash, and spruce. Two years later he ordered another 59,000, at a cost of £126.

With the exception of Ray Wood, which pre-dates Castle Howard, and the great lime avenue, which was planted by the founder *c.* 1714, the credit for the glorious woods on the estate belongs to the 5th Earl. He planted an enormous number of new trees and re-stocked those which had been neglected, such as Pretty Wood and Coneysthorpe Banks. The account books show the comparative prices of these magnificent hardwoods, many of which are still standing. One order, for example, lists:

10,000	oak	at	36s.	per thousand	£18	0s. 0d.
12,000	larch	at	36s.	,,	£21	12s. 0d.
14,000	spruce	at	15s.	,,	£10	10s. 0d.
500	ash	at	20s.	,,	£5	0s. 0d.
500	ash	at	38s.	,,	£9	10s. 0d.
6,000	oaks	at	28s.	,,	£8	8s. 0d.
400	oaks	at	16s.	,,	£3	4s. 0d.

Total: 56,000 trees at a cost of £76 4s. 0d.

Since trees are commonly planted at an approximate ratio of 1,000 per acre, that particular order would, in time, have provided some fifty or sixty acres of woodland.

In later life the 5th Earl became something of a tyrant, at least in the

eyes of the younger generation. Lady Morpeth's sister, Harriet Cavendish, later Countess Granville, loved staying at Castle Howard, but
disliked Carlisle and thought his wife silly. The Earl was not yet sixty
in 1807 when Harriet wrote that: 'Il régne en despote', and was 'par
force the mainspring of every smile and frown that *publickly* appear
on our faces.' The following year she reported from Castle Howard
that she was:

... bored to death. The dinners are insufferable – I am promoted to Lord
Carlisle's right hand – We none of us speak – He sits like a nightmare upon
our powers of articulation, and if Lady Carlisle did not laugh incessantly we
should be taken for a meeting of quakers waiting for the spirit to move us.

Despite her feelings about her hosts Harriet seems to have had no
qualms about accepting their hospitality for literally months on end.
Five years later, and married to Lord Granville Leveson-Gower,
Harriet is less frightened of the Earl but equally acid about the
company at Castle Howard. Writing from there in 1813, to her
brother, the 6th Duke of Devonshire, she described her arrival:

We found upon arriving here at half past four, among the statues, G. [her
sister, Georgiana Morpeth] in a bedgown and dishevelled, and Lord M.
[Morpeth] 'pacing with hurried steps his room along'. The Earl had put off
dinner for an hour, as four was the usual time. However this has been the
only disturbance. He is in high good humour. We dine at five and he lets
Granville shoot.

   To make the scene present to you I will give you a sketch of us at dinner.
Lord Carlisle, star-shining, lip-projecting, with a dish of his own, a sort of
solid soup, by his side which he offers to a chosen few. Next to him G
looking amiable and resigned, and very pretty. Lady Julia Howard by her
side with a wreath of white roses, more rouge than ever and innumerable
jewels. Granville looking very good tempered between her and Lady Carlisle
with a camelia japonica and a red pink in her cap, trying, like a busy bee, to
extract conversation from us all by nodding and staring at us. Harry Howard
is aide-de-camp at the joints of meat and never by any chance opens his lips.

Carlisle was always surrounded by family at Castle Howard, even if they sat around in crushed silence. Harry Howard was one of his younger sons and Lady Julia his unmarried sister. She was a remarkable spinster who lived to the age of ninety-nine, harrying four generations of Howards. Reputedly a very ugly woman, she nevertheless insisted on decking herself out like a freak. Harriet, however, rather admired her, as can be seen from a letter she wrote to her sister, in 1822, deploring her own lack of energy:

Relaxation is my bane, Lady Morpeth. All my habits and tastes lean that way and in consequence I am going to wage war upon them all. I dread a languid yellow old age, hot, perfumed, and dawdling, and I prefer our Julia's course, active, smart, burnished and braced.

Lord Byron, another kinsman of the 5th Earl's, attacked him in print. Carlisle was the poet's first cousin once removed through his mother's family, and was appointed Byron's guardian by the Court of Chancery in 1798. It was not a charge he wished for and it turned out to have bitter repercussions. Annoyed because he thought his guardian was taking insufficient trouble over him, particularly about his introduction to the House of Lords, Byron vented his temper in public. His satirical poem 'English Bards and Scotch Reviewers' (1809) was already at the printer's when he insisted on changing one couplet referring to Carlisle for another. In the original version Byron had written a pleasant compliment to his guardian:

> On one alone Apollo deigns to smile,
> And crowns a new Roscommon in Carlisle.

After a mammoth row Byron deleted these lines and substituted a piece of typical and gratuitous malice:

> No muse will cheer with renovating smile
> The paralytic puling of Carlisle.

The same poem, which is full of cheap gibes at contemporary authors, contains another vitriolic volte-face along the same lines. In 'Hours of Idleness', which had been published in 1808, Byron praised his guardian's literary works, saying that they had '. . . long received the meed of public applause; to which, by their intrinsic worth, they were entitled'. But in 'English Bards', published only a year later, Byron wrote, referring to the tragedies, which, though published to critical acclaim, had not been produced in the theatre:

> So dull in youth, so drivelling in his age,
> His scenes alone might damn our sinking stage;
> But managers for once cried, hold, enough!
> Nor drugged their audience with the tragic stuff.

Some years later Byron had the grace to apologize, and included a complimentary reference to Carlisle's third son, Frederick, who was killed at the Battle of Waterloo, in *Childe Harold*: '... no nobler breast than thine, young, gallant Howard!'* The Earl, however, was not pacified. He not only disliked and disapproved of Byron's character but thought him a bad writer and a plagiarist – 'Lord Byron's Don Juan is most disgusting and it has not even the poor merit of original depravity ...' Carlisle considered that Byron had stolen the ideas for *Don Juan* from *The Marriage of Figaro* and other sources.

Harriet Granville always exaggerated; Byron resented his guardian; both were prejudiced against the Earl. There were plenty of other people, only too delighted to receive an invitation to Castle Howard, who found their host perfectly agreeable. Sydney Smith, for example, the charming clergyman, scholar and wit, draws a far more

---

* The complete stanza is No xxix:

> ... Yet one I would select from that proud throng,
> Partly because they blend me with his line,
> And partly that I did his sire some wrong,
> And partly that bright names will hallow song;
> And his was of the bravest, and when shower'd
> The death-bolts deadliest the thinn'd files along,
> Even where the thickest of war's tempest lower'd
> They reach'd no nobler breast than thine, young, gallant Howard!'

sympathetic portrait of Carlisle in his numerous letters. He was given the living of Foston Rectory, only a few miles from Castle Howard, in 1814, and became a life-long friend of the whole Howard family. The 5th Earl, delighted to find such good company near at hand, hastened to call at the rectory. Saba, the rector's wife, described their arrival:

Our infant colony was still in so rude a state, that roads, save for a cart, had hardly been thought of. Suddenly, however, a cry was raised, that a coach and four, with outriders, were plunging about in the midst of a ploughed field near the house, and showing signs of distress. Ploughmen and plough-women were immediately sent off to the rescue; and at last the gold coach [as Lady Carlisle used to call it], which had mistaken the road, was guided safely up to the house, and the kind old Lord and Lady, not a little shaken, and a little cross at so rough a reception, entered the parsonage. The shakes were soon forgotten, and good-humour restored . . . Lord Carlisle drove off, and made us promise to come and stay with him at Castle Howard.

Sydney Smith's early impression of Carlisle was that 'the old Earl is young, athletic, beautiful and merry . . . he has many good points, and I must do him the justice to say that he keeps his bad ones tolerably well out of sight'. And of his heir, Lord Morpeth, who was a near contemporary, the rector wrote: 'I like Lord Morpeth – a man of excellent understanding, very polished manners, and a good heart; but I should suspect very irritable and very sensitive – the last to a fault'. Carlisle, on his side, found in Smith an amusing and cultivated neighbour, a man of the utmost probity, on his own intellectual plane, with whom he could discuss everything from local problems to abstract ideas. The rector was no sycophant. Soon after meeting the Earl he wrote that 'He is fond of quizzing me, but I give him as good as he brings, so all goes on very well.' And, on another occasion, when they disagreed on a matter of principle, Smith wrote back swiftly to Carlisle, that 'My opinions, and the free expression of them, I will surrender to no man alive – nor will I hold myself accountable to any man for the exercise of this right.'

Most of the letters relevant to the 5th Earl, however, are written in a much lighter vein, discussing such matters as the price of coal, or the latest problem for the bench. In 1815 he wrote to his friend and patroness, Lady Holland, that the Earl:

has broke out this year into a fit of most extraordinary politeness towards his neighbours. Among the rest he paid a visit to a family whom he had not visited since the capture of the Bastille, and apologized for not having called before . . . We have stayed at Castle Howard for two or three days . . . I soon found myself at ease at Castle Howard, and if he is not capricious, which I suppose he is, Castle Howard will make an agreeable variety to my existence.

It did. The rector became completely at home in the house, reading in the library and fishing in the lake: 'We had a miraculous fishing, catching 105 perch, each longer than any of Mr Wrangham's fingers, and quite as rapacious.'

In 1821, Carlisle wrote to the rector congratulating him on an unexpected inheritance. The letter shows both the Earl's sensitivity to the economic difficulties of others, and his scorn for the parsimonious ways of richer men. As for the reference to the Castle Howard housekeeping budget, it certainly shows the extent to which the old man has reformed since his spendthrift youth. 'Foston', he wrote admiringly,

in neatness and ostensible comforts will hardly perceive the benefit of this addition to your income . . . I have ever regarded the establishment at Foston with admiration and surprise, *not being above knowing to a shilling the monthly consumption, and expenses, of this house*; and I have thought of my friend Fitzwilliam [another extremely rich landowner] who has erased the word Comfort out of the Wentworth Dictionary, as neither he nor any one about him could ever comprehend its meaning.

Carlisle often sent presents of produce from the estate to the rectory, which must have helped the Smiths' housekeeping. They were carefully chosen: Smith's letters gracefully acknowledge not only standard gifts – venison, game and exotic fruits, such as grapes and pineapples from the splendid castle greenhouses – but also the receipt of more mundane fare. The Earl bothered to send cucumbers, and even cauliflowers as well. Smith reciprocated by sending a basket of 'what I think is the model of all potatoes' to Carlisle's daughter-in-law, Georgiana. He adds a charming rider – 'Pray do not let Flinn eat them in the Stewards Room'; and tells her where they may be bought, in case 'your happiness depend upon potatoes as much as mine does'.

Smith's concern for the elderly couple is clear. He wrote to the Countess with his usual sage compassion, inquiring 'whether my Lord and you keep up health and spirits with tolerable success – a difficult task in the fifth act of life, when the curtain must ere long drop and the comedy or tragedy be brought to an end'. And on the 5th Earl's death, in 1825, at the age of seventy-seven, Sydney Smith, charitable to the last, mourned 'the loss of so good a neighbour and so kind a friend'.

Nevertheless, there is no doubt that by the last years of his life the 5th Earl had become a distinctly cantankerous and bitter old man. In some notes written around that time, tersely headed 'On Marriage', he vented his spleen on the modern girl. Parents attempting to arrange an alliance are, he feels, doomed to betrayal by their silly daughters. On dealing with a proposal for a daughter's hand he says that:

. . . a slight repugnance [on the part of the daughter] shd not immediately be yielded to; a decided one shd not be opposed by force.

The first objection, personal appearance, lies not with them [i.e. the parents] if it weighs not with the person most concerned. But a young person shd not be married out of her nursery; she shd know + see something of the world, + be able to better judge for herself. – Give her 2 yrs all these advantages; What is the common result of such experience? To learn from other girls how to attract some particular poor object, the more unfit, the more romantic and irresistible; to fail in every scheme, to scare away every proper suitor, + for fear of being put upon the shelf, in despair take up with something that she herself, with all interested for her, utterly disapproves. Tis tiresome to hear such a match must be happy! The parties suit each other so well! They are so like each other — They had better be quite different. If one shd be placid, the other shd be animated etc, etc, With the same habits + pursuits, the same ideas, the same ways of considering all things, life wd stagnate + ennui would not wait the passing away of the honeymoon. In short, all that parents can do in their choice of husband for their daughter is to secure good temper, integrity of character, common sense, and an income to reach all the rational wants + comforts of life. To attempt more is only to provoke disappointment.

Just which of the Howard girls had caused this outburst Carlisle does not specify, but it really cannot have been his eldest daughter-in-law, Georgiana Morpeth, the future 6th Countess — surely the most dutiful, but also the most interesting, of all the Carlisle wives.

7

'. . . Reform Bill Carried by a Majority of 109'

Lady Georgiana Cavendish was born in 1783 and married Lord Morpeth, later the 6th Earl of Carlisle, when she was just seventeen. She was the eldest daughter of the 5th Duke of Devonshire and the legendary Duchess Georgiana. The young 'G.', as she came to be known in order to differentiate her from her mother, grew up at Devonshire House, at that time synonymous not only with glamour, wealth and privilege but also with an extraordinary degree of moral licence. The Devonshires lived for years in a *ménage à trois* with Lady Elizabeth Foster, surrounded by their various children, both legitimate and illegitimate. In addition to 'G.', her sister Harriet and the Cavendish heir, Lord Hartington, the Duke fathered two children by Lady Elizabeth Foster, and the Duchess had an extra daughter – by the future Earl Grey. Moreover, as often as not, they all lived together under the same roof. To complicate matters even further, the Duchess's sister, Lady Bessborough, who collected the eighteenth-century equivalent of toy-boys, believed in keeping her lovers in the family: she had a brief affair with the young Lord Morpeth, before he married 'G' – who was, of course, her niece. Lady Bessborough also carried on a liaison with Lord Leveson-Gower for twenty years, and when that came to an end she married him off to G.'s sister, Harriet Cavendish. Surprisingly, all these curious arrangements were not only accepted by society without question, but seem to have worked rather well.

All the same, it is probably no coincidence that the next generation rebelled against such blatant immorality. With the notable exception of Caroline Lamb, a first cousin of G.'s, the Devonshire House girls became patterns of propriety in later life, and exemplary wives. And *their* daughters, of course, grew up under the influence of Victorian morality: thus, in just two generations, society's view of adultery turned a complete circle.

Georgiana Cavendish, as a child, was described by a contemporary as 'gentle, pliable and serious'. Moreover, she was extremely well educated – much better, in fact, than her twentieth-century counterparts are today. Miss Trimmer, the girls' governess, had impressive academic qualifications, but even more importantly she came from noted Evangelical stock and was a woman of strong religious principles. The Duchess, who had a surprisingly pious streak in her nature, felt that Miss Trimmer's teaching and moral precepts would prove a salutary counter to the dubious example of the Devonshire House set. Miss Trimmer, in fact, proved an excellent tutor and a most sympathetic confidante, loved and admired by the whole family.

The Duchess herself, despite her frivolity, was a clever woman, almost an intellectual. She put the highest possible premium on her daughters' education and kept a constant check on their progress. Thus, when G. was only nine years old, her mother was already writing to her, from Pisa, that she was 'glad that you are reading the Illiad', and adds that she will try and find a copy in Italian and re-read it herself, so that they may discuss the book together on her return. And a year later Georgiana learnt the news of the French King's execution in a letter from her mother written entirely in French – all the Cavendish correspondence, even gossipy letters between the sisters, is larded with phrases in both French and Italian, and scattered with quotations from the classics. They were a literate society.

At the age of sixteen Georgiana was presented at Court, and a magnificent ball was given in her honour at Devonshire House. She wore a 'dress of white crepe trimmed with blonde and silk cords and tassels, diamonds in her hair which was beautifully dressed and three white feathers'. The Duchess, only too aware of the pitfalls of society, and with no intention of encouraging her daughters to follow in her

131

own scandalous footsteps, was inordinately strict with Georgiana. She was hardly allowed out of doors, even in her own grounds, without a footman in attendance. Furthermore, Georgiana was never allowed to wear make-up, even though the other débutantes took it for granted. While her brother Hartington was writing that most of 'the girls blush Mdlle Martin Rue St Honoré', the Duchess was busy assuring Georgiana's grandmother, the strait-laced Lady Spencer, that she 'need not have feared about the rouge, I would not on any account have let her wear any'.

The ball cost a fortune, but exactly how big a fortune remains unclear. The Duchess, who was always economical with the truth when accounts were in question, thought it cost no more than £400. 'The world,' however, she wrote to Lady Spencer, 'says £1,000, but I am sure not.' Whatever the true figure, it was a suitably lavish affair. The main ballroom was decorated with pink artificial roses and the supper tables were laid with 400 places, each surrounded by its own array of expensive delicacies. There was a 'canvas room', or marquee, hung with fishing nets and festooned with 'Exotics', including orange trees from the Devonshires' glasshouses at Chiswick. This last room was lit 'by the hoop lustre bound with roses holding 18 wax candles and the effect was like magic'.

Georgiana, despite her inherent reserve, was not in the least crushed by all this splendour, and the young Lord Morpeth noticed her at once: he thought her 'the most distinguished person at the ball'. The Duchess was soon reporting to her mother that Morpeth '. . . is extremely kind to her and has given her leave to make use of his name whenever she did not want to accept a partner – and he has been attentive to her on all occasions. I think he is afraid of remarks if he asked her to dance.' It is, of course, equally possible that Morpeth felt embarrassed about courting Georgiana considering that he had so recently been making love to her aunt.

Nevertheless the affair prospered, and in the spring of 1801, three months before her eighteenth birthday, Georgiana married Morpeth. He was twenty-eight at the time, a private, shy man, of great good nature and a modest approach to life: even in his salad days Morpeth had exhibited no signs of the extravagant wild behaviour which had so tarnished his father's image twenty years earlier. Apart from that hiccup with Lady Bessborough, he seems to have been an exemplary young man, of high morality – a perfect consort for the thoughtful and pious Georgiana. And in fact the marriage, which lasted for more than forty years and produced twelve children, was one of singular harmony.

Both sets of parents were delighted with the match. Apart from the obvious suitability of a marriage between the Cavendishes and the Howards, it was an important alliance between two great Whig families at a time of great political moment – the Napoleonic war was at its height. Besides, the couple were clearly in love with each other and the families had been close friends for years, indeed for generations. Thirty years previously the 5th Earl of Carlisle had been a member of Duchess Georgiana's court – he once wrote a rather bad ode to her coiffure, a monstrous erection of pink ostrich feathers:

> When on your head I see those fluttering things,
> I think that love is there and claps his wings.
> Feathers helped Jove to fan his amorous flames,
> Cupid has feathers, angels wear the same.
> Since then from Heaven their origin we trace,
> > Preserve the fashion – it becomes your Grace.

Apparently the headdress in question was 'not less than three-quarters of a yard High' and 'an ell wide'.

The Duke settled £30,000 on his daughter while the Duchess spent a fortune on her trousseau: the haberdasher's bills alone came to £3,368 9s. 6d. Carlisle was equally generous. Receipts at Castle Howard, dated February 1801, from Rundell and Bridge, the most fashionable and expensive of the London jewellers, obviously represent handsome wedding presents to Georgiana. They include an opal and emerald necklace, and a sapphire and diamond ring. He, too, contributed handsomely to the marriage settlements. A note in the Castle Howard archives gives the details:

133

The Lady's Fortune

on his marriage £10,000 capital to Morpeth plus an income of £1000 p.a., until his father's death . . . And it is further proposed, in ease of the Carlisle estate, that in case the Lady shall survive Lord Morpeth that a Rent charge of a thousand shall be secured to her, out of her Father's Estate, for her life, in part of the provision to be made for her by way of a jointure.

The Duke of Devonshire offered the Morpeths Londesborough, his house in Yorkshire, but Georgiana, still only seventeen years old, was deemed too young to set up her own establishment and they went to live with the Carlisles at Castle Howard instead. This was a common enough arrangement among the aristocracy of their generation, and stately homes such as Castle Howard were certainly large enough to allow for a modicum of privacy, but it cannot have been easy for the young couple. As has already been demonstrated, the 5th Earl became increasingly autocratic in later life and seemed to delight in finding fault with the younger generation. He was obsessed with punctuality, which can hardly have suited a Cavendish – mealtimes at Devonshire House were notoriously unpredictable. Nevertheless, Georgiana was able to rise above her father-in-law's bad temper: she became pregnant at once, with the first of her twelve children, and was fully preoc-cupied for years with her nursery. In any case she was an adaptable girl, with ample previous experience of tricky situations and com-munal living from the years when she lived with her parents. As far as Morpeth was concerned, however, remaining in the shadow of his formidable father was clearly a mistake. He was a gentle, charming character, devoted to his wife and family, but he was insufficiently ambitious to please the 5th Earl.

Morpeth was a clever man, with a fine, inquiring mind, but he was far more interested in literature and the arts than in current affairs. He wrote a number of odes and sonnets, which were well received on publication, and was a considerable classical scholar – but he was a most reluctant politician. Predictably, however, Morpeth duly conformed to family tradition and took his seat in the House of Commons, in 1795, at the age of twenty-two. As had become the custom for the Carlisle heirs, he represented the local Whig interest, standing for the family borough of Morpeth, the Northumberland town from which his courtesy title derived. He was of such a retiring disposition, however, that he took little part in debates, either in the Commons or, later, in the Lords. In spite of this passive attitude Morpeth went on to hold a number of reasonably important Government posts over the next thirty years. His inherited status within the Whig hierarchy guaranteed advancement, and after his marriage he was backed by the powerful Cavendish factor as well. Morpeth was soon promoted to Government and, in 1806, was made a member of the Privy Council in the Ministry of All the Talents and a commissioner for the affairs of India. In 1824 he was appointed Lord-Lieutenant of the East Riding of Yorkshire, one of the traditional family sinecures; on succeeding to the title the following year he entered the Lords as a member of Canning's Cabinet, in the post of chief commissioner of woods and forests. As the 6th Earl of Carlisle he continued to play a minor role in politics, twice holding the office of Lord Privy Seal, until ill health forced him to retire in 1834. Gout was always the bane of the Howard family, and it had virtually crippled the 6th Earl by the time he was sixty. On his retirement Carlisle was appointed a trustee of the British Museum, a position for which he was admirably suited, and in 1837 he was invested with the Garter.

Morpeth and Georgiana had to wait until 1825 to inherit the title and assume control of Castle Howard. By that time he was fifty-two, already old by contemporary standards, and she, though ten years younger, had borne twelve children. Her health was uncertain and she had suffered for some years from bouts of depression. Had Morpeth inherited the title when he was younger he might well have opted for a more academic style of life from the start, and eschewed politics altogether. In that case there would have been no parental pressure to influence his choice of career, and he would also have been financially secure. As it was, Government office at least provided an easy route to independence. The Morpeths were probably only too thankful to escape from the gloomy atmosphere of Castle Howard, and the constant carping of the old Earl. They installed themselves, with their rapidly growing family, in a rented house in Park Street, and for the next twenty years divided their time between London, Yorkshire and the usual round of country house visits.

Morpeth may have appeared a reluctant politician in the House of Commons but he lived in such stirring times, politically speaking, that he could not fail to be excited by events. Besides, he was married to Georgiana, who, like all the Cavendishes, was passionately interested in current affairs. The 6th Earl's lifetime spanned four reigns, from George III to Queen Victoria, and saw the most momentous changes there have ever been in the English Constitution. It was the age of triumph for the Whigs, crowned by the passing of the Reform Bill in 1832. This was a measure which would eventually – after nearly 100 years – bring about the universal franchise in practice today. They were the men who succeeded, in spite of fierce and violent opposition, in passing all the great reform laws – the abolition of slavery, the reform of the Poor Laws and the Municipal Reform Act. In effect, this was the generation which took the first steps towards modern democracy, and Carlisle was one of its leaders: whether he actually spoke in the House or not was irrelevant.

Georgiana kept notebooks and diaries all her life and several of them survive. Among her personal papers there is a red leather box which holds six little matching leather notebooks, embellished with gold lettering and engravings, all crammed with her tiny, spidery handwriting. At the same time her sister Harriet, by then the Countess Granville, was writing her famous series of letters to Georgiana, long and lively screeds, full of indiscreet remarks about almost every major figure on the social scene. Both sources give a fascinating insight into the daily life and times of a great lady during the first half of the nineteenth century. Georgiana and Harriet, thanks to their Cavendish origins, belonged to the very innermost circles of society, but they were also both married to men in the forefront of politics. The aspect of the sisters' lives which most surprises the modern reader, conditioned to think of such aristocratic ladies in terms of elegant leisure, is how extremely busy they were. What modern political wife, with a large young family and two houses to run, would find the inclination, let alone the time, to attend debates in the House of Commons day after day? Or, having listened to a speech, bother to comment on its delivery in her private diary? Georgiana did both.

The earliest extant diary is headed 'Friday. my 33rd birthday – July 12th 1816 –'. It was a summer of intense social activity. On Sunday she wrote 'Dinner at Ld Bath's'; on Tuesday, 'we went to Woburn'; on Thursday, 'we arrived at Castle Howard'. The following week, and the one after that, there was a large house party at Castle Howard, including her sister, doubtless in her usual acerbic mood. As soon as the guests had gone, on Monday 19 August, the whole caravanserai was off again, to Naworth this time. Georgiana was a devoted mother who took her vast brood of children with her whenever possible, so it is not surprising that they took two days to travel the 100-odd miles between Castle Howard and Naworth. By the spring the family had moved back to London, and her diary begins to read like a political *Who's Who*. The week before Easter she attends three dinner parties, all of them given by leading Whig aristocrats – 'dinner at Ld Grey's', 'Ld Holland's', and 'Ld Lansdowne's'. But the diary is also laced with pious or philosophical exhortations to herself – single words to remind herself that life is not all dissipation, for example – 'Fortitude', and 'important employment'. Later, she clearly suffers from a bout of guilt and writes 'inevitable evil', or 'cheerful endurance'. In October she writes the single word 'Duty!' in the middle of a week at Castle Howard, an outburst triggered off, perhaps, by the latest row with her father-in-law.

That same autumn the family went on to visit, in turn, Chatsworth, her childhood home in Derbyshire, Lowther and Corby Castles in Cumberland, and Cawdor Castle in Wales. They returned to London and the house in Park Street for Christmas; made a short trip north again in the early spring, and were back dining at Carlton House and

Cleveland House, the very centres of political life in London, by May. It was a frenetic life; and considering the discomfort of travel in the eighteenth century, even without the added factor of Georgiana's frequent pregnancies, it seems to have been unnecessarily exhausting.

Fifteen years later the pace was the same; so are the names in the little red diaries. But by then her husband had inherited the title (in 1825), and 'G.' had become the 6th Countess of Carlisle, chatelaine of Castle Howard. She was, of course, brought up in a highly political family, and she married into another one – but, even so, the interest she showed in contemporary issues, and the amount of time she spent in the Visitors' Gallery, is remarkable for a woman with such heavy family commitments. Georgiana must have been aware that she was witnessing history in the making, during the autumn and winter of 1831–2. Her diary at this time switches continually, from social life to the latest war news, from the children to eager political comment, and back again to straight gossip. Thus, in one week in September, the diary, which she carefully notes was bought on 'Wednesday, Sept 14th, 1831, starts: 'Dined at Ld Melbourne's – met the Hollands, Ldy Stanhope, George Lambs, Sr Frdck, Ld Grey, Ld Godwich, Duke of Richmond, Ld Seaford', and a 'Mr Allen' – who was, in fact, the popular and erudite librarian at Holland House. Next day, the 15th, in the morning, she drove to see 'Georgiana' (it is unclear which Georgiana but by then it may well have been a granddaughter) at Roehampton, and in the evening 'dined at Devonshire House – met Ld and Ldy Shrewsbury, Ldy and Miss Hunloke, Gowers, Dovers [Lady Dover, also called Georgiana, was one of her married daughters], Blanche [another daughter, who married her cousin, the Earl of Burlington, later the 7th Duke of Devonshire], Ldy Chirton'. On the 16th 'Dined quietly at home'; the 17th was 'Ld C[arlisle]'s birthday – the Cawdors [Caroline, Lady Cawdor was a cousin], Dovers, Harriet [Granville, her sister] + Ld Clifden dined with us'; on the 18th, Sunday, 'drove over New London Bridge with the Children – dined with Ld Stafford [yet another relation] – news of Warsaw being taken by the Russians – met the Gowers and Cawdors; 19th, dined and stayed quietly at home all day – 3rd reading of

Reform Bill in House of Commons – Game Bill in Hse of Lords'. On the 20th she stayed at home again and merely notes that 'Augustus married Miss Elphinstone'. On the 21st she notes first that 'Blanche dined with us' and then *'Reform Bill carried by majority of 109'*. On the 22nd she opens with more of the exciting news: *'Reform Bill carried up from the H of C to H of Lords'*, – and then goes on to report on the same page that she has attended the launch of a new ship, the *Thunderer*, at Woolwich. And so it goes on: 'my children went to Brighton', 'Ld C was gouty', 'Ld Brougham defended himself from Ld Londonderry's attack', and 'Ld Gower sent me a Goose' . . . plus a great many more dinner parties, and a constant litany of famous Whig names.

Georgiana spent hours in the House listening to the debates. On one occasion a row blew up, which she clearly reports from first-hand observation: 'Ld Carlisle was at the House of Lords where Ld Londonderry nearly challenged Ld Brougham for what he said to him, resenting his mode of questioning – it was however amicably settled + likely to lead to greater peace in future.' This sanguine note is followed by a terse statement that she has engaged a cook, and then that '. . . the Duke of R. [Rutland] expects to carry the bill by the 5th – Ld Mulgrove to lose it by the 15th'. The entry for 2 October first mentions driving to Roehampton, then a dinner, again with Whig grandees, and finishes 'more debate on the Reform Bill'. Another entry is more explicit about the protagonists fighting the Reform Bill: she had obviously stayed to listen to the whole debate, and wrote in her diary that Lord Grey had spoken admirably for two and a half hours and 'Ld Harrowby also spoke for 2 hrs, very well + much cheered by his party . . . Ld Melbourne answered him + spoke well . . . *the Duke of Wellington long and tiresome'* . . . Christmas in London again – dinner at Princess Esterhazy's when she 'met the Seftons, Hollands, Ld Palmerston + Talleyrand', among others . . .

Both Georgiana and her sister Harriet were well-known figures at Court, but appear to have reacted rather differently to Royal favour. Georgiana was very popular with King George IV and Lady Conyngham, his fat and jolly mistress, chiefly because she adored gossip. Lady Conyngham called Georgiana 'the most perfect of human beings and her *best* and *dearest* friend'. Harriet, on the other hand, was bored by the King and quite prepared to show it. Madame de Lieven, one of Harriet's cleverest friends, described the latter's behaviour in society thus:

... She [Harriet] cannot bear any kind of constraint; and her sole pleasure in society is to get into the most obscure corner of a drawing room equipped with her lorgnettes, so that she can see how ridiculous all the surrounding faces are, and accompanied by someone she can laugh with. She has never learned to be polite. I have often seen the King of England call her to sit by him – and two minutes later she would leave him because she did not find him amusing.

But then Harriet was an intellectual snob and had never suffered fools gladly, Royal or otherwise. Harriet herself, in one of her letters to Georgiana, makes it quite clear that the King preferred her sister's company and easy freedom of speech. The King had beckoned Harriet to his side and said – 'My dear, tell me something about the Cowpers and Lambs': Harriet, presumably not wanting to air the family scandals – Lady Caroline Lamb was a first cousin – prevaricated, causing the King to complain crossly: 'Bless me!! if G had been here she would have told me all about them! every particular!'

Harriet was Georgiana's closest friend and confidante, and, luckily, liked Morpeth, but she had never made any secret of her dislike of the 5th Earl. After his death in 1825 Harriet, once again at Castle Howard, rejoiced in the change of atmosphere:

Nothing can be more agreeable, more easy than the genre de vie here ... We take daily drives and the beauty of the place shakes me more than ever. The comfort of the house is ever a new delight. I cannot believe in the laisser aller and independence of all.

Over the years Sydney Smith had become not only a close friend of all the Howards, but their ex-officio spiritual mentor and general counsellor. In 1826 he told the new master of Castle Howard to spend

Gambling in the Great Subscription Room at Brooks's Club, St James's Street, by Rowlandson and Pugin. The 5th Earl lost a fortune at cards in the eighteenth century

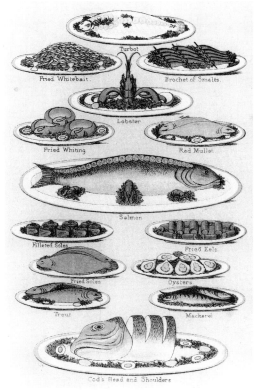

Plate from Mrs Beeton's *Every-Day Cookery and Housekeeping Book*

The artist Edward Burne-Jones with one of the children of the 9th Earl and Countess

The frontispiece of *A Picture Song Book* (1910) by George Howard, 9th Earl of Carlisle (1843–1911), with the Earl presenting his book to three of his children

The south parterre at Castle Howard *c.* 1870, with the Atlas Fountain and *parterre de broderie* laid out by William Nesfield in 1852–3. The parterre was removed by Rosalind Carlisle

Rosalind, 9th Countess of Carlisle
(1845–1921), by Aimé Jules Dalou, 1872

Rosalind Howard

Three generations: Lady Stanley of Alderley (seated), her daughter
Rosalind (sitting on the steps) and her granddaughter, later
Lady Mary Murray, 1891

Portrait of George Howard, 9th Earl of Carlisle,
painted in 1880 by Sir William Blake Richmond

View on the Nile, Luxor, by George Howard, 9th Earl of Carlisle

George Howard and his six sons (ascending the steps): Charles, Hubert, Christopher, Oliver, Geoffrey, Michael, *c.* 1883

Canvassing for one of Geoffrey Howard's political campaigns. He entered
Parliament for the first time in 1906 as the Liberal Member for one of the
Cumberland seats

Liberal Party gathering at Castle Howard in 1922, with Geoffrey Howard
in the centre

The Tapestry Room in the Victorian era, with the Vanderbank tapestries of the Four Seasons

The Music Room, Castle Howard

The fire of 1940, which devastated much of the south-east front of the
building

less time hunting: 'As I am an adviser by trade, allow me to recommend moderation in pursuing the pleasures of the chase. The fox was given to mankind not for business, but for amusement.' But it was Georgiana who needed him most, who had turned to Smith for comfort and counsel ever since the rector had come to Yorkshire. Smith, who suffered from melancholia himself, understood and sympathized with Georgiana's moods of shattering despair. In September 1819 he wrote to her that:

Everybody is haunted with spectres and apparitions of sorrow, and the imaginary griefs of life are greater than the real. Your rank in life exposes you the more to these attacks ... I like in you very much that you are a religious woman, because, though I have an infinite hatred and contempt for the nonsense which often passes under and disgraces the name of religion, I am very much pleased when I see anybody religious for hope and comfort, not for insolence and interest.

Smith was a singularly considerate man; knowing Georgiana's innate shyness and need for reassurance he ends his letter on just the right note: '. . . As for me, I will promise never to quizz you – that is, only a very little, and to your face, and in a low voice, and not before strangers; and for the rest, you will always find me a discreet neighbour and a sincere friend.'

And it was to Lady Georgiana Morpeth that Smith addressed his famous maxims for dealing with depression. They were written in 1820, when she was at Castle Howard:

Nobody has suffered more from low spirits than I have done, so I feel for you.
1. Live as well and drink as much wine as you dare.
2. Go into the shower-bath with a small quantity of water at a temperature low enough to give you *a slight sensation of cold* – 75 or 80 degrees.
3. Amusing books.
4. Short views of human life not further than dinner or tea.
5. Be as busy as you can.
6. See as much as you can of those friends who respect and like you.
7. and of those acquaintance who amuse you.

8. Make no secret of low spirits to your friends but talk of them fully: they are always the worse for dignified concealment.
9. Attend to the effects tea and coffee produce upon you.
10. Compare your lot with that of other people.
11. Don't expect too much of human life, a sorry business at the best.
12. Avoid poetry, dramatic representations (except comedy), music, serious novels, melancholy sentimental people, and everything likely to excite feeling or emotion not ending in active benevolence.
13. Do good and endeavour to please everybody of every degree.
14. Be as much as you can in the open air without fatigue.
15. Make the room where you commonly sit gay and pleasant.
16. Struggle by little and little against idleness.
17. Don't be too severe upon yourself, or underrate yourself, but do yourself justice.
18. Keep good blazing fires.
19. Be firm and constant in the exercise of rational religion.
20. Believe me, dear Lady Georgiana,
    very truly yours
    Sydney Smith.

The rector's advice to the Howards could also be eminently practical: he made a serious study of medical lore and became a noted herbalist, often consulted by his parishioners. Smith wrote a charming poem on the subject for the Hon. Mrs Henry Howard, titled 'The Poetical Medicine Chest', which illustrates his knowledge of basic medication.

> With store of powdered rhubarb we begin;
> (To leave out powdered rhubarb were a sin),
> Pack mild magnesia deep within the chest;
> And glittering gum from Araby the blest;
> And keep, oh lady, keep within thy reach
> The slimy surgeon, blood-devouring leech.
> Laurel-born camphor, opiate drugs prepare,
> They banish pain, and calm consuming care.
> Glauber and Epsom salts their aid combine,

Translucent streams of castor-oil be thine,
And gentle mana in thy bottles shine.
If morbid spot of septic sore invade,
By heaven-sent bark the morbid spot is stayed;
When with black bile hepatic regions swell,
With subtle calomel the plague expel.
Anise and mint with strong Aeolian sway,
Intestine storms of flatulence allay,
And ipecacuanha clears the way.
I know thee well, thou antimonial power,
And to thee fly in that heart-rending hour,
When feverish patients heave their laden breath,
And all is sickness, agony, and death!
Soda and potash change their humours crude,
When hoven parsons swell with luscious food.
Spare not in eastern blasts when babies die
That wholesome vigour of the Spanish fly.
From timely torture seek thy infant's rest,
And spread the poison on his labouring breast.
And so, fair lady, when in evil hour
Less prudent mothers mourn some faded flower,
Six Howards valiant and six Howards fair,
Shall live and love thee, and reward thy care.

Since health, or rather the lack of it, is one of the most constant themes throughout contemporary diaries and correspondence, it seems appropriate, at this point, to glance at the state of medicine in general during the eighteenth and nineteenth centuries.

Of course many of the diseases rife at that time no longer exist today, or are easily dealt with by modern medicine. Scrofula or 'King's Evil', 'green sickness', and 'St Anthony's Fire', for example, have long since vanished from the medical scene. But in the past vast numbers of people suffered from these and other illnesses unknown to us which were horribly painful, disabling and often unsightly. Bad health was a constant and inevitable factor of daily life on a scale which would be unimaginable in the twentieth-century civilized world. Gout, dropsy, worms, rickets, spinal deformities, skin ulcerations, repeated miscarriages and venereal disease may not have been fatal but they put an end to a pleasant life. Moreover, many of the so-called 'treatments' were even more agonizing than the illness itself: the 6th Earl of Carlisle's mother-in-law suffered agonies towards the end of her life when her eyesight failed and the doctors applied leeches direct to her eyeballs. The most barbaric surgery was often inflicted upon patients quite unnecessarily and to no good purpose. Septicaemia was rife and usually fatal – and the only anaesthetics available were laudanum and the brandy bottle.

A 'Domestic Medical Guide', written at the beginning of the eighteenth century and still popular 100 years later, suggested that a family medicine chest should include laudanum, calomel, antimony and extract of lead – all potentially dangerous drugs which today would be available only on prescription. Among the standard medicines to be recommended were such weird-sounding substances as 'Agaric of Oak, Ash coloured Ground Liverwort, Burgundy pitch, Elixir of Vitriol, Crabs Claw prepared, Tincture of Mars, Flowers of Sulphur, Liquid laudanum, Snake root, and Sweet spirits of Nitrate'. Others mentioned were clearly homoeopathic remedies – 'Syrup of Poppies, Tamarind, Cinnamon water, Yellow basilicum and Wild Valerian root'.

Some of the remedies suggested by other sources seem purely absurd, such as that put forward by the Revd Edmund Pyle, who wrote in all seriousness that he:

... took Mrs Stephen's mixture ... I swallowed two ounces of soap a day, for six months together. Besides the oyster shell, or egg shell powder, in small beer, to the quantity that will lie on a half-crown with each dose of soap; I think the doses were 3 or 4 in the day.

Unfortunately the record does not say what particular malady eating soap was supposed to cure – its effect was presumably that of a daily emetic. And around the same time Lord Byron, always an exhibitionist, started a vogue for slimming which involved eating nothing but biscuits soaked in vinegar.

Superstition has always been the enemy of scientific progress. It is, therefore, not surprising that one of the most important medical discoveries ever made – vaccination against smallpox – should have met with bitter opposition at the start. Edward Jenner, who had been experimenting with cowpox as a vaccination for some time, first published the idea as early as 1796 but it was not accepted, even by the medical profession, until well into the next century. Superstition, too, was responsible for the extraordinary success of the 'quacks', one of the more frightening aspects of contemporary medical fashion.

Quacks, referred to as 'nostrum-vendors', were as popular and powerful as qualified physicians. Indeed the two were not mutually exclusive propositions – the doctors of the day relied heavily on the quacks and their wares. Nor was the use of these quack medicines confined to the more gullible sections of society; on the contrary, testimonials from celebrated clients were quoted freely in all the advertisements. 'Mr Ward's Drops', which Sir Thomas Robinson had advocated so strongly for his father-in-law's gout, were also endorsed by Lord Chesterfield and Henry Fielding. Byron was a great believer in Acton's Corn Rubbers, and the poet Cowper in Opdeldoc Ointment, for rheumatism. And both Horace Walpole and Fanny Burney swore by the dangerous fever powders peddled by Dr Robert James.

In the context of modern thought it seems almost unbelievable that there was no legal restraint whatsoever upon these quacks, nor were they obliged to declare the ingredients of their patent medicines. The success or failure of a particular brand was determined by fashion, faith and word of mouth alone – scientific analysis was seldom mentioned. The public often had no idea what drugs they were taking, let alone the quantities involved, in all these dubious concoctions which they swallowed so blindly. Even the most respected – and expensive – doctors prescribed patent medicines which had been prepared to secret formulae. Roy Porter cites the case of Doctor James's powders in his book *Health for Sale*:

. . . Most famously (or notoriously) of all Doctor Robert James, with his Cambridge M.D., became a public celebrity with those best-selling febrifuge powders, for which Horace Walpole had such a 'superstitious veneration', but which may have hastened the deaths of Dr Oliver Goldsmith, John Howard, and Laurence Sterne, amongst others, for they were amongst the most potent antimonial preparations of the day. James . . . had knowingly fudged the formula of his patent – to maximize secrecy – with the result that the unpredictable mixture of ingredients would readily prove a health hazard.

Handbills advertising these pills and powders were posted in shop windows and published in all the papers. They made the most outrageous claims; a typical bill proclaimed that a Pill against *all* Diseases would, among other things, cure the:

. . . chief signs of Scurvey, Putrefaction and Stinking of the Gums, Stinking-Breath, Blackness and Looseness of the Teeth, sudden Flushings, Heat and Redness in the Face and Body, much Wind and unsavory Belchings . . .

Many of the quack remedies traded on snob-appeal, for example, 'the Duke of Portland's Powder', for gout, 'Lady Moor's Drops' and the 'Countess of Kent's Powder'. Others made a fortune out of venereal disease – not surprisingly, in view of contemporary mores. As Porter writes:

The figure of the syphilophobe, fearful of every little twinge in the back, and convinced his nose was daily disappearing, looms large in the medical anecdotes of the time.

Scores of remedies were on offer, coyly addressed to those who had 'been sporting in the garden of Venus', or had 'anchored in a Strange Harbour' etc., etc., and *ad nauseam*. Bills headed 'A Most Infallible, and Sure Cheap Secret Safe and Speedy Cure for the Pox', or 'Venus Deceiv'd . . . an Account of the Seat, and Nature of a Clap', guaranteed cures in only seven doses.

These unsavoury mixtures were not cheap; the average cost of a bottle of medicine was one shilling – the price of a dozen pints of ale, or a labourer's wages for a day. Doctor James's powders were an even more expensive poison, at 2s. 6d. for two sachets, while one of the most popular cures for venereal disease, 'Kennedy's Lisbon Diet Drink', which cost 10s. 6d. a bottle, was clearly beyond the reach of any but the most affluent lechers.

'Miracle' cures for infertility were equally popular at a time when so many men suffered from syphilis or gonorrhoea, and so many women from the results of attempted abortion. (The demand for these particular drugs was confined, of course, to a very small number of ladies who needed to give their husbands an heir: in the case of 99 per cent of the population, however, there was nothing the women wanted less than continual pregnancies and many of them ruined their health with quack contraception.) James Graham, who was clearly a charlatan, became the sexual guru of the 1780s, numbering among his clients such leaders of fashion as Catharine Macaulay and Georgiana, Duchess of Devonshire. Graham set up a 'Temple of Health and Hymen' in Pall Mall, where, among other attractions, society could watch him being buried naked in mud. With only his head poking out of the mud, the 'doctor' regaled the company with a lecture on health, *risqué* enough, according to a contemporary account, to call up the 'chaste blushes of the modest ladies'. Graham's most notorious claim to fame was the 'Celestial State Bed', said to aid fertility, which was on offer to couples at £50 a night. This ludicrous contraption featured electric shock treatments to the sound of music, and sounds more suited to an expensive brothel than a medical centre:

The Grand Celestial Bed, whose magical influences are now celebrated from pole to pole and from the rising to the setting of the sun is 12ft long by 9ft wide, supported by forty pillars of brilliant glass of the most exquisite workmanship, in richly variegated colours. The super-celestial dome of the bed, which contains the odoriferous, balmy and ethereal spices, odours and essences, which is the grand reservoir of those reviving, invigorating influences which are exhaled by the breath of the music and by the exhilarating force of electrical fire, is covered on the other side with brilliant panes of looking-glass. On the utmost summit of the dome are placed two exquisite figures of Cupid and Psyche, with a figure of Hymen behind, with his torch flaming with electrical fire in one hand and with the other, supporting a celestial crown, sparkling over a pair of living turtle doves, on a little bed of roses.

The other elegant group of figures which sport on the top of the dome, having each of them musical instruments in their hands, which by the most expensive mechanism, breathe forth sound corresponding to their instruments, flutes, guitars, violins, clarinets, trumpets, horns, oboes, kettle drums etc . . .

At the head of the bed appears sparkling with electrical fire a great first commandment: 'BE FRUITFUL, MULTIPLY AND REPLENISH THE EARTH' . . . [the] Superior ecstasy which the parties enjoy in the Celestial Bed is really astonishing and never before thought of in this world: the barren must certainly become fruitful when they are powerfully agitated in the delights of love.

The public loved the Bed, and Graham made a fortune – a sufficiently apt comment on the mood of the period.

8

'. . . As Her Majesty is Coming to Castle Howard'

By the beginning of the nineteenth century ostentatious display of any kind had come to be considered a sign of vulgarity, rather than a necessary statement of status. The feckless attitude to life which had been the hallmark of the aristocracy in the previous century – and which had played such havoc with the Howard finances – had been replaced by more prudent and sober values. Extravagance and waste were cardinal sins in Victorian England: conspicuous consumption not only distasteful, but immoral. Nevertheless, the sheer scale upon which the great houses were run increased, if anything, rather than diminished, during the first half of the nineteenth century: in one month alone, October 1847, *a total of 2,138 meals* were served at Castle Howard. Of these, 395 were eaten in 'the Parlour' – i.e. by the family and their guests – and 1,743 by the 'household', or staff. Nor are these staggering figures unique; the pattern is repeated during the whole of the 6th Earl's tenure of Castle Howard. Admittedly the 6th Earl and Georgiana had a vast family, and by 1825, when he succeeded to the title, several of their children were married, and would often be accompanied by their own broods, complete with separate nursery staff, when they came to stay, thus swelling the numbers even further – but, nevertheless, the catering records indicate an unprecedented amount of entertaining.

The Carlisles had a surprisingly efficient comptroller, or steward, at the time: meticulous records were kept from 1825 to 1849, written in a series of notebooks and headed respectively 'larder book', 'game book', 'dairy book' and 'cellar book'. Their author took the trouble not only to record the quantities of food consumed in a particular month, but what it was, and whether it was served to the staff or to the family and their guests. These notebooks illustrate clearly the scale upon which the great aristocrats continued to live in Victorian England. For example, in the autumn of 1834 the quantities of meat consumed at Castle Howard were as follows:

	October	November	December
Beef	1,217lb	1,256lb	1,326lb
Mutton	1,906lb	2,061lb	2,195lb
Veal	143lb	76lb	49lb
Pork	204lb	465lb	491lb
Bacon	82lb	70lb	35lb
Ham	71lb	91lb	11lb
Total	3,623	4,019	4,107 = 1.83 tons!

The figures quoted for game during the same season are, comparatively speaking, low for such a large estate. They are listed under the heading 'Consumed or Given Away' – an indication of the prevalent custom of giving game away as presents to both gentry and tenants:

	October	December
Hares	40	49
Rabbits	86	80
Geese	18	11
Partridges	88	13
Pheasants	27	63
Snipe	4	2
Woodcock	1	34 + 10 wild duck

This could well have been a period when the resident complement of the household was predominantly female and there were few available guns. Just over ten years later, in 1847, the game book indicates, under the heading of game 'Consumed or Given Away', a series of much larger shooting parties:

	October	December
Hares	43	41
Rabbits	166	123
Geese	51	11
Partridges	189	2
Pheasants	40	57
Snipe	22	10
Woodcock	7	41

In 1847, too, the amount of meat consumed was much greater:

	April	August	October	December
Beef	1,989	2,301	2,278	2,196
Mutton	2,297	1,469	1,839	1,740
Lamb	–	128	80	–
Veal	109½	140½	101½	168
Pork	75	–	83	341
Ham	125	173	114	47
Bacon	333	204	158	182

The same dedicated hand recorded in the Dairy Book that in the month of April, 1847, 1,886 meals were served at Castle Howard, and in December 2,055:

April	Dined in Parlour 290
	Dined in Household 1,596
December	Dined in Parlour 370
	Dined in Household 1,685

There is a further note to the effect that, in the same month:

The Parlour used 68½lb butter and 95½ pints cream
The Still-room used 48¼ lb butter and 91 pints cream
The Kitchen used 15 lb butter.

These figures by no means represent the total amount of dairy produce consumed by the Castle that month. They refer only to the quantities brought in from the home farm: in addition, 107 lb of butter were *bought* for the household, plus 100 half-pints of cream and 336 pints of milk.

The vast quantities of food consumed in the 1830s and 1840s can only be interpreted as evidence of continuous entertaining. In 1825, when the household was in mourning for the death of the 5th Earl, the totals were a fraction of the amounts quoted above. Even in the Christmas month of that year only 328 lb of beef and 531½ lb of mutton were needed in the kitchens, and there was a comparable reduction in consumption of everything else.

Drink was another matter altogether, and the state of the cellars at Castle Howard has swung from one extreme to another, according to the temperaments of the various owners. When the house was built, at the beginning of the eighteenth century, a lavish supply of drink was expected to be on offer to all comers throughout the day, and the quality of the wine was of paramount importance. Since one of the reasons why Charles Howard, 3rd Earl of Carlisle, built the house in the first place was to enhance his status, it was clearly incumbent upon him to lay down a good cellar. Besides, like most of his contemporaries, he liked wine and drank heavily until overtaken by gout. The accounts for February 1702 show that he bought half a hogshead★ of Burgundy for £25, as well as large quantities of champagne and Canary wine. (Canary, incidentally, was a light sweet wine imported from the Canary Islands, which had come into fashion during the sixteenth century and was regarded as an innocuous ladies' drink, useless to anyone of serious alcoholic intent.)

★ One hogshead equals 52½ gallons.

All through the eighteenth century the drink continued to flow at
Castle Howard. The cellar lists include all the obvious wines, such as
claret, Burgundy, champagne, 'Old Hock', red port and Madeira, but
they also mention some which are virtually unknown today. For
example 'Mountain', a sweet white wine made from grapes grown in
the mountains of Malaga, and 'Frontiniack', a similar French wine,
both of which were again very popular with women. 'Arrack', a
rather coarse, sweet liqueur, made from rice or coconuts, was another
favourite of the period which has since gone out of fashion.

From the 1770s to the 1820s port appears to have been the most
popular drink at Castle Howard, probably because it was considerably
cheaper than imported French wine. Port cost 3s. 6d. a bottle as
compared to claret and champagne, which both cost 7s. a bottle. This
was the period when the 5th Earl was attempting to economize – but
hardly to the point of abstemiousness in the light of the quantities
ordered. In 1778, for example, an order was placed with the firm of
Watlington and Bainbrigge for two pipes of red port – and one pipe
equalled 105 gallons. In 1805 the records show that the cellars
contained *229 dozen, and eight*, bottles of port, and the rate of consumption continued to rise over the next few years until it reached nearly
100 bottles per month. By far the largest proportion of all this port
was drunk in the Steward's Room, as can be seen from the relevant
figures in the Cellar Book. In one month, in 1821, for example, the
Steward's Room drank 94 bottles of port, whereas the Dining Room
accounted for no more than 17. Ale was, of course, the standard fare
of the servants, in preference to water, which was often dangerously
tainted. Both beer and ale were home-brewed at Castle Howard and
drunk in huge quantities: records written in 1858 show that, in
August alone, thirty-one employees drank *114½ gallons of ale, plus 49½
gallons of beer.*

Nevertheless, by 1848, when the 7th Earl inherited Castle Howard,
Queen Victoria's influence had already begun to dictate a more sober
approach to life. Sherry, a lighter drink than port, replaced the latter
as the most favoured drink, and the total amount of alcohol consumed
at Castle Howard began to decline. But wine for the family and

guests, and beer or ale for the staff, were still served at every meal; champagne appeared for parties, ladies sipped their ratafia and the gentlemen still lingered over their port in the dining-room. All this came to an abrupt end in the 1890s, when the 9th Earl succeeded to the title – or rather when his wife, Rosalind, became the chatelaine. The 9th Countess of Carlisle was a formidable character and a dedicated teetotaller, to put it mildly: she closed all the pubs on the estate and virtually banned alcohol at Castle Howard.

In 1825, when the 6th Earl inherited the title, no less than forty-six servants were employed on a full-time basis, the largest complement in the Carlisle records. In addition there were an unspecified number of peripheral, part-time staff who would be mobilized to assist when the occasion demanded. A few key figures remained constant in each residence, but the majority moved between London and Castle Howard in the wake of their employers. Thus the stationary household kept at the London house consisted of only four servants – house-keeper, housemaid, porter and one extra maid. The Castle Howard permanent indoor staff was obviously larger, including, besides the housekeeper, seven maids of different kinds and an 'Usher of the Hall' – presumably a male general factotum, in the absence of the butler and footmen. These skeleton staffs were considered sufficient to keep the respective houses in order while the family were away; whenever the Carlisles were in residence the household was automatically augmented by the travelling servants. It was clearly cheaper to move the servants than to keep the various houses fully staffed all the year round. The Carlisles' travelling retinue comprised twenty-three ser-vants, and included some of the very lowliest in the hierarchy:

House steward	Under coachman
Groom of the chamber	Postillion
Cook	Groom
Valet	Steward's room boy
Lady's maid	2 stable helpers

Young ladies' maid	Laundry maid
3 Footmen	Upper kitchen maid
Under footman	Under kitchen maid
Under butler	Housemaid
Head coachman	Nursemaid

It must have been exciting for a young country girl, newly arrived in service as a junior kitchen maid, to find herself chosen to accompany the Carlisles to London. The possibility of travel was one of the inducements to a life in service with a great family. And, wherever they were, the servants were certainly well fed: records dated 1830 estimated that the following allowances of food and drink per servant, per day, were required:

Meat	$\frac{1}{2}$lb
Bread	1lb
Ale (men)	1qt
(women)	$\frac{1}{2}$qt (sexual discrimination, as usual)
Small beer (men)	1pt
(women)	$\frac{1}{2}$pt
Tea	qt oz (tea was still an expensive item)
Sugar	$1\frac{1}{2}$ oz

The most complete record of the wages paid to the various servants at Castle Howard was compiled thirty years later, in 1880, by the trustees of the 8th Earl. However, the amounts are unlikely to have increased to any marked extent during the interim, and the figures tally with those quoted by Mrs Beeton for a comparable household during the mid nineteenth century. By far the highest paid member of the staff was the house steward, whose job at the time the records were compiled involved even greater responsibility than usual, since the titular head of the family was absent owing to mental breakdown. The steward is listed as George Martin, whose salary is given as £105 a year; this amount is exactly double that of the next mentioned, in order of seniority – John Duthie, Groom of the Chambers, who was paid £52 10s. a year. Mrs Martin, the housekeeper (presumably the steward's wife), was the highest-paid woman member of the staff, at £50 a year, and the cook, Mrs Hibberd, came next at £45 a year. The wages of the more menial female servants, however, were much lower: 'Three housemaids at £16 16s. 0d.; £13 13s. 0d. and £12 12s. 0d. per year respectively, with 9s. per week Board Wages all year round.' Six other girls are mentioned, their jobs unspecified, whose wages range from £24 to £13 13s. As usual, the male staff fared a great deal better than the women:

> James Mansfield, under butler £35
>
> Frederick Knight, footman £28
>
> 'John Bedell £45 12s. 6d. per year, as Brewer and Usher of the Hall. One suit of Clothes (not livery). No board Wages, but fed in Servant's Hall.'
>
> William Robinson, watchman £45 12s. 6d. per year, or 2s. 6d. per night. One suit of clothes per year (not livery).
>
> Thomas Crother 24s. 6d. per month, 'for Sleeping at night to be in readiness on the premises in case of fire'. [It is a tragedy that no successor was employed in this post: in 1940 Castle Howard was nearly destroyed by fire.]

A scullion is mentioned, at 14s. per week, and 'A man for attending to the stoves, carrying luggage etc 17s. per week'.

The most valued member of the outside staff seems to have been the head gardener, who was paid £90 a year. The head coachman earned £40 a year and the second coachman £28, both on a permanent basis: the groom was paid £1 a week, when on call, and the children's pony boy 18s. a week. The stable yard was capable of catering for at least 100 horses and five coaches or carriages, for the use of the family and guests, riding, hunting or driving. (The servants' horses, and carthorses, were stabled elsewhere on the estate.) A 'Yardman' was employed, at 2s. 6d. per day, and a house carpenter at 3s. 6d. per day. The post appears to have been an expensive item: in the 1830 accounts there is a record that the Malton postman was paid 6d. a day 'for carrying letters to and from Office and Castle, Dinner in the Servant's Hall'. But ten years later there is another account which puts the postman's wages at 2s. per day, and his total annual cost at £88 8s. 2d. The breakdown of this figure gives an interesting insight into comparative values at the time:

The expenses of the post (mail) 1840
The keep of a horse £25
The keep of a cow £10
Rent of house and garden £5, equals £40 a year – *expenses* of postman
Year's *wages* of Postman, at 2s. per day = £36 10s. 0d.
Uniform (Castle Howard livery) £11 18s. 2d. = £48 8s. 2d.
Total cost of postman £88 8s. 2d.

The 1830 accounts end with a charmingly evocative entry: 'Henry Wright an Old Woodman has always been employed at the Castle in preparing wood for the Bakehouse and Kindling for fires at 14s. per week.' And a note was added to the records, possibly in justification of these relatively high wages, that: 'The above have been many years in the service connected with the Castle and Residential Establishment.' In fact many of the Castle servants came from families who had worked for the Howards for generations – as can be seen from the frequent repetition of the same name on tombstones of different dates in the local graveyards. These people were born on the estate, went into service at the Castle as soon as they were old enough, and retired at the end of their working lives to one of the tied, rent-free, cottages reserved for employees. For such, Castle Howard became their whole life, their whole *raison d'être*. The Howard servants were fortunate in their employers: a retainer such as the 'Old Woodman' would never have been dismissed simply because he had outlived his usefulness. *Noblesse oblige* may have been a costly force but it was a boon to the working classes – and anyway created a benevolent circle, a mutual loyalty between employer and employee.

In August 1850, Queen Victoria and her family spent two nights at Castle Howard, the first reigning monarch to visit the house since it had been built 150 years before. By this time the 6th Earl of Carlisle had died (in 1848), and had been succeeded by his eldest son George, the 7th Earl – an old friend of Prince Albert's. Since the 7th Earl remained unmarried, Georgiana Carlisle, who outlived her husband by ten years, carried on as chatelaine of Castle Howard. A vigorous matriarch in her sixties, Georgiana was well accustomed to entertaining on the grand scale and, in any case, though of a different generation from the young Queen, had known the Royal family all her life. The family were in particularly close contact with the Court in 1850 since Carlisle's sister Harriet, now the Duchess of Sutherland, had recently been appointed Mistress of the Robes to Queen Victoria. The time was ripe for a Royal visit to Castle Howard, and an invitation was duly dispatched. Carlisle suggested that the Royal party come to stay on their way to Scotland: on 27 July 1850 Prince Albert replied with a formal letter of acceptance:

. . . we cannot refuse your kind invitation and . . . we shall with pleasure stay two nights with you . . .

We shall leave [Osborne] . . . on Tuesday 27 August and reach Castle Howard that evening . . .

The smaller your party and the less of pomp and ceremony the better the Queen will like her stay under your roof.

The Carlisles, however, had no intention of hiding their light under a bushel on such an important occasion. The first visit of a reigning monarch was a landmark in the history of Castle Howard, and both mother and son were determined to make the most of it. Work began at once on gilding the cupola of the main dome, and the acorn on the dome of the East Wing; the rooms for the Royal party were all redecorated, and new carpets and furniture either bought or hired for the occasion from York. A few days before the Queen arrived, Carlisle raced into the town yet again to buy a new billiard table. The obligatory red drugget for the Queen's reception, however, was kept to a minimum and ordered on sale or return: Carlisle thought it rather a waste of money. The whole household was involved, under the direction of John Henderson, the agent, assisted

The Queen and her family spent two nights at Castle Howard in August 1850.
The royal visit became a three-day fiesta for all the local villages and 15,000 people
gathered to cheer the Queen when she toured the grounds.

by the butler, Mr Mayor, and Charlotte Parker, the housekeeper. Mrs
Parker despaired at the state of some of the furnishings in a letter to
the Countess dated 5 August:

As her Majesty is coming to Castle Howard I take the liberty to write to
your Ladyship to name a few things necessary to be had – New chintze
covers for the Music Room, the old ones are very much faded and worn,
long muslin curtains would be a great improvement to this room and to the
Drawing Room as well as the rooms upstairs that Her Majesty is to have.
Fire irons and fenders are much wanted for the Blue Silk Room and Green
Ivery, the fenders now are only painted ons. I have made some new toilet
covers and linings for rooms, but they are not good enough for Her Majesty.
I could get some pretty figurd net at Malton with some white or pink sattin
to line it . . .

By 1850 a number of bathrooms and lavatories had been installed at Castle Howard, albeit of a somewhat primitive nature. For the Queen's visit 'a dozen new large foot tubs' were made by the estate carpenter and orders given to 'see particularly that all the water closets are in proper order, especially the two which are on the Queen's floor'.

Carlisle's particular concern was to show off the Castle's newly acquired gas lighting. Gas burners had been installed in various key positions on the ground floor at the beginning of the year, and Carlisle decided to extend the system to the Royal apartments upstairs. A London gas specialist, Mr Leslie of Conduit Street, was imported to devise a plan of illuminating the dome. Mr Leslie wrote to the agent:

I have seen Lord Carlisle . . . and we have determined the plan. I am to make a ring for the balustrade to which I am to attach 15 seperate [*sic*] letters GOD SAVE THE QUEEN. These will contain about *2,000* of my seperate tubes. The inclination of each letter will be such that the whole sentence may be read below. I do not know the distance under ordinary circumstances that the Dome of Castle Howard can be seen, but I have no doubt that some people will see it who never saw it before. It will have a beautiful effect, internal as well as external.

Georgiana, meanwhile, went off to seek the advice and help of her brother, the Duke of Devonshire, who had experience of entertaining the Queen from her visit to Chatsworth. He told Georgiana that 'what H.M. chiefly cares about is for there to be a sufficient number of *tables* to put all her *things* upon' – the Victorian mania for clutter was in full spate. Devonshire also offered the services of Joseph Paxton, the famous Chatsworth head gardener, who proved 'most amiable and liberal in offers of assistance during the Queen's visit by sending [Castle Howard] flowers and fruit'. Best of all, the Duke lent Castle Howard the Chatsworth musicians – Mr Coote, and his band. The six players were paid a fee of 10 guineas each, plus travelling expenses of £20 for the group. Their instruments were a piano-forte, a harp, a clarinet, 'cornet a pistons', a 'cello and a flute.

Near-panic appears to have attacked the staff a couple of weeks before the Royal party arrived. Lord Carlisle was still in London making final arrangements about the lighting, and Georgiana still at Chatsworth on 8 August, when the butler in town wrote to the agent at Castle Howard:

This is not the time to talk but to act . . . His Lordship has just told me that Lady Carlisle [and] Lady Mary will be at C.H. on Monday next. In the first place you will be *good* enough to *kill* − or slaughter 3 sheep on Saturday, 1 bullock on Monday and 2 fine *fat* bucks . . . I shall send on Saturday Large and a helper, and 2 horses, a footman and Steward's room boy.

Henderson replied that: 'We have 20 men in the house now and they will not finish this week, paint as they may . . . if I durst ask you to put your journey off for two days I would do so.' The family in fact arrived *en masse* on 15 August, accompanied by a mountain of luggage, hampers of wine and 'a great many boxes, very heavy', full of provisions for the Royal visit.

Lord Carlisle spent the intervening days experimenting with the new gas lighting while Lady Carlisle fussed about the sleeping arrangements − with reason. Castle Howard would be stretched to its limit. For a start, the Royal party consisted of fourteen guests accompanied by fifteen servants. The Queen brought four of her children, along with their governess and tutor, and her private Chaplain, as well as various aides-de-camp and ladies-in-waiting. Prince Albert's secretary had already written with precise instructions about the children's rooms: the Prince of Wales and his tutor, Mr Birch, were to be given separate, but adjoining rooms, but the Princesses could share a room with the nurserymaid. The nursery party were to have a separate sitting-room, and another room should be reserved for the governess. The letter added that: 'The Queen does not actually make a point of these rooms being very near Her own, but She is anxious that they should not be *near anybody else's*.' The Royal servants, whose accommodation also had to be taken into account, included, among others, two pages, three valets, three footmen, three dressers and a hairdresser.

And, of course, there was the rest of the Howard family itself, all clamouring to come and stay for the Queen's visit. By 1850 most of Georgiana's children had married and produced numerous progeny of their own – whose claims to Royal notice their parents doubtless wanted to assert as early as possible. Children came back into fashion with the advent of Queen Victoria. No longer banished to the servants' quarters, they were given light and airy rooms as their nurseries; they were courted and petted, dressed up and paraded in the drawing-room after tea. Nanny became one of the most powerful figures in the household, an autocrat in her own domain, who often seemed almost a part of the family itself, a fixture in their lives, who would be passed on from one generation to the next. This was the age of Alice in Wonderland and Hans Christian Andersen, of Sunday school in white gloves and embroidered religious texts over the nursery beds.

After ruthless editing of the guest list the final total still came to an extra sixteen members of the family, or their friends, who would be staying at Castle Howard. In the end, the party consisted of: the 7th Earl of Carlisle and the Dowager Countess, Georgiana; the only unmarried daughter of the house, Lady Mary Howard; the four married daughters, with their various appendages (Lady Caroline Lascelles and her husband William; Harriet, Duchess of Sutherland, with her daughter; Lady Dover, plus two daughters, a nurse and her father-in-law, Lord Clifden; and Lady Elizabeth Grey with her husband); Mr and Mrs Edward Howard; and Charles Howard, whose wife had died tragically at the age of twenty. Charles brought his little son George, who later became the 9th Earl of Carlisle. And, finally, just one outsider – Mr W.H. Prescott, an American historian who was a particular friend of the host.

The Queen's visit was a major event for the whole county. Both *The Times* and the *Daily News* considered her brief stay at Castle Howard worth sending a special correspondent from London to cover in detail. (They arrived at the same time as fifty-six brace of grouse from Naworth.) And the York Superintendent of Police estimated that more than 15,000 people gathered in the park to watch her drive by when she toured the grounds with her hosts – and many of them would have walked all the way from York. The Royal visit became a three-day fiesta for all the local villages: stalls sprang up all along the Queen's route, the ballad-singers were out in force, and the pubs were packed. The crowd, according to the Earl's diary, were 'perfectly behaved'. At that time Queen Victoria was at the height of her popularity and the enormous crowd roared their applause whenever they saw her. At one point during the visit, when the Queen and her children came out on the steps of Castle Howard to wave to the waiting crowd, her reception was so tumultuous that the police became alarmed. The Earl reported that: 'Here the people, to use the expression of the York Superintendent of Police, became wild, and if she had stayed a minute longer than she did, I think they must have been upon her.'

The Queen and her party had left Osborne at 8.00 on the morning of Tuesday 27 August and arrived at Castle Howard station★ dead on time, at 6.00 in the evening. (They had stopped on the way to pay a visit of condolence to the ex-Queen of France, whose husband, Louis-Philippe, had died the previous night – the journey from London itself took only six hours.) The arrival of the Royal party was described by the local paper:

The early part of the day was wet, cold and disagreeable, a mist worthy of the Grampian Hills enveloping the landscape, and a drizzling rain descending. Notwithstanding the unfavourable state of the weather, however, numbers of people flocked in from the surrounding district to witness her Majesty's arrival. Trains laden with loyal subjects arrived from Scarborough; and we encountered one indefatigable lady who had come all the way from Bath to have a good view . . .

By and large, the visit was a success, despite one or two hiccups. On the first evening the Queen got lost, according to the Earl's diary, 'and I

★ Castle Howard station was a private halt, constructed by the railway company as part of the deal they made with the 7th Earl at the beginning of the nineteenth century. It was not closed down until shortly before the Second World War.

The arrival of Queen Victoria at Castle Howard station. The station was a private halt built in 1845, and the Howard family retained the right to stop any passing train, even an express, until shortly before the Second World War.

found her alone in a crowd of guests and servants'. She seems to have been a fairly bossy guest, who went round opening windows and asking for the fires to be reduced: Prince Albert slightly upset the Earl as well by asking all sorts of pertinent questions about the various treasures in the house which Carlisle was quite unable to answer. The military band of Dragoons, who had been brought in to play during dinner the first night, were wasted, because the Queen felt music would be inappropriate the day after Louis-Philippe had died. Fortunately she did not decide to go into full mourning, so the rest of the entertainment was able to continue as planned. It was an innocuous, pleasant programme, typical of country house entertaining at that time: the Royal party watched a cricket match, admired the greenhouses, toured the house, drove in the park, inspected the farm and planted trees. The

Queen was particularly interested in the mausoleum and told Carlisle that she was thinking of building one herself because 'the Royal family think the vault at Windsor so gloomy'. On the first night the party was confined to the immediate family circle and their guests – thirty-five, in all; but in the course of the visit the Queen was introduced to all the neighbouring gentry at various great receptions. Fifty guests, including the Archbishop of York, were invited to lunch on the second day, and that evening Mr Coote's band was permitted to play. According to the Earl, 'there was not a moment's cloud on the Royal brow' that night. He added, however, that:

The only thing to be a little regretted, and chiefly for her own sake, is that in the evening and in general society she has not the way of putting a room quite at its ease.

On the last morning seventy more people were asked to breakfast, and afterwards the Royal party took their leave of Castle Howard:

[The Queen] was most kind and amiable to my mother, told her all her daughters were so very dear, and that it was a perfect picture of a united family, and she gave her a bracelet.★

Carlisle's only regret about the visit was that there had been no buns for the schoolchildren, but that, he added, 'was Henderson's fault'.

The festivities continued even after the Queen and her entourage had left: taking advantage of the musicians' presence at Castle Howard, Carlisle gave an enormous ball that night for all his friends and neighbours. Dancing took place in the north end of the gallery, and in the Octagon, while supper was served for forty at a time in the south end. Unhampered by the restraining presence of the Queen, the ball carried on until three in the morning.

Queen Victoria was clearly disappointed in the gardens at Castle

★ As has already been mentioned in a previous chapter, the Queen also left £100 to be distributed in tips among the household staff, and a further £50 for the stables.

Howard, finding the design somewhat bleak and boring – as indeed, they were by Victorian standards. She wrote in her diary that: 'There are no flowers about, & but a few gravel walks, but Ld Carlisle intends to have a flower garden, where now there is nothing but grass, with an obelisk in the centre.' Originally, there had been rather more in the way of obelisks. When the founder of Castle Howard laid out the gardens at the beginning of the eighteenth century he had ignored the prevailing 'cult of unadorned nature', opted instead for a highly elaborate parterre, and filled the grounds with ornamental statuary. John Tracey Atkyns had described the main parterre in 1732: '. . . Entirely different from the common parterres that swarm with (topiary) evergreens: a long square laid out in two slopes one below the other', each having 'four obelisks, 40ft high, an Ionic pillar in the middle 50ft high with a gilt vane on top. The squares are filled up with 4 large gilt vases . . . All these together are placed in such a form as to have a pretty effect.' Not everyone agreed with Atkyns: Lord Oxford wrote in 1725 that 'It must be easy to guess what a figure this [the parterre] must make except to those who are in love with Obelisks', and added that Ray Wood was 'the most beautiful thing about the place'. And Philip Yorke, when he visited Castle Howard twenty years later, felt the same: 'In general the gardens are overcrowded with Vanbruggian statues and obelisks, particularly a lawn before the house.' However, by the time Queen Victoria arrived in 1850, this description was clearly out of date, and there can have been little trace of such flamboyant clutter.

The 7th Earl decided to employ W.A. Nesfield, a well-known landscape gardener, to design a new floral parterre for the South Front, 'with a stability of character in accordance with that splendid fellow Vanbrugh'. The idea was to replace Vanbrugh's column, which had stood in the middle of the lawn, as well as the various statues and vases which still remained. These included two large stone oval tazzas, probably designed by C.H. Tatham, which had been bought by the 5th Earl. In the end, however, Nesfield reported that 'his Lordship seems pleased with the new design which has been arranged so as to *leave standing* the large oval tazzas and the heavy

The reception for Queen Victoria in the Great Hall. The 7th Earl installed gas lighting in honour of the Queen's visit; part of the greeting 'God Save the Queen' can be seen above the balustrade.

grouped statues'. The 9th Countess later demolished the whole of Nesfield's elaborate parterre and re-designed the garden once again, but the great tazzas, virtually immovable, are still standing today. At the same time yew hedges were planted to frame the lawns, and herbaceous borders were created and filled with the colourful flowers so loved by the Victorians.

By the time he had finished working at Castle Howard, Nesfield had brought about the most radical alterations to the grounds of Castle Howard since the 5th Earl had created the Great Lake to the north of the house, during the 1790s. (This, incidentally, finally achieved an ambition which had been outstanding since the beginning of the eighteenth century, when the South Lake was made. In March 1724, Hawksmoor wrote to the 3rd Earl urging him to consider 'how Beautiful a Body of water at Connysthorpe could look to ye North front'.)

Nesfield's greatest contribution to Castle Howard was the baroque Atlas fountain, which came from the Great Exhibition of 1851 and replaced Vanbrugh's column in the middle of the South Lawn. The five figures supporting the globe were carved in Portland stone by John Thomas and transported to Castle Howard railway station by steam train. The fountain is fed by a reservoir in Ray Wood, which today holds half a million gallons of water.

In 1857 the first *Guide Book to Castle Howard* was published. It is a typically Victorian eulogy, full of unnecessary superlatives, but it includes a section on the walled garden which gives an account of its size and contents at the time:

The Gardens

Occupy an area of twelve acres, surrounded by a wall upwards of twelve feet in height, the whole being divided into six compartments, in order to obtain additional space for the various kinds of wall fruit trees. The HOT-HOUSES, twelve in number, produce the finest pines and grapes; and the collection of ornamental stove-plants, although not very numerous, is choice and select. The CONSERVATORY or GREENHOUSE is sixty feet in length by fifteen feet in breadth, and contains a magnificent display of curious and rare exotics, the gorgeous beauty of many of which, as well as the stove-plants, cannot fail to render them objects of attraction to every spectator.

A collection of hardy herbaceous plants, numbering about six hundred species, occupies a large plot of ground near the south-east corner; and a broad border which runs by the boundary wall on the north side for its whole length, as well as other borders of similar dimensions, are planted with various kinds of ornamental flowering plants, native and foreign, which fill up the seasons with their varied charms, and offer incense to Flora . . .

Of the immense number of vegetable forms which have been found on the surface of the globe, the collection at Castle Howard comprises upwards of 1,000 species, including such as are cultivated for culinary use, or elegance in the dessert: and presuming these to be tolerably familiar . . . we shall . . . proceed to give an account of those which are more peculiarly adapted for ornament . . .

The Selected List published with the *Guide Book* includes hundreds of plants from all over the world, the following among them: *Agave americana*, popularly supposed to flower only once in 100 years; *Altingia excelsa*, from Norfolk Island, described by the *Guide Book* as 'a most superb plant, growing to an enormous size, and never losing the bright imperishable foliage with which it is covered, as with a coat of mail'; *Humea elegans* – 'A beautiful plant . . . of brilliant crimson flowers'; '*Night-flowering Cereus*', whose flowers open only at dusk and last no more than a single night, but which makes 'a most magnificent appearance by candle-light'; *Melocactus communi* - 'Turk's Cap, or Melon Thistle' – which looks like 'a large fleshy green melon . . . set all over with knots of strong thorns . . . Linnaeus remarks that this plant resembles a hedgehog . . .'; *Musa cavendishii* – 'A splendid plant, native of China', which must have been brought back by a member of the Cavendish family, who were, of course, closely connected to the Howards; *Richardia aethiopica* – a specialist, greenhouse, version of the common 'cuckoo pint' flower; and *Strelitzia reginae*, 'Canna-leaved Strelitzia', which originates from the Cape of Good Hope.

There was a Japanese quince, an 'Elastic Gum Tree' from Mexico, a 'Cock's Comb Coral Tree', a 'New Zealand Tea' tree, an 'Ice Plant' and an Arabian Coffee tree. There were date palms, pomegranates, lemon trees, orange trees, figs, vines, and every conceivable species of apple and pear tree. Oleanders, magnolias and camellias flourished in the hothouses and conservatories; sage, rosemary, cow parsnip, ribes and the castor oil plant outside. It is not surprising that the head gardener was the highest-paid outdoor worker on the estate. The gardens were one of the great glories of Castle Howard in the nineteenth century.

9

'The Perfect Victorian'

By the end of his life George Howard, 7th Earl of Carlisle – or 'Morpeth', as he continued to be called by his colleagues even after he had inherited the title – had served in the Cabinet under three premiers, spent fourteen years in Irish administration and sat in the Commons for seventeen years. Nevertheless his political career must, in the end, be deemed a failure.

In 1838 Morpeth seemed to be one of the brightest young stars in the Whig firmament, on course for a truly brilliant career, and a candidate for the highest office. In 1838 the Duke of Sussex spoke of him as a future leader of the party and a possible premier: as Lord Greville put it, in amazement – 'a man young enough to be the son of half the Cabinet ministers, and not in the Cabinet'. (In fact, he joined the Cabinet the following year, but had to resign his office when he was defeated in the general election of 1841.) But less than ten years later all this promise had evaporated; he had achieved no more than two minor positions in Government and was unlikely to be considered for further office. Two overriding factors were responsible for Morpeth's comparative lack of success as a politician: first, his failure to give active support to the party during the years when the Whigs were in opposition; and, second, a fatal tendency to compromise in the name of expediency – with the result that he too often ended by pleasing neither side. His political decline, and its causes, were summed up by Lord Campbell in 1847:

I am sorry that Lord Morpeth, our First Commissioner of Woods and Forests, one of the most amiable and excellent of men, has rather gone down in the world lately. He had a brilliant reputation at the conclusion of Lord

Melbourne's Government, and I remember the Duke of Sussex prophesying to me that Morpeth would one day be Prime Minister. Losing his election for the West Riding of Yorkshire in 1841, he was too long out of Parliament. His travels in the United States of America rather cooled his zeal in the popular cause. But he has been most damaged by his *sanitary* measures, which he brought forward with pomp, and was obliged with disgrace to abandon. He may rally again, but I would not give much for his chance of the Premiership.

Over the past few years, Morpeth had been involved in a number of proposed reforms, including the Child Labour Act and the Sanitary Acts. In both cases his initial zeal for reform had evaporated in the face of political expediency. Once again, over both issues, he had been too pragmatic for the idealists and yet too liberal for the businessmen.

Nevertheless, Morpeth's political career had its minor triumphs, and even though he may never have realized his ultimate ambitions, his whole attitude to life in general, and to Parliament in particular, is of interest since it is so typical of his class and time. In many ways the 7th Earl of Carlisle was a prime example of the Victorian liberal aristocrat. He was a man of absolute integrity, of strong religious faith and strict moral principles, who dedicated much of his life to public service, and who believed passionately in the freedom of the individual. At the age of nine Morpeth was already concerned with political issues and religious tolerance. He wrote to his father urging the cause of Catholic civil rights: '. . . in the middle of your speech you must say, Shall we, who are protestants be tyrants? Shall we oppress others because we are of a different religion?' And, in a rousing speech to the electorate of Bradford, in 1830, he voiced the guiding principles which were to last the rest of his life:

All my principles may be summed up in one word, and that word is *Freedom* . . . Freedom civil and religious . . . not the Freedom which seeks to destroy the Constitution, but the Freedom which seeks to preserve and improve it . . . Freedom, wherever we can assist it – in foreign countries, if we can lend it a helping hand – but above all, Freedom in our own dominions – in our own West India Islands . . . Freedom in the operations of commerce, in the expression of opinion, and in the worship of God.

(This, incidentally, was the year in which Morpeth also set himself the task of copying out large sections of both the Old and the New Testaments – 250 closely written pages in all. His approach to the Church was as practical as it was intellectual: for example, he took an active and personal interest in the various livings at his disposal, often attending several services on the same Sunday at different churches on the estate, in order to judge the performance of the various vicars.)

Morpeth had first entered Parliament in 1826, representing the borough from which he derived his name. His maiden speech, on the subject of Catholic emancipation, was a triumph, described by Lady Holland as 'the most complete success for a maiden speech ever heard'. In 1830 he was forced to fight an election for the first time – as opposed to being returned automatically by one of the family 'rotten boroughs' – and won easily. And during the furore over the Reform Bills, which was to dominate the next few years, Morpeth played an active and eager part in the Commons – while his father, the 6th Earl, tended to remain a quiescent spectator in the Lords.

In the spring of 1835 Morpeth was appointed Chief Secretary for Ireland, in Lord Melbourne's administration, a job which he held for six years and handled surprisingly well. Much of the credit for his success was due to a heroic programme of entertaining the Irish MPs and their families, both in London and at his magnificent house in Phoenix Park, Dublin. London society had tended to snub the Irish, deeming them uncouth ruffians whose manners were unfit for a ladies' drawing-room. Morpeth's natural geniality, and his complete lack of snobbishness, made a welcome change and went a long way towards smoothing his political path. He quickly became Dublin's most popular host, giving regular political dinners, receptions, balls and breakfasts, to which he invited not only the friendly Irish politicians but all the leading figures of society as well. Morpeth found all this entertaining distinctly wearing, but regarded it as an investment in his political future. He wrote to his mother describing one of the gala balls, which had been a tremendous success with his guests, that he himself 'felt rather out of conceit with it for all the first part . . . thought it hot & squeezed, that I was overrun by fat wives of Colonels . . . and that I have been very stupid . . .' And that Christmas he wearily reported to Lady Carlisle that 'There is no end to the dinners, & I have now every moment of evening as well as morning pledged till I sail [for England].' Thanks to the high profile he had exhibited in Dublin, Morpeth's political future seemed secure – but fate intervened. In 1841 the Whigs were defeated and he was thrown, quite suddenly, into the political wilderness – as his forebears the 3rd and 5th Earls of Carlisle had been before him. At this crucial point in his career, instead of remaining in London, supporting his colleagues and fighting back from the Opposition benches, Morpeth opted out of politics altogether. He went off to America and Canada for a year, and when he came back from his travels went to live at Castle Howard for a further two years. Morpeth did not return to the political scene until 1844, and by then it was really too late. Although he was given a few minor jobs in the Government his career had lost its momentum, and it never really recovered.

Although Morpeth did not inherit the title until 1848, his father, the 6th Earl, had been an invalid for the last five years of his life, and virtually paralysed with gout. As a result the management of Castle Howard and the estate had devolved increasingly upon Morpeth, as the heir-apparent, working in conjunction with the agent, James Loch. During the years he spent rusticating at Castle Howard Morpeth was able to concentrate on improving the various properties. His father gave him a free hand and he was on excellent terms with Loch, the Scotsman who had been in charge since 1824. The agent had already proved his worth: in 1827, three years after his employment, the annual income from rents was £37,167. By the time of his death, in 1855, estate and mine rents together brought in £55,732 and the total income had risen to £82,098. Loch's success was due to meticulous management coupled with investment and modernization. Much of the land was switched from corn, always an unreliable source of income, to stock farming, conducted according to the latest scientific methods. The coal mines and quarries on the Naworth estate were leased out instead of being worked by their own employees, which proved much more profitable, and a new programme of forestry was put into effect. Under Loch's management the average annual income from timber rose to £6,000 per year and at one point, in 1840, reached £11,220.

The greatest expense around this time was the cost of Castle Howard itself. Maintenance and repair bills for the house alone often came to more than £1,000 a year. And, with the 6th Earl living permanently at Castle Howard since his retirement, the running costs of the household were unusually high, even though the kitchen could rely on a constant supply of produce from the estate. Loch, who hated extravagance of any kind, imposed a rigorous economy campaign: this was readily sanctioned by the Carlisles, both of whom had been haunted by their respective parents' debts for years, and had no desire to follow their example. (The 7th Earl must have been unique among the Howards in that he positively disliked gambling – when *rouge et noir* became the rage he tried it once and found it boring. Nor was he ever in the least wild or extravagant, even as a young man: Sydney Smith remarked of Morpeth in his youth that 'he lacked indiscretion'.)

At the same time Loch decided to increase investment in the railways. Morpeth had been one of the first great landowners to see the potential of the new railways and Loch was equally enthusiastic. They had taken an active interest in the development of the Newcastle–Carlisle railway since its conception in 1827, and their initial investment had already paid off handsomely. They arranged for the new lines to pass through the poorest agricultural land on the estate, thus enhancing its value in real terms, as well as earning compensation. Moreover, part of the agreement between landowners who permitted the railways to cross their estates was the use of a private station, or halt, built at the company's expense. The Castle Howard station, which was built in 1845, enabled travellers and goods to avoid the long drive out from York, and continued to operate for almost 100 years. The Howard family reserved the right to stop any train passing through the station, even an express, until shortly before the last war.

The 7th Earl was an energetic host, who entertained frequently both at Castle Howard and at his town house in London. Carlisle House had long since passed out of the family's hands, and No. 10 Grosvenor Place had been bought in its stead – a comfortable, rather than luxurious, house within easy walking distance of the House of Commons. 'The London Day Book 1853–1855' gives some indication of the size of the household during the tenure of the 7th Earl. For example, during the period between 22 May and 18 June – less than a month – a total of *730* people were fed at Grosvenor Place. In one week alone *223 couverts* were served, and these statistics were not unusual. Although the 7th Earl was a bachelor it was often a predominantly female household: his mother, his sister, even his old great-aunt Julia, who lived to the age of ninety-nine, all continued to use the house as their London base.

At the beginning of the London 'season' the records show that thirteen members of the staff were served daily in the servants' hall, plus between seven and nine in the steward's room, and a further two to three 'casuals'. At a dinner party in May 1853 there were seventeen guests, and the complement of staff was increased to thirty-one in all; the following week Carlisle gave another, even larger dinner for nineteen, with a corresponding increase in the number of staff, to thirty-four. The pattern was repeated, with a dinner party nearly every week, throughout the summer:

Dined in Parlour April 21 – May 21	95
Dined in hsehold April 21 – May 21	715
Total	810

It was a formidable number of meals to prepare with the limited facilities of a London house. And when the family returned to Castle Howard during the summer months, their social life continued at the same pace. The housekeeper's book lists some of the comings and goings; many of the house guests stayed several weeks and all the numerous Howard children came to Castle Howard for the whole of their long school holidays – plus their usual complement of governesses, tutors, nannies and nurserymaids. The guest list for August 1855 reads like the pages of Debrett, or a roll-call of the Whig aristocracy – Cavendishes, Granvilles, Greys, Cokes, Lascelles, Grenfells, Laboucheres . . . the Duchess of Sutherland, the Dean of Lichfield, Lord Burlington, and Lady Elizabeth Grey recur throughout the pages – many of them, of course, related to the Howards.

They were an unusually united family. In 1830 Thomas Moore wrote of the 6th Earl and his children that they were 'softeners' on society: 'There are so many of them and all so gentle and good tempered that they diffuse a kindly tone around them.' And the 7th Earl, in his turn, was always preoccupied with the welfare of his brothers and sisters. Like most Victorians, Carlisle placed a high premium upon family solidarity and never rejected even the most tiresome of his relatives. His brother, Henry Howard, for example, was a constant problem – he was a compulsive gambler, like his grandfather, and Carlisle was always having to pay his debts. He was clearly devastated when his brother Frederick, who had been an officer in the army, was killed in an accident in 1833; and equally so by the death of his sister Blanche, who had married the Earl of Burlington, two years later. And by 1850 William Howard's mental health had deteriorated to such an extent that he could no longer take care of himself and had to be kept under constant supervision. He was eventually removed by Carlisle to Ticehurst Asylum, near Tunbridge Wells, said to be the best and the most compassionate of such institutions at the time. Lord Ashley, the great authority on asylums, was a personal friend of Carlisle's.

Of the other siblings, his sisters Harriet, Georgiana, Caroline and Elizabeth were all married; Edward, who later became Admiral Lord Lanerton and the comptroller of Castle Howard during the 8th Earl's mental breakdown, had married Diana Ponsonby; and Charles had married the enchanting Mary Parke, who was to die so tragically at the age of twenty. In 1852 he notes with delight and relief in his diary that his remaining sister Mary is to be married at last, to Henry Labouchere, a former political colleague of Carlisle's. Since the death of their respective spouses both his sister Georgiana and his brother Charles have returned to the family circle, and are spending much more time at Castle Howard, while Elizabeth and her husband, the Revd Francis Grey, living at Morpeth, have become neighbours at Naworth. Harriet is Queen Victoria's Mistress of the Robes, and all the other siblings are suitably settled, with the sad exception of his brother William, by now demented but peaceable – as he was to remain for the rest of his life.

It was concern for his family, too, which prompted Morpeth's interest in the extraordinary craze for Mesmerism which suddenly swept Victorian society in 1844. This strange pseudo-scientific practice had, in fact, been around for some time, having originated in Paris at the end of the previous century, but had remained dormant in England until suddenly taken up by the popular author Miss Harriet Martineau. She wrote an account of her life as an invalid, which had a huge success, and when, a few months later, Miss Martineau recovered completely, she attributed her miraculous cure to Mesmerism – which thus acquired a quasi-medical status. The most unlikely people became converted to the cult, including such respected intellectuals as Lord Palmerston and the Revd Sydney Smith.

Morpeth was fascinated by Mesmerism, and he carried his interest to potentially dangerous lengths. He began to experiment with mesmerizing his tenants at Castle Howard, in the name of alleviating their various aches and pains; he also attempted to cure several of the 'Malton paupers' – presumably with little success, since there are no records of astonishing recovery. When the supply of willing 'guinea-pigs' on the estate ran out, Morpeth cajoled various members of his own family to offer themselves for treatment. One evening his experiments succeeded to an alarming degree with his newly married – and already neurotic – sister-in-law, Mrs Henry Howard. After only a few mesmeric passes, Mrs Howard turned rigid and, on recovering her senses, said that she had been unable to move her hands; she apparently continued to act extremely oddly for the duration of her visit. Morpeth was frightened into abandoning his experiments on the family, and thereafter confined his efforts to those of his tenants who continued to believe in the cult as strongly as he did himself. It was, of course, the medical possibilities of Mesmerism which attracted otherwise rational men such as Morpeth: his mother, whom he adored, had always suffered from acute bouts of depression, while his father had been a prey to gout for most of his adult life. He was never interested to anything like the same degree in the other contemporary crazes, such as spiritualism and phrenology.

Morpeth was a compassionate man, possessed of a strong social conscience. During his years in London as a politician he had joined a number of philanthropic societies, and through one of these, the Metropolitan Association for Improving the Dwellings of the Industrious Classes, he met two of the great reformers of the day – Joseph Toynbee and Charles Dickens. Both men took Morpeth on walking tours through the terrible slums of London, upon which his laconic comment was that they gave him 'startling views about health'. At least he was impressed by Dickens, of whom he wrote in his diary that:

The 1st appearance has much to be got over; a great length of spare locks, & a moustache; the observing eye is fine. He seems to have much good feeling, & is altogether a more grave & earnest man than I had prefigured to myself.

After he inherited the title, the 7th Earl adopted a rather more leisurely way of life than had been possible as a Member of Parliament. Though he continued to spend much of his time in London it was the social life, coupled with his philanthropic obligations, which drew him to the metropolis, rather than politics. He became President of the Royal Society of Literature and gave a lecture on the poetry of Alexander Pope, and another on Gray's *Elegy* – his favourite poem. Carlisle had always written poetry himself – typically restrained, conventional little verses, about nature, God, innocence and other suitably acceptable subjects. Never, either in his diaries or in his creative writing, did the 7th Earl allow himself to express his own emotions. And yet his behaviour shows that he was not a cold man; it was the habitual reserve of the Victorians, a dedication to the creed which insisted that any indication of passion, any display of emotion, was vulgar. No gentleman allowed his feelings to show, whatever the provocation. It is difficult to imagine what Victorian dinner parties were like, considering that money, politics and sex were all taboo as subjects of conversation.

In spite of his habitual reserve there is no doubt that the 7th Earl was immensely popular, the kind of good-mannered, cultivated and amusing bachelor who is always in demand at parties. And though most of his writing, even in his diary, is so discreet that it verges on the boring, there are occasional glimpses of the lighter side of his nature, that sense of fun and quiet mockery which must have been part of his charm − as, for example, his account of his two sisters' very different reactions to the ceremony of the Garter, always an occasion of maximum pomp and splendour. Carlisle was made a Knight in 1855 and invited his sisters Harriet and Caroline to watch the Investiture:

The ceremony produces different effects upon minds of different mould; the Dss of Sutherland [Harriet] thinks it very thrilling and elevating; Ly Ellesmere [Caroline] could barely conquer her propensity to laugh; the delivery of the old chivalrous charge by the Bishop of Oxford in his earnest pregnant accent is on Harriet's side; Ld Fitzwilliam walking backwards in very long robes is on Ly E's.

The 7th Earl adored dressing up, and did full justice to the occasion by decking himself out in numerous diamonds, including a 'diamond badge hanging down to his knees, like a sabretache'.

Such frivolity was rare: *au fond*, Carlisle was a serious man of high moral tone who was easily shocked. It is hardly surprising, therefore, that he was almost passionate in his disapproval of the customs and behaviour he encountered on his tour of the Eastern Mediterranean during the 1850s. His diary is full of critical comments about the people and places he visited. In the Balkans, for example, he found the local inhabitants 'models of picturesque filthiness', who did not seem to have progressed in civilization since Trajan's conquest. And his overall verdict on the area was that:

The more I see of these countries ... I feel more strongly that any change which should disturb the stagnant mass would seem to give a chance of eliciting something better than the present state of fetid, mouldy putrefaction.

The litany of criticism continued: in Turkey there were 'banditti-haunted mountains, torpid laws, a corrupt administration, a disappearing people', and as for their morals, the less said the better. And, when it came to Constantinople, friends had already told Carlisle all the 'shocking details' of Turkish vice before he even got there. On arrival in the city he heard that the local equivalent of a Punch and Judy show, which he was expected to attend, was particularly indecent – so he simply refused to see it. Carlisle may have been a prude, but at least he practised what he preached – unlike so many of the Victorians who relished low life and were happy to indulge in vice, as long as it was in secret. In Lesbos he caught smallpox, and in Egypt fell ill again, with a fever which effectively put an end to the tour. By 1854 he was back in London, in time to be appalled by the Government's handling of the Crimean War. Florence Nightingale later became a personal friend.

The 7th Earl's final – and most successful – foray into political office came relatively late in his life. In 1855, to his great delight, Carlisle was made Lord Lieutenant (or Viceroy) of Ireland, a post which he held, with only one short break, until 1864, when ill health forced him to retire. Carlisle was an outstanding success in Ireland on all levels. He was generally acknowledged to have been an excellent ambassador, able, popular and tactful. His resignation, when it came, was regretted as much by the Irish as the English Government.

As far as the social life implicit in the job was concerned, Carlisle was in his element, and the Viceregal Lodge became the focal point of the gayest season Dublin had ever known. He was told by his aides that his court was much more fun than the Queen's, and the popular newspapers took to calling him 'Buck' – a nickname which delighted the Earl. The sheer scale of the entertainments is redolent of Royalty: at a morning levée there are 1,300 guests; at an afternoon drawing-room 1,730 – and on that occasion the receiving line continued for three hours. He introduced alfresco tea parties, held on Saturday afternoons in the Lodge gardens, to which 6–700 guests would be invited, including children – an idea which was an instantaneous success with the family-minded Irish. And, above all, there were the great dinner parties and magnificent balls, when more than 1,000 guests would be invited. Night after night these parties went on – and Carlisle was no reluctant spectator. On the contrary, blazing, as usual, in the family diamonds, he led off the dancing and usually stayed to the end. Considering that the Earl was already in his fifties the chronicle of social activity shows that he must have had considerable stamina, as well as enjoying parties. It must be remembered that Carlisle had spent years in political 'exile', neglected by the Party and passed over for office by younger men. There can be little doubt that much of his pleasure in Dublin derived from knowing that he was once again in a position of power. The 7th Earl certainly made the most of his years of glory.

Nevertheless Carlisle adhered to his customary puritan standards. At the very first drawing-room he held in the Viceregal Lodge some of the guests got drunk on the punch – so he served nothing but tea and ices at the second. (The shades of teetotalism were already beginning to close on Castle Howard.) And at the end of the first year in Ireland, the Earl admonished himself in his diary against succumbing to the snares of vanity:

Here ends 1855. It has embarked me in a new position; I have been too anxious for this species of prominence; at all events my ambition has been satisfied. Let this be thoroughly borne in mind by me through my whole future life.

May God guide my judgement, and be to me the Supreme Enabler.

The 7th Earl had little in common with his more boisterous

ancestors. For a start, he never cared for horses or racing, and disliked rough sports. He neither gambled nor had affairs, and avoided excess of all kinds. As a boy he was a shy and gentle creature, a quiet introvert who lived in a world of his own. When he was nine, and spending a few weeks at Althorp, his cousin Sarah reported that he turned pale when led into a cross-country gallop on a strange pony; and added that 'he talks of beauty, and poetry, and even novels, till I long to send him for the summer to the sea . . .' At Eton he joined the theatrical and debating societies, keeping well away from the riots which broke out in 1811. (The boys pelted the headmaster with rotten eggs, smashed the windows and let off home-made bombs all over the school.) He went skating and swimming at school, though his mother wrote that she was terrified of his drowning; and he developed a liking for cricket – presumably because it was a relatively gentle game as far as Eton was concerned. In later life he organized cricket matches at Castle Howard which became one of the joys of the summer – elegant, gracious affairs, which often lasted for several days.

As a young man, when he first made his début on the London scene, he was said to be good company and always popular, but to have little success with women. A contemporary described him as 'rather clumsy, overweight and shy'. All the same, it is, in fact, surprising that he managed to stay single, for the young Lord Morpeth was outstandingly eligible. His only tentative foray into the world of flirtation seems to have occurred in 1833, when he courted Lady Anne de Grey, the daughter of Whig neighbours in Yorkshire, whose mother was a friend of *his* mother's. Lady Anne would have made a most suitable wife, but she was a very pretty girl and much sought after; Morpeth was too slow and she turned him down in favour of a man who was his polar opposite in character – Lord Fordwich, whom a contemporary had christened the 'King of the Scamps'. The rejected suitor thereafter abandoned all thoughts of marriage and settled instead for the pleasant and undemanding role of popular bachelor.

In 1858 Georgiana Carlisle finally died, at the age of seventy-five. It was a mortal blow to the 7th Earl, who had always been particularly close to his mother – in retrospect, dangerously so. She was the recipient of his confidences, his mentor and his chief correspondent – they exchanged letters several times a week until her death. His mother's influence remained the dominant factor in Carlisle's life until he was well into middle age, and may explain why he never married.

The 7th Earl thus became the last of the line to inherit the title directly from his father; after his death the succession passed first to one of his brothers, and subsequently to a nephew – who, in his turn, became the last Earl of Carlisle to live at Castle Howard.

The 7th Earl's health collapsed in 1864, and it became clear that he could no longer continue in office. He suffered from intermittent attacks of dizziness and a species of paralysis, which affected his speech as well as his mobility. Carlisle's departure from Dublin was a sad occasion: instead of a farewell speech to the crowds who had come to see him off, the Earl could barely manage one coherent sentence. His final words to the Irish, who had been witness to the 7th Earl's one political triumph, were these:

I leave, after my term of office, undimmed by one particle of personal bitterness either on the present or the crowded memories of the past.

Less than four months later he died at Castle Howard and was buried in the mausoleum. On his death Harriet Martineau dismissed Carlisle's achievements, and wondered at his popularity:

Such regret as is felt at the departure of this nobleman is something rare in the case of a man who has not rendered himself necessary to his country by his statesmanship, nor commanded homage by his genius, nor established or continued a great family ... [He] left no enduring work behind him to make him known to future generations, or to illustrate his own time.

Diana Oliens, however, in *Morpeth – A Victorian Public Career*, points out that 'Morpeth' had been the perfect Victorian, the epitome of a set of values which it has since become fashionable to decry. In her summing up she wrote that:

Carlisle spent a lifetime of diligent work in public service. Though never a shaper of great events, he lived up to his assertion, made in 1830, that the aristocracy could never be so well employed as when it was honorably engaged in the service of the people. He demonstrated the length and limit of what could be achieved in Victorian government by a man of excellent connections, high principle, and the best of intentions.

And *The Times* wrote in its obituary that Carlisle's career had been in keeping with the family motto: '"Volo non valeo",★ and . . . he was one of the most popular men in this country, because of the "volo", and despite the "non valeo" . . . a good, kind nobleman in the best sense of the word . . .'

The death of the 7th Earl of Carlisle not only broke the direct line of inheritance but also, in a sense, signalled the beginning of the end of a way of life for the Howards, and indeed for Castle Howard itself. Aristocratic privilege was already threatened; the balance of power had begun to shift, away from the wealth implicit in land towards the riches of industry; and the concept of socialism was already in the air. The next generation of the Howard family would be riven by irrevocable feuds; within sixty years the estates would have been split and Castle Howard would have ceased to be the home of the Earls of Carlisle.

★ 'I am willing but not able'. The words are taken from the *Confessions* of St Augustine, chosen by the founder of the family, Lord William Howard.

'No Time for Faded Grandeur'

The 8th Earl never lived at Castle Howard: the 9th never cared for it. In 1885, barely twenty years after the death of the 7th Earl, the poet Wilfrid Scawen Blunt was appalled at the way standards had been allowed to lapse in the daily routine of the great house:

... life in this house is that of a Bedouin camp ... Everything cut down to the barest necessity of existence; no one to open the gates at the lodge, not a servant to be seen except at meals and no footman with the carriage. Gardens neglected ...

The days of pomp and splendour, of glitter and opulence, had gone for good. Nevertheless, the closing years of the nineteenth century were far from barren in the history of the family fortunes, largely thanks to the Howards' enlightened patronage of contemporary artists – particularly the Pre-Raphaelites and their followers.

Since the 7th Earl of Carlisle died without issue the succession passed to his eldest brother, William Howard, who held the title from 1864 until 1889. The 8th Earl had originally chosen a career in the Church and was allotted one of the family livings in Yorkshire;★ however, as has already been explained, he had a mental breakdown early in life which grew progressively worse. By the time the 8th Earl inherited the title he was confined to a lunatic asylum, where he remained for the rest of his life. He was thus never more than the titular head of the

★ A sinecure which he retained almost to the end of his life, thanks to an anomaly in ecclesiastical law.

family and was unable to take any part in the management of the estates. Castle Howard passed into the hands of the next brother in line – Admiral Edward Howard, who was created Lord Lanerton in 1874.

Lord Lanerton retired from the Navy, after a most distinguished career, in order to assume control of Castle Howard. He was a man of strong religious feeling and devout faith who took a particular interest in the ecclesiastical affairs of the Howard estates. He rebuilt the church at Slingsby, one of the neighbouring villages, and repaired many of the other churches on the estate. But, above all, Lanerton was responsible for the complete renovation and the glorious Pre-Raphaelite decoration of the private chapel at Castle Howard.

The private chapel is, and always has been, an Anglican one, although many other branches of the Howard family are Roman Catholics. In Lord Lanerton's time, as in all Victorian households, the entire staff were summoned to join the family in daily prayers every morning, and regular services were held in the chapel. (Nowadays there are approximately fourteen services a year, timed to coincide with major church festivals, and the chapel is also used for private weddings, baptisms and funerals.)

The alterations to the chapel, initiated by Lord Lanerton, were begun in 1870, under the direction of the architect R.J. Johnson. It was decided to enlarge the existing chapel, mainly by lowering the floor and by changing the entrance to the room. The area designated, at the end of the West Wing, was originally described by Tatham's drawings (which had been commissioned by the 5th Earl in 1800) as a 'columned dining hall', but it had never been used as such. Both the pillars of the existing room, and the ceiling – which was a copy of the one designed for the Chapel Royal at St James's Palace – were retained, although redecorated. The artist W.H. Hughes was commissioned to paint the frescoes on the south wall, depicting the Old Testament prophets, and he also painted the large picture above the altar, *Christ at the Pillar*, for which he was paid £110. The lovely stained-glass windows in the chapel were designed by Sir Edward Burne-Jones and executed by the firm of Morris and Co. in 1872.

They are generally considered to be the finest examples of Pre-Raphaelite stained glass in the world, and have become one of the major attractions of Castle Howard. The organ was made by the celebrated firm of Harrison and Harrison, at a cost of £835 10s., and was originally powered by a hydraulic engine. In 1953 this mechanism was replaced by an electric motor.

Lord Lanerton died in 1880, but the 8th Earl lingered on for another nine years. Castle Howard passed to the heir presumptive, George Howard, son of yet another brother of the previous generation – his father, Charles, had been fourth in the line of succession but also predeceased the 8th Earl. George Howard, however, was an artist, and had little desire to take on the role of aristocratic landowner. In any case both George and his wife Rosalind preferred Naworth to Castle Howard, and always regarded Cumberland as their home, rather than Yorkshire. In fact, during the early years of their marriage most of their time was spent either in London or on long trips abroad: the grand life implicit in Castle Howard held little appeal for either of them and they went there as seldom as possible. Nevertheless the future 9th Earl, and in particular his Countess, had enormous influence upon the fortunes of Castle Howard.

George Howard inherited his artistic talent from his mother, Mary Parke, a daughter of Lord Wensleydale. She died giving birth to George, in 1843, at the age of twenty, but in the course of her short lifetime she established a lasting reputation as a serious artist in her own right. Mary was a pupil of the artist De Wint and painted in the Victorian water-colour tradition. She was an exceptionally prolific artist, considering the brief time at her disposal, and her works are much sought after today. Although George never knew his mother personally, he grew up surrounded by her paintings; a desire to emulate her example was obviously one of the factors which influenced his decision to opt for an artistic career.

In 1864, at the age of twenty-one, Howard married Rosalind Stanley, daughter of Lord Stanley of Alderley. Several books have already been written about the consequences of this marriage and the character of the 9th Earl's wife. Opinions differ, but in this particular context it is sufficient to say that Rosalind Carlisle was a formidable woman, whom even her own daughter described as having 'An Eye like Mars, to threaten and command'. She was a year younger than her husband and at the time of their engagement the dominant element of her character was more or less quiescent: nevertheless, even at that stage she was capable of reproving her fiancé for laziness: 'I don't think you are very capable of applying yourself to hard study,' she wrote, a few weeks before the wedding. George was in love with her – as, indeed, Rosalind was with him – and replied adoringly:

You seem to me the perfect idea of guardian angel and saint combined, yet better than any saint because you are pure and noble, not by denying the human element of your nature but by raising it, purifying and ennobling it. If anything could make my life of any use you will.

The young Howards began their married life at Naworth, and the medieval castle remained, for both, even after they separated, a symbol of the romantic and physical side of their life together and of the happiness they had once shared. For the marriage was an undoubted success during the early years; it was not until after they had produced eleven children that the relationship turned sour and terrible rows began to spoil not only their own lives, but those of all around them.

The newly-weds loved Naworth, but they had no desire to live there all the year round: George wanted to live in London, so that he could pursue his painting studies at the South Kensington School of Art, where he worked under both Legros and Costa. Accordingly, in 1865, Philip Webb was commissioned to build a house for the Howards in Palace Green, Kensington. George Howard had already become a member of the Pre-Raphaelite circle centred around Dante Gabriel Rossetti, Edward Burne-Jones and William Morris – all of whom contributed to the building and decoration of No. 1 Palace Green. It took five years to complete and was an unusual house for its time, in as much as it was built in brick, whereas the normal practice was to face a new building in plaster to create the appearance of Portland stone. Despite the initial controversy, No. 1 Palace Green came to be regarded as one of the most beautiful houses of the late nineteenth century.

In 1889, the year George Howard succeeded to the title and became the 9th Earl of Carlisle, *The Studio*, a contemporary art magazine, devoted a long article to the house, headed 'The Cupid and Psyche Frieze by Sir Edward Burne-Jones, at No. 1 Palace Green':

It would seem a rash statement to affirm of the decoration of any single apartment that it was absolutely the best example of the style it obeyed. Yet if ever it were safe to speak thus unreservedly, it might be concerning the beautiful morning-room at the Earl of Carlisle's town house, Palace Green; representing, as it does, the united efforts of Burne-Jones, William Morris, and Philip Webb . . .

The room at first sight appears by no means gorgeous, nor even sumptuous – indeed its momentary effect is somewhat austere; but as the eye lights on the frieze which surrounds it, the coffered ceiling with decorated beams above, and the panels of the dado below, rich in gold and silver, the whole appears to glow like a page of an illuminated missal; and yet so well is the balance kept by the plain masses of peacock-blue paint that, even when the eye has focused all the gorgeous decoration in detail, the breadth of treatment of the whole still retains a splendid simplicity . . .

. . . Below each panel runs a long quotation from the poem, inscribed in thin Roman letters of gold upon the dull peacock-green of the woodwork. The woodwork . . . was at first entirely in white; but this pigment was found to mar the effect of the paintings, and so it was replaced by the present colour . . . The scheme of the paintings, although frequent use of white in the robes of the figures keeps the whole fairly light, is not in a high key; here and there, as for Psyche's box and for her lamp, raised and gilded gesso is used, but only sparingly. The panels below are filled with a beautiful design by Morris, worked in flat gold and silver. The corbels and the 'styles' of the decorated panelling immediately below the frieze are covered with a simple diaper in red, upon a burnished gold ground. The spandrels of the brackets supporting the beams of the ceiling are painted with conventional foliage, the free acanthus-like leaf which Morris loved, in golden browns and russets ... The panelling of the ceiling itself is enriched with a Morris design painted in soft colours. A very fine chimney-piece, grate and fender, after Mr Philip Webb's designs, a superb gilded cassone with old Italian painting in its panels, and an old metal coffer are the most notable objects in the room, where no superfluous furniture or *bric-à-brac* intrudes to destroy the air of repose ...

The writer goes on to elaborate the furniture and other works of art throughout the house, and ends by pointing out the originality of the building and praising Lord Carlisle's innovative decision to build a genuinely contemporary house, rather than following the Establishment pattern, which was to copy the architecture of the previous century:

... Yet all these objects of art do but play their part in adorning a quiet and restful home. The house is in sharp contrast with the average town mansion, where Louis XIV, XV, and XVI, varied by a trace of Adam, reign supreme. Compared with the average Park Lane palace it looks severe and simple; but it is pre-eminently an artist's home, which not only genius has enriched, but good taste has controlled ... splendid things fall into the scheme simply and unobtrusively. Even its good taste is not unduly evident, but becomes the more apparent the more closely you observe it. By thus avoiding emphasis of all kinds, the treasures it holds seem but ordinary fittings, until more curious inspection shows many of them to be unique masterpieces. The majority of these are modern – a singularly pleasing exception to the average 'palace' of today, which, if it holds masterpieces of any kind, is singularly careful that they shall be of goodly age, hall-marked as it were with official approval of their sterling value.

George Howard had expectations of wealth, but was far from rich during the early years of his marriage – at least in comparison with his peers. His income in 1864 was £1,000 a year, 'Not Much', as his future mother-in-law, Lady Stanley, remarked doubtfully when the engagement was proposed. However, both sets of parents, as well as

George's uncle, Lord Carlisle, helped with financial contributions from time to time, and, in any case, neither of the Howards had expensive tastes. For example, neither spent much money on their appearance: in 1864, the year they married, their joint expenditure on clothes came to no more than £100 10s. George had already adopted the distinctive 'uniform' which he was to wear for the rest of his life: a large, floppy tam o' shanter, worn with an outfit consisting of soft collar, large bow tie, waistcoat, tweed jacket and knickerbockers. Rosalind, though beautiful in her youth, abhorred vanity and usually dressed in plain, loose-fitting, dark gowns, which may have been cheap but did little to enhance her looks.

By 1870 the Howards were installed in Palace Green, which at once became a centre for all the most illustrious artists of the period. Later, after George had joined the Etruscan School, founded by the Italian painter, Giovanni Costa, the house also served as the nexus between crosscurrents of European, as well as British, artists. A typical dinner party, in January 1871, included William and Jane Morris, Edward and Georgiana Burne Jones, and Mr and Mrs Carnegie, of American library fame and money. On that particular occasion both Rossetti and Webb declined. Other guests who came often to Palace Green – and also to Naworth, though seldom to Castle Howard – included Lord Leighton, Sir John Millais, Browning, Thackeray, Gladstone, Arthur Balfour and the George Trevelyans. The Howards gave a dinner party for Princess Louise and Lord Lorne when they announced their engagement (she was a painting friend of George's, and he was a cousin), and when Costa and his wife came to England they gave another, in the Italian artist's honour.

Rosalind's account books illustrate the life the Howards led at Palace Green. Housekeeping expenses between October 1870 and July 1871 came to £385, and in one week, during June, they had three dinner parties, on successive nights – for twelve, fourteen and thirteen people respectively. The drink bill for nine months in 1871 was £60 1s. – at this stage in their lives neither had turned teetotal – and included sixty bottles of manzanilla, 132 bottles of sherry, thirty-four bottles of champagne, seven of brandy, 180 bottles of light claret at

22s. a dozen, 'plus a further 72 bottles of the same', and thirty-eight bottles of 'best claret at 4/6'.

The lists of furniture bought for Palace Green, and the prices the Howards paid for it, show just how greatly the price of antiques has risen – in little more than 100 years. Many of the items mentioned could, today, cost up to 1,000 times their purchase price in the 1870s. Among the more tantalizing pieces listed are:

A Chippendale mahogany side table £6 8s. od.
A Sheraton inlaid side table £7 15s. 6d.
16 Sheraton chairs, inlaid, £16; covered in morocco for a
  further £16.
Satinwood sofa table with 2 flaps and 2 drawers £4 5s. od.
Turkey rug for the dining-room £28 16s. od.
Indian rug for the library £24 10s. od.
Persian rug for the sitting-room £18
14 Chippendale carved mahogany chairs for the library £15;
  covered in morocco for a further £16
Sofa for the library, 'ebonised, with brass ornaments', £12.

The drawing-room furniture included an Empire sofa, which cost £10, a round, inlaid, satinwood table made by Sheraton for £5, a pair of black and gold bamboo chairs at £2 5s. each, and two Queen Anne gilt carved mirrors for £18. In the sitting-room there was a Charles II walnut bureau, which cost £28 1s. 6d., and a 'Pier looking glass over the chimney piece', bought for £12, 5s., while the windows were covered with 'embroidered curtains dated 1600', marked at £27 in the accounts. Among the pieces bought for Rosalind's bedroom there were two wardrobes, one of them Chippendale, which cost the princely sum of £30 4s., and an oval Pembroke table, 'mahogany, with satinwood border', bought for only £2 4s.

It is surprising that the Howards, who insisted upon contemporary, rather than classical, design when building the house, and whose greatest extravagance was in buying 'modern' art, should furnish their house with so much antique and eighteenth-century furniture. It seems most unlikely that, even then, second-hand furniture was regarded as an economy, particularly since there is a note beside one of the most expensive pieces bought for the house, clearly intended to justify its price, to the effect that it 'belonged to Ldy Ellenborough'. The piece in question was an antique, and it cost the Howards £37 1s.

George Howard was a serious artist, and he made a small but steady income from his paintings. He sold his first picture, a water-colour of an Italian landscape, in 1865 for £25. Rosalind was delighted, and wrote triumphantly that he was: 'No longer an amateur, for better or worse he has taken his stand amongst the artists.' A few years later his income from painting had risen to £218 15s. in one year, and by the 1880s the price of his water-colours had doubled, from around £25 a picture to an average of £50. An oil painting of Mentone fetched £71 13s. 3d. in 1883: today, even a small water-colour by George Howard can cost hundreds. At first, however, Rosalind had been unsure of her husband's talent. She wrote in her diary, in 1869:

He has not any inventive genius and can one be a great painter without that? I think he is getting on but I don't know that he will ever be a really first rate painter and yet I see that daily he is becoming more engrossed by painting. He thinks and talks of nothing else now; he seems to care less about politics. All the friends he seeks out and cares to talk to if they are not artists are people who care to talk art.

There is a querulous note already in this particular comment of Rosalind's: doubtless she had realized that George would always prefer art to current affairs, and that, though sympathetic to the Liberal cause, he would never feel as strongly about politics as she did. (Encouraged by his wife, Howard did, in fact, stand for Parliament in 1880, and spent five years as the Liberal member for East Cumberland. In 1886 Gladstone brought in the Bill for Home Rule for Ireland: a general Election was called, and Howard, who was opposed to the Bill, relinquished his seat.) In any case Rosalind was quite wrong about her husband's artistic potential: he was already well on the way to being recognized as one of the finest painters of his generation.

And George's own friends, of course, welcomed his dedication to work; had he behaved like the usual aristocratic dilettante they would never have taken him seriously. Stopford Brooke, staying at Naworth during the summer of 1872, confirmed this view of Howard:

It is not strange and yet it is, how entirely this place is apart from modern life and its associations when one is outside the house, and even in. G.H. is so unlike a mere modern gentleman, and so much one of the artist band who belong to all time, in manner and in thought, that the illusion is still supported. I suppose it is on account of this that this place rests me (almost) more than any I know.

George, himself, thought otherwise. The following autumn he complained strongly that the constant social life at Naworth, centred round his wife's political ambitions, stopped him painting: 'Gladstone and Mrs next week. I get no time to do anything I want to do with all these people here.' Gladstone, on the other hand, was delighted with his visit and charmed by his host: he wrote in his diary that 'George Howard made the most clever sketch of me in the forenoon.'

It was the Howards' custom to spend several months every winter on painting trips travelling around Europe. They particularly favoured Italy, where George fell in love with the landscape and produced some of his finest work. Year after year they returned, staying in different *pensiones* or villas all over the peninsula, from San Remo on the Ligurian coast to Naples and Capri in the South. George first explored the Campagna with Costa in 1866; ten years later he was again in the company of Costa when he wrote of his life in Rome:

Every day I work – very slowly though. Once a week I ride on the Campagna – which is more heavenly than anything you can imagine. Yesterday I rode where the whole country looked like a Cumberland moor covered with asphodel instead of heather.

One summer the Howards rented a villa at Oneglia, where he painted the women washing clothes at the river, in the evening light. This picture was exhibited at the Grosvenor Gallery in 1878 and provoked Walter Crane to write: 'I congratulate you more particularly on the twilight at the river's mouth. One can almost hear the distant sound of the waves where the river meets the sea.' The Italian pictures firmly established George Howard's reputation, both with the general public and among his fellow artists. In August 1879 Stopford Brooke wrote to George reporting a marvellous accolade for Howard's work from Burne-Jones, regarded as the ultimate arbiter by the Pre-Raphaelites:

I dined with Burne-Jones – the talk fell upon your work. When I told you at Oneglia what he had said, it seemed as if he did not say much to you personally about it, and though I am a little shy of saying to you all he said for I do not know quite whether you will care to hear a report of a conversation, yet I give it to you because it was all so pleasant. He not only said over again what I told you – that it was *years* ago since you had passed clear away from the amateur to the artist, but went on to say that your drawings were simply the best water colour work that was done at the present day; the most refined, the most poetic, the most 'erudite' (many of them) in technical treatment of certain things – trees, distant roofs and buildings . . . He spoke with real enthusiasm of the beauty of the trees – and of many other things. He said, not only that the Italian drawings should one and all be bought by everyone who cared for Italy, and that no other Italian drawings were to be compared to them – but he said that for himself there were some of them which were quite enough to make him sit down in a corner and cry with pleasure . . . I can never forget them . . . it is no small thing for me to say that there are many of these drawings, among the multitude of drawings that are now produced, which have [meant?] so much to me, and which are so vividly before my eyes that I can never forget them – There is that sunset at Oneglia, and a drawing at Monte Oliveto, and four or five of the Roman drawings and of the Venice ones and others. (He did not mention all, nor did I press him.)

He said – lest you should think I have nothing to say on the other side – in his figures, the faces have not the true roseate tint of pure flesh. They are not exquisite. It is not flesh colour, it has a 'brick dust' look – I think that was the word. He ought to make them as pure and fine as the rest.

In 1880 Lord Lanerton died and George inherited Castle Howard.

Song written in 1878 for Rosalind Carlisle during a visit to Oneglia in Italy,
illustrated by William Morris.

(Though not, of course, the title, since his uncle, the 8th Earl, was still alive.) Neither he nor Rosalind were particularly pleased: from George's point of view it was an enormous inheritance which he had neither the desire nor the training to manage, and which could only interfere with his painting. Rosalind wrote to her mother that: 'Personally we feel sorry about having these extra responsibilities thrust upon us.' Initially they compromised, making occasional visits to Castle Howard, but continuing to regard Naworth and Palace Green as their real homes. As time went by, however, Rosalind began to see the point of being a chatelaine on such a grand scale, and eventually took over the management of all the estates herself. George quietly continued painting, travelling abroad more and more often alone, only too happy to leave his financial affairs in the hands of his wife.

It was a mistake, as Dorothy, Lady Henley, one of Lady Carlisle's daughters, points out in the book she wrote about her mother:

... politics apart, present day [1958] assessment of her professional work is critical. In the view of a ... qualified agent 'her capabilities were poor. She had no knowledge of forestry; to employ three men for 2,000 acres when wages were £1 per week was inefficient; to buy oak for gate-making when thousands of young oak were screaming to be thinned was not clever; she completely neglected the eighteenth century Follies, Temple, Mausoleum, Bridge etc; she was often told that the roof of the Temple needed repairing but she said it was unnecessary.'

Rosalind was a Radical who had long disapproved of the luxurious image of Castle Howard. The amount of money spent upon maintaining it in Lord Lanerton's day had been a constant source of annoyance to her for years. She referred scornfully to the 'satined walls of the bedrooms' and had complained to the trustees about 'the bad decoration and greenhouses and such freaks as repainting the frescoes in the salon'. One of Rosalind's first acts on assuming control of the house was to cover the priceless Pellegrini murals in the High Saloon with William Morris wallpaper. (This was later removed, but the Pellegrini paintings were lost in the fire of 1940.) 'We must make things ship-shape and *délabré* finery is not pleasant to see,' she wrote to George. The 'Radical Countess' had no time for faded grandeur.

The inventory records, however, indicate that Rosalind was surprisingly influenced by fashion in interior decoration. Thus, when the craze for Oriental artefacts swept the country during the 1880s, she indulged in an orgy of shopping at Liberty's and Swan and Edgar, the two leading London stores at the time. Castle Howard was filled with 'palampores' (cotton hangings, made in India), Turkey carpets and Oriental china, including '48 Japanese eggshell plates', 'tall Imari jars from Swan and Edgar' and 'Oriental jars, to be fitted up as gas lamps'. The account books show an incredible attention to detail, noting, for example, which shops would deliver free, and which charged extra for the use of a packing case. Every scrap of linen in the house was meticulously counted and its condition at the time of writing noted. There was to be no waste in the Radical Countess's household, and certainly no margin by which a light-fingered member of the staff could take advantage.

Rosalind's authoritarian behaviour and passion for economy could be carried to ludicrous lengths, as Lady Henley recalls:

My mother constantly shamed her family by embarrassing demonstrations during travel. Mary [the eldest daughter] described the way she would arrive at an Italian hotel at midnight with six children or attendants, and mountains of luggage, and expect rooms to be ready though she had not ordered any, and if the rooms were not satisfactory she would go off and try another hotel. This was still happening when I was taken to Venice: after we had all got into a hotel late at night and everything seemed settled and the luggage carried up, my mother found out that candles were 'extra' in the charge. So we were all bundled into another gondola and a hotel found which 'included' candles!

The Howards' income during the 1880s averaged between £17,000 and £18,000 a year, a huge amount at the time, and there was really no need for all this anxiety about money. The accounts for a trip to Egypt, for example, show just how cheap travel was at the end of the nineteenth century:

> 1887. Journey to Egypt, with 5 children for 3 months: Total
>   cost £1024.
> Hotel life for 79 days at 12/3 per day per person
> Tickets to First Cataract and back to London £532.
> Donkeys, Expeditions etc. £72.16.0
> Luggage to Cairo and back £30
> *Less*, saved in housekeeping, wages and stable expenses at
>   Naworth £472 thus reducing expenses of journey to £552.

George had no more liking for luxurious living than his wife, but he did, however, have one consistent extravagance, which was liable to cause a deficit at the end of the year – contemporary art, particularly paintings by his friends. For example, the year that he inherited his father's estate (1880), the total amount spent on paintings came to *£2,044*. This figure included: £1,240 for the magnificent Burne-Jones *Annunciation* . . . £200 to Walter Crane, as part payment for the morning-room frieze at Palace Green . . . W. Richmond's portrait of Rosalind, which cost £210 . . . Two pictures by Legros – an oil at £125 and a water-colour at £30 . . . and a Costa for £120. All through the 1880s George continued to increase his collection of contemporary paintings. In 1881 he bought another Burne-Jones, a circular water-colour entitled *Dies Irae*, for £450, and a painting by Costa, of Lerici, for £120. The same year he bought a bust of his current hero, Mazzini, for £50, and commissioned a carpet for the drawing-room at Naworth from William Morris. In 1882 he commissioned Burne-Jones to paint a fresco for the library at Naworth, paying him £500 on account, while in 1885 the bills for paintings include £240 for another Italian landscape by Costa, and a copy of Watts's portrait of Tennyson by Miss Hawkins, one of his Pre-Raphaelite friends, for £37 10s.

It is clear from the accounts of the period that the needs of Castle Howard came low on the list of financial priorities. Even after they inherited the house, the Howards continued to spend far more time at Naworth, which the family had always preferred. For example, housekeeping expenses averaged £21 a week at Castle Howard, £25 a week at Palace Green and £30 at Naworth. Another set of household figures, dated 1888, confirms the pattern: the expenses at Castle Howard for a month are given as £77 17s., whereas the equivalent figure for Naworth is £139 11s. – virtually double: similarly, the amounts spent on furniture for the two houses in the same period are respectively £35 and £173.

In the same context, the figures quoted for the garden at Castle Howard explain Rosalind's decision, at the end of the nineteenth century, to abolish Nesfield's pretty floral parterres. The total cost of the garden in 1888 came to £790 19s. 5d., and the following year it was £805 4s. There was an occasional profit, such as the £17 from the sale of peaches and £58 11s. from the pigs, but nothing significant. The account book notes that the total included the wages of the head gardener, at £115 6s. 3d. a year, and those of the labourers, which came to £467 10s., but fails to specify how many men were employed. In any case, this kind of garden was clearly labour-intensive as it stood, and it did make more economic sense to concentrate on lawns rather than flower-beds. Castle Howard was certainly not unique in this decision – virtually none of Nesfield's parterres have survived to the present day.

The money went elsewhere – much of it on Rosalind's charitable works. For example, she had long been distressed by the plight of working-class women condemned to live in the new industrial towns, and in 1883 she converted the inn in the Castle grounds into a guest house for ailing women. Every month – except one, when the Matron had a break herself – twelve women were given a month's holiday in the country. This practice, which cost between £300 and £400 a year, was maintained right up until the First World War. Another of her innovative ideas was to arrange country holidays for town children: over 500 were selected by the Leeds Charity Organization Society and billeted on the local cottages. (One cannot help wondering how that worked out.) She wrote to the *Leeds Mercury*, asking for subscriptions towards the cost of the scheme, in emotional vein:

. . . As I sit under the apple tree in the garden under these old castle towers, I hear the song of the birds, carolling on every side, and the warm sunshine and the soft wind fills the heart with the sense of the blessedness of summer; the flowers are blooming; all the earth is newly dressed in her garment of rich foliage . . . freshness and beauty is in every blade of grass . . . Then send, oh send, us your children quickly, that no single day of this bounteous season may pass away and not shed its fullest radiance on the little children who are so buried in the grimy towns that often their only contact with great mother earth is the pleasure of making mud pies near the street gutter, or perhaps, in some happier cases, to cherish a few pale window plants.

Unfortunately Rosalind, like many women philanthropists, found it easier to love and understand other people's children, particularly if they were underprivileged, than her own. Her relationship with her sons in particular was disastrous and tragic. One after another she quarrelled with Charles, Hubert, Christopher, Michael and Oliver: the rows were about politics, money, drink, girls, ideas – anything and everything. Moreover, by some bitter twist of fate, these very five sons all died prematurely, predeceasing their mother, who was left to mourn their estrangement. Only Geoffrey remained in her life to the bitter end – and it was indeed bitter. The girls fared better in their dealings with Rosalind, who was, after all, one of the original feminists, but even they were not immune to their mother's fearsome rages. Dorothy Henley described her mother's reaction to the announcement of her engagement to Francis, who, though a future Baron, was also a brewer, and moreover was connected with the Stanleys, whom Rosalind had grown to hate:

My mother received me grimly sitting in the South Parlour [at Boothby, in Cumberland]. That evening she was insane, with the insanity of rage uncontrolled . . . There sat my mother in the black dress of her widowhood . . . She cursed all that was to be mine, my life, my children, my husband. I was to suffer the deaths, the humiliations, the miseries and infidelities she had suffered; it was even in Biblical and mediaeval language. Insanity may be hard to define in a court of law, but she was crazy then. It was spell-binding. But not for long: suddenly there came a grotesque anti-climax. She said 'And don't let him come here offering me his samples!' I walked out of the room; left the house; and we did not meet for ten months.

One of the main reasons for the split between the Howards is mentioned in this quotation: during the 1880s George Howard almost certainly had an affair, and fell in love with his pretty, flirtatious sister-in-law Maisie Stanley. Venetia Stanley (with whom the Prime Minister Asquith corresponded at such length) was generally thought to be George's daughter. The other great cause of dissension between the couple was the question of Home Rule: Rosalind was passionately in favour, George was not. In 1886 he became a Liberal Unionist, in company with five of his sons, an act which was regarded by

Rosalind as unforgivable treachery. Nevertheless, the following year the family went to Egypt together for most of the winter, presumably in an attempt to preserve the marriage. Neither George nor Rosalind wanted a scandal, so there was no official separation – the couple simply avoided each other. George tended to live in London or at Naworth, while Rosalind stayed in the country dividing her time between Castle Howard and Naworth, but there was no hard and fast rule and, in fact, they often coincided under the same roof. Lady Henley described the atmosphere at Naworth towards the end:

For whiles all would appear happy and smooth. Then suddenly clashes would come. My mother would shut herself up in her own quarters and send my father innumerable letters, many by me, to the other side of the house, and I brought back his written answers. This absurd system was entirely hers; to my father it was distasteful. These quarrels were not primarily political, I am certain, but personal, and often concerned my father's friendships.

There was an unwritten agreement that George should be responsible for the older children – though Mary and Cecilia married in 1889 and 1891 respectively – and Rosalind should have control of the younger ones. In practice, as they came of age, all the boys, except Geoffrey, shared their father's political views on Home Rule and other such explosive subjects, and therefore kept out of Rosalind's way. (In fact, neither George, nor the majority of his sons, were all that interested in politics anyway.)

In spite of her difficult nature, Lady Carlisle was in many ways an admirable woman. She was a genuine philanthropist, a passionate Liberal, and one of the founders of the great crusade for Women's Rights. Lady Carlisle was not known as the 'Radical Countess' without reason. A complete list of the causes she espoused – and for which she worked with tremendous energy all her life – would make daunting reading. At Castle Howard, among many other activities, she served on the local district council, supervised the Friendly Society, inaugurated a Temperance Association, launched a Coal and Clothing

Club and a Widow's Charity; and the pattern was repeated at Naworth. She was a member of the National Union of Women Workers, the British Women's Temperance Association, the Women's Liberal Federation, and Women's Suffrage – although her views on the last named issue were somewhat qualified. She was a formidable advocate, an articulate and intelligent speaker and motivated by genuine belief. The problem with Rosalind – and the reason she made so many enemies – was that she appeared both arrogant and intolerant. As early as 1876 Lady Paget, whom Rosalind had never liked, wrote spitefully that:

Mrs Howard had an expression of hardness in her light blue eyes and her complexion was too florid for beauty . . . Both she and her husband hoped that they were extreme Radicals. She put her ideas into practice by being the veriest tyrant at home.

Lucy Cavendish, a cousin, was more perceptive when she wrote in her diary five years later: 'This description of Rosalind's customs and manners at Castle Howard make one despair of her ever knowing how to be gentle, humble or considerate; and yet she *is* kind and affectionate.' Rosalind seems to have been literally incapable of seeing that anyone who disagreed with her might, in fact, not only be worth listening to, but might have a valid point of view. And, in any case, that they were entitled to their own opinions.

Lady Carlisle's character invited apocryphal stories. One of the better ones, still in circulation today, arose from her attitude to Temperance – an issue, incidentally, with which her husband was in complete agreement.

The inns on both estates were closed, and when they inherited Castle Howard it was said, and widely believed, that Rosalind had thrown all the rare wines in the cellar into the lake. (In fact, wine continued to be served to guests at Castle Howard until 1903, when the Countess was elected President of the National British Women's Temperance Association.) Needless to say this story caused considerable outrage, and was brought up again in the popular Press in 1916. Lady Carlisle was accused of wasting wine that might have saved the lives of wounded soldiers in hospital. She replied with the truth:

I see in to-day's issue that I have destroyed 1,500 bottles of old vintage at Castle Howard. The so-called wine in the 800 bottles that have been thrown away was sour stuff condemned as worthless and undrinkable 50 years ago and was left as rubbish at Castle Howard by our predecessors. Not even a dipsomaniac under the influence of his worst drink craving would have touched the mixture of fungus and smelly liquid.

As a peer who was also an artist of considerable standing in his own right, George 9th Earl of Carlisle was an influential member of the Establishment. He became Chairman of the Trustees of the National Gallery, after serving on the Committee for twenty-two years, and made them a magnificent donation of some of the finest classical paintings in the Howard collection. Philip Webb rightly said of the 9th Earl that he was 'A constitutional caretaker of precious things'. As one of his many contributions to the artistic world he was involved in commissioning murals for the House of Lords, in which context he employed, among others, the artist Byam Shaw. Carlisle was a generous and imaginative patron of the arts, and he took a particular interest in helping the young. In 1908 he was elected President of an international congress for the development of teaching art and its application to industry – a subject which had always been dear to his heart – and he was also on the selection committee which chose the masters for the famous South Kensington School of Art.

George Howard, as he signed himself, was a compulsive, dedicated artist, never seen without a sketchbook in hand. During the last twenty years of his life he went on a number of long painting safaris, to India, the West Indies, and South Africa as well as all over Europe. Today George Howard's paintings, of landscapes, friends and family, fill the walls of the Museum Room at Castle Howard.

The 9th Earl of Carlisle died of heart failure at the age of sixty-seven in 1911. King George V sent a message of sympathy to Geoffrey Howard on hearing 'the sad news of the death of your father whom I knew so well'. And his old friend Wilfrid Scawen Blunt commented sadly: 'George Howard Lord Carlisle is dead. He was one of the best of men, as well as one of the most domestically tried.'

The 9th Earl left a will which caused a good deal of speculation and controversy, and led to the break-up of the Howard estates. His eldest son Charles, who became the 10th Earl, inherited only Naworth Castle and a small amount of surrounding land in Cumberland, which had already been entailed: the whole of the rest of the estate, including Castle Howard, was left outright to Rosalind Carlisle, who would thereby remain free, on her own death, to dispose of it however she wished. She had quarrelled irrevocably with Charles many years before, and in any case he predeceased her. In her own will Rosalind decided to bypass Charles's son, another George,★ who had become the 11th Earl and the new titular head of the family, and instead, after favouring various of the grandchildren in turn, left Castle Howard and the rest of the estate to her eldest daughter, Lady Mary Murray. However, by the time Rosalind finally died in 1921, at the age of seventy-six, Lady Mary was firmly established with her own family in Oxford, where her husband Gilbert Murray was Professor of Greek: neither of the Murrays had any desire to live at Castle Howard, or to run an estate of such magnitude, and so Lady Mary gave it back, lock, stock, and barrel, to her brother Geoffrey. At the same time, the family decided by mutual agreement that their mother's will was inequitable and were able to modify the terms to a certain extent. Alternative provision was made for the other siblings, and for the descendants of those who had died, including the new Earl of Carlisle and his children. Thus, Castle Howard passed out of the hands of the Earls of Carlisle for ever, but remained in the Howard family.

★ George Howard, 11th Earl of Carlisle, was born in 1895, died in 1963 and was succeeded by his son, Charles, the 12th Earl, who still lives at Naworth Castle.

I I

'A Losing Battle for Survival'

Wealth and austerity are relative concepts. Thus, though the magnificence and display so loved by earlier generations of Carlisles had long since vanished from Castle Howard by the beginning of the twentieth century, the family continued to live in a style which seems the height of elegance and ease when compared to the standards prevalent today. Furthermore, the discrepancy between one person's estimate of his own wealth and position, and other people's perception of the same, can be very different – and tends to illustrate character rather than fact. Though Rosalind Carlisle was herself convinced that she had imposed a regime of Spartan economy upon Castle Howard, in the eyes of the next generation the house remained a powerful symbol of aristocratic splendour.

Gilbert Murray O.M., the classical scholar who later married the 9th Earl's eldest daughter, Lady Mary Howard, described his first encounter with Castle Howard and its chatelaine in a broadcast on the B B C to commemorate his ninetieth birthday:

... The next great influence on my youth befell me in my last year at college when I was on a picnic with the Sidgwicks [Arthur Sidgwick], and talking I remember to a little girl who was trying with her small paintbox to paint the river a proper blue, when suddenly an impressive lady whom I didn't know said to me in a severe voice, 'Mr Murray are you a teetotaller?' 'I'm afraid I am,' said I. She followed with questions on Home Rule and Woman's Suffrage, to both of which I pleaded guilty. The lady proved to be the famous temperance enthusiast and radical, Rosalind, Countess of Carlisle, and the incident led to several summer holidays at Castle Howard.

It was a striking experience, a great house, many guests, lots of cricket and tennis and unceasing political discussion, much of it novel and exciting, touched by the old Whig tradition, which held that all Tories were born bad but rapidly became worse as they grew up. However, there was also an atmosphere of art and culture and knowledge of foreign literatures, which was new to me and greatly impressive. Castle Howard taught me much, and besides, gave me a wife who seemed the answer to all my ideals, and who through good and evil days in a long life has never once failed in courage, never once missed an opportunity of doing a kindness ... [Lady Mary Howard, the eldest of the 9th Earl's eleven children]

The socialist principles indicated in this quotation, which were so strongly advocated by Lady Carlisle and her circle, must also be judged in the context of contemporary society, if they are not to seem absurd. Before the First World War – and in some cases even afterwards – it was taken for granted that a household comparable to Castle Howard would employ a large number of living-in servants. Labour was still cheap and the class system still ingrained in the public consciousness; furthermore, domestic service was a means of providing employment on the great estates, and *noblesse oblige* was still regarded as important.

Many of the Tory establishments so despised by the Countess continued to flaunt their status with spectacular parties, liveried footmen, and other symbols of conspicuous consumption: in comparison to such, the standard of living at Castle Howard was indeed relatively modest. Nevertheless, the Carlisles' breed of socialism in the early part of the twentieth century certainly did not entail forgoing the comfort implicit in keeping a comparatively large domestic staff: nor was there any question of the family regarding their servants as anywhere near their social equals.

As long as Rosalind Carlisle was alive (and, in fact, for a few years after her death), Castle Howard continued to employ twelve full-time living-in servants, as well as a number of daily and part-time staff. This figure is just over a quarter of the one given for the size of the 6th Earl and Georgiana's household, some 100 years earlier, but it still represents a formidable amount of leisure by present standards. By this time, of course, many of the functions of former domestic posts had become obsolete, for example that of the postillion. The head coachman and his satellite grooms had been replaced by a chauffeur, and neither a house steward nor a groom of the chambers were any longer deemed necessary. Footmen, too, had disappeared from the scene, along with the splendid liveries which had been worn by the male staff in the past. But there was still a butler in formal dress and the family as well as their guests still changed for dinner every night as a matter of course. The resident housekeeper, who was paid £90 a year and had her own private sitting-room, still ruled the roost below stairs: and the cook, paid £52 a year, still had a scullery maid and a kitchen maid working under her. Three resident housemaids, in descending order of rank and wages (ranging from £52 a year to £24 a year) cleaned the rooms and looked after the fires, with the help of a daily charwoman to scrub the floors. And there were others, the very name of whose jobs evokes luxury, if not grandeur, and a most nostalgic image of gracious living – for example there was a 'sewing maid', full-time and paid £50 a year, and a 'parlour-maid', doubtless complete with frilly white apron and starched cap, who would have come into her own at tea-time, serving muffins and seed cake from a silver tray.

Leisure, before the First World War, was still a serious business. It must be remembered that the modern concept of escaping to the country to relax in peace after a hard week in the office was not applicable to this generation. Few of the Castle Howard guests at this period needed to work for their living: the great estates had not yet been decimated and the majority of the upper classes could still count upon an unearned income. And since the great Victorian credo that 'the Devil finds work for idle hands' continued to haunt the twentieth-century conscience, it was important to organize the days in meticulous detail – the mornings in study, or other worthwhile activities, and the afternoons in planned entertainment.

Boating had always been popular with the Howards, and at the end of the previous century the 9th Earl had founded the Castle Howard Boat Club. Membership was later extended to include tenants and neighbours, and at one point the club had fifty-eight full members, of whom seventeen were ladies and twelve juniors: the fee was 5s. a year for the Gentlemen and 3s. for Ladies and Juniors. The Carlisles built a new boathouse on the edge of the North Lake as well as donating a number of gondolas, skiffs and other small craft to the club. Some of the larger pleasure boats which plied the lake in the summer could hold a dozen passengers – the minutes of one of the Boat Club meetings mention a number of craft for hire at thirty shillings, presumably for a whole day. The Castle Howard Regatta, held annually in August, became a major social event which lasted well into the twentieth century and consistently rated coverage in the local papers:

The extensive and picturesque lake at Castle Howard, which, thanks to the privileges permitted by the Earl and Countess of Carlisle, has now become a popular resort for boating during the summer months, was on Saturday afternoon a picture of gaiety and excitement, when large crowds of people lined the banks adjacent to the boathouse, to witness the annual aquatic sports in connection with the Castle Howard Boating Club ... (*Malton Messenger*, 20 August 1893)

The races and games started at one o'clock and went on until dusk, while 'an excellent tea was provided in a marquee adjacent to the boat house' and the Castle Howard Brass Band played on the lawn. This particular year, however, the *Messenger* took exception to the bad sportmanship of the crews:

... The boat-racing was on the whole very good, although there was no excuse for the lack of pluck on the part of one or two of the crews who shewed a decided disposition to hoist the 'white feather'* on finding themselves outstripped. The swimming competition was an excellent one

* A symbol of cowardice at the time. White feathers were distributed to reluctant soldiers during the Boer War.

and loud were the plaudits and encouragements of the spectators on the banks as the first two contested their last few yards by inches.

There were foot races and high-jumping competitions, and an annual tug-of-war between two teams of married men and single men which always went down well with the crowd and caused a good deal of ribaldry. Prizes were given out by Lady Carlisle and included brass pewters and a pound of tobacco. The regatta ended with dancing on the lawn, to the strains of the brass band playing polkas and waltzes. It must have been an enchanting sight. (Almost exactly 100 years after the festivities described above, the local Yorkshire press was able to report the revival of boating on the Great Lake: a new pleasure-boat, christened *The Dame*, after Dame Christian Howard, was launched in 1991. It is a Victorian-style vessel, 18ft 6in. long and powered by an electric motor.)

Cricket, once played on the grand scale with its own 'Home' and 'Village' teams, was still a regular feature of summer life at Castle Howard during the early years of the twentieth century. Lady Henley, describing the matches of her youth, wrote that '. . . Castle Howard cricket was still enormous fun, but it no longer had the glamorous addition of a "Lady Carlisle's XI", with many God-like young cricketers in white flannels staying in the house for special and formidable two-day matches.' Lunch was served in the Grecian Hall, a fine stone-vaulted room which opened on to the garden, and the family and village teams all sat down together. Teas were spread out on long tables under the lovely walnut trees which surrounded the cricket grounds. Occasionally, however, even something as relatively harmless as cricket could lead to trouble: the Harrow Wanderers once broke off their match in the middle and walked off the field after an angry row with Lady Carlisle about the lack of drink.

Bertrand Russell, who was a nephew of the Carlisles and also a constant visitor at Castle Howard, described the tenor of life and the *dramatis personae* of a house party during the summer of 1904:

Castle Howard

This place is a large 18thc house, embodying family pride and the worship of reason in equal measure. It is a family party – the Murrays, whom you know: Cecilia and Roberts [Charles Roberts, Cecilia's husband] – she, devoted to all her family, especially her mother, placid usually, but capable of violent sudden rage, in which she utters magnificent invective, though at all other times she is a fat, good humoured saint and (oddly enough) a Christian: Roberts, tall, thin, nervous, quivering like a poplar in the wind, an idealist disillusioned and turned opportunist; Oliver Howard, lately back from Nigeria, where he administered brilliantly a lately-conquered district, containing a town of 500,000 inhabitants, in which he was almost the only white man. He is smart, thin, delicate, conventional with a soft manner concealing an oriental cruelty and power of fury, of which his mother is the occasion and his wife the victim – at least probably in the future. He is very beautiful and his wife is very pretty: both are Christians; she too is very smart and conventional, but she has real good nature, and is on the whole likeable. They are very openly affectionate; in him, one dimly feels in the background the kind of jealousy that would lead to murder if it saw cause. Being very like his mother in character, he differs from her in every opinion, and relations are painfully strained. – Then there is Dorothy, who seems to me just like my grandmother Stanley – crude, sometimes cruel, plucky, very honourable and full of instinctive vitality and healthy animalism, oddly overlaid with her mother's principles.

The shadow of Rosalind Carlisle's dominant personality loomed heavily over this generation: they were a lively, talented group but so many of them seem to have been doomed from the start. Some of the boys' problems, at least, may have been caused by their parents' disastrous decision to dispense with sending the younger sons to school. While it was still the custom for girls of their class to be educated at home by governesses, boys were usually sent off to boarding school from the age of eight. George Carlisle, however, had hated Eton, and though Matthew Arnold's influence prevailed upon him to send the eldest son, Charles, to Rugby, and Christopher went to Clifton, the other four boys were taught at home by a succession of tutors. The experiment was a shattering failure. Lacking the

212

discipline of a public school the Howard boys became wild and violent, made the lives of their tutors a nightmare and reduced the schoolroom to a state of anarchy. Of course this state of affairs meant that they learnt very little – or rather that they learnt only that which they wished to learn. Eventually, their parents became alarmed at the boys' obvious ignorance and called in one of H.M. Inspectors of elementary schools to set them an exam. In the more esoteric subjects, which appealed to them, such as foreign languages, astronomy and higher literature, the children passed with flying colours, but the Inspector found their knowledge of the basics of education 'to be virtually Nil'.

One after another these attractive boys, so bright with promise, came to grief. The litany of tragedy began in 1896 when Christopher Howard died of pneumonia at the age of twenty-three. He was a handsome, gentle and sweet-natured young man, adored by his sisters and his mother's favourite – but he got drunk one day with his fellow soldiers in the 8th Hussars, and Rosalind never forgave him. Only two years later Hubert, who had begun his career as a barrister, went off to fight in the Boer War and was killed at Omdurman: he was only twenty-seven at the time. Hubert, like Christopher, was much loved by his siblings, but the Countess considered him a bad influence on the younger ones and discouraged their meeting after he went to London and joined the smart set. He fell passionately in love with a girl his mother thought unsuitable, and, besides, Hubert was also a compulsive gambler, particularly at cards – he once lost £500 at a sitting. His sister Dorothy wrote of him: '. . . poor Hubert, the gallant, brave, intelligent loveable Hubert, who made an almost Saga-Hero impression on his contemporaries in his short life – a bad influence!'

Oliver was the next to die prematurely, at the age of thirty-three, in 1908. Oliver Howard was, as Russell has indicated, a tricky character, but he had many fine qualities and showed great potential, sadly never realized because of his untimely death. Even so, he led a wild and adventurous life, roaming the world in search of excitement. As a boy Oliver had wanted to be a jockey and used to drink gin in secret, hoping to stunt his growth. He became a magnificent horseman and rider, and at one point went off to work on a ranch in Canada, where his skill and bravery with the horses earned the highest praise from even such critics as the seasoned Canadian ranchers. From there he joined the Colonial Service and went off to Nigeria, with his pretty wife Kitty. Nigeria was known at the time as 'the white man's grave' and it was there that Oliver fell ill and died. He was said to be the best-looking of the Howard boys and was the only one who cared about his appearance, always elegant and well-dressed.

Michael Howard, too, led a doomed and tragic life, cut short when he was still in his thirties. He was a clever child, with a flair for mathematics and chess, who might have made much of his life had he not taken to drink. After a spell in the Army, Michael, like Oliver, became an adventurer, searching the world for fulfilment. He worked his passage to Australia, as a stoker, and later to British Columbia where he worked on a fruit farm and for a time remained sober. One of Michael's most bizarre escapades concerned a stint in Nicaragua, when he went off to fight in one of their revolutions – apparently quite indifferent to the issues at stake, and motivated solely by a love of adventure. As it happened, Michael's side won and he was rewarded with eighty hectares of land in Nicaragua – which needless to say, he never went near after leaving the country. In 1911 he married, and had three children before returning from his travels to fight in the First World War. He died in France in 1917, at the age of thirty-seven.

The eldest son, Charles Morpeth, also died relatively young, of cancer, at the age of forty-five, in 1912. As in the case of his brother Hubert, it was his choice of a wife which led to the initial breach with his mother, but it was Rosalind's violent objection to his political career when he joined the Unionists which made reconciliation impossible. 'Charley', as he was known, was born in 1867, and was only nineteen when he got engaged for the first time – to Kitty Lushington, the daughter of a Liberal neighbour and an ideal bride in the eyes of his parents. But Kitty broke it off, and Charley's next choice, Rhoda Lestrange, was anathema to Rosalind since she had been brought up in the Tory household of Lord Muncaster. Rosalind not only refused to go to the wedding herself but forbade her younger daughters to act as bridesmaids. (During the same month the Countess gave a grand wedding at Castle Howard for the cook, complete with gun salute and family photographs on the front steps.)

Geoffrey was the only one of the boys who not only survived his parents but remained on good terms with both of them. And it was he who became, in 1921, thanks to a chain of events which have already been explained, the new owner of Castle Howard. Born in 1877, Geoffrey Howard was the fifth son of the 9th Earl of Carlisle, and it is his grandson, Simon, who is the present incumbent of Castle Howard.

Geoffrey Howard appears to have been a less complicated character than his brothers. Lady Henley wrote of him that

... His live-and-let-live temperament, his essential good nature and moderation, his shrewd common-sense, and his outlet into politics that were congenial to my mother, made it much easier for him to live with her ... he was liked and happy in all he did. Popular in society, his gaiety caused him to be called 'the drunkest teetotaller ever known'.

Geoffrey became a politician, first entering Parliament in 1906 as the Liberal member for one of the Cumberland constituencies. In 1910 he lost the Cumberland seat but was re-elected as the member for West Wiltshire; the same year he was made Personal Private Secretary to the Prime Minister, Asquith, who referred to Geoffrey as 'a very sound Liberal and an old friend'. The Prime Minister went often to Castle Howard, where he could 'rest his nerves and think in the peace and quiet of the country': the visitors' books of the period indicate a number of house parties composed of politicians, artists and other intellectuals as well as numerous Howards. The guests included Winifred and Ben Nicholson (she was Geoffrey's niece), as well as those two formidable pillars of the Liberal Party, Margot Asquith (Countess of Oxford) and Lady Violet Bonham-Carter. Geoffrey

Howard went on to become Vice-Chamberlain of the Household from 1911 to 1915, and then Junior Lord of the Treasury. In 1923 he said of his political views, in a speech to the electorate, that 'He was a Liberal, a Radical and all that implied, and during the 23 years that had elapsed since he fought his first election at the age of 23, he had found himself not diminishing but increasing that Liberalism and Radicalism.'

Geoffrey Howard made a most felicitous marriage, to the charming Kitty Methuen, a daughter of the famous Field-Marshal, Lord Methuen. When she died in 1935 one of her friends wrote to *The Times*:

It is difficult to pinion and hold fast within the rigid limits of the written word even a fleeting vision of the grace and gaiety of Kitty Howard . . . She brought with her wherever she went the light and laughter of spring and a music to which life danced . . . She scattered happiness broadcast with both hands. There was no conscientious purpose or direction about it it. Like careless *largesse* it slipped through her fingers – her heart's overflow. No moment shared with her could possibly be flat or dull . . . Her delicious, irresistible gaiety swept one along on its sparkling current.

And another obituary mentioned that Mrs Howard ' . . . had the tradition of the great hostesses of the past, and so far as modern conditions allowed, made Castle Howard one of the most hospitable, as it was also one of the happiest, houses in the country'.

If these quotations still evoke an image of gracious living and financial security they are misleading. In 1935, when they were written, the country was in the middle of the Depression, and Castle Howard had, in fact, been fighting a losing battle for survival ever since the break-up of the estates in 1921. Whatever the moral arguments for or against primogeniture, it is a system which has the indisputable advantage of keeping the wealth of an estate intact. After the property was divided among the 9th Earl's eleven surviving children, Geoffrey Howard, the new owner of Castle Howard, could no longer count on the income from the Naworth estate, and much else besides had been given away to support the rest of the family. Although the *intention*, at the time of the division and re-distribution, had been to provide Geoffrey with a sufficient income to support the Castle Howard estate, it proved a fallacy. By the time of his death, in 1937, moreover, so many other factors had helped to change the pattern of aristocratic living almost beyond recognition: the 1914 war, heavy taxation, death duties and, finally, the Depression had all played their part in the decline of even the wealthiest families' fortunes. The Howards were by no means unique among their generation in finding themselves unable to maintain a house the size of Castle Howard.

At the time of Geoffrey Howard's tenure of the house no less than 130 rooms were still in use. Most of the basement and ground floor were taken up by the servants' quarters and domestic offices, which had been enlarged and improved by Rosalind Carlisle at the end of the previous century – the level of the South Lawn had been lowered at the back of the house in order to admit more light. The butler slept next door to the safe-room and his own pantry, while the housemaids had their own kitchen. Other service rooms included another, larger, pantry, a 'sweep's room', a 'china room', a 'linen room', a 'brush room', and an ominous-sounding space referred to simply as 'dark hole'. Apart from the large kitchen there was a scullery, a larder, a store room, a still room, a wine cellar, a laundry and a separate drying-room. A short staircase led up from the basement to a small dining-room, sometimes used for the children's meals, and next to that there was a large gymnasium. The two schoolrooms, one for the girls and one for the boys, were on the ground floor alongside various household offices, and there was also a billiard room.

The principal reception rooms ranged along the south side of the house on the ground floor, looking out on the gardens and the Atlas fountain: the main rooms were called respectively the (large) Dining-Room, the Canaletto Room, the Garden Room, the Drawing Room, the Music Room, the Tapestry Room, the Orleans Room and the Museum Room. The Long Gallery stretched the length of the West Wing, with the China corridor and various bedrooms and dressing-rooms behind it – and the chapel, with its magnificent Burne-Jones windows, occupied the north-west corner. The only bathroom on the ground floor is in the East Wing, somewhat oddly placed next to the Old Library, but there were several separate lavatories and a cloakroom.

The two main bedroom suites on the first floor were on either side of the High Saloon and looked over the South Lawn. Both had their own dressing-rooms but only Mrs Howard's had a bathroom: her husband's suite included a converted 'closet', with a wash-basin for shaving and another lavatory. The 'Kit-Cat Room' led off the South Gallery on the eastern side of the house, and the two main guest suites, known as 'Lady Cawdor's Room' and the 'Admiral's Room', were also in this part of the house. Again each of these bedrooms had its own dressing-room but neither had a private bathroom. Guests wandering along the corridors in search of the nearest bathroom, clad in their dressing-gowns, spongebag in hand, were a familiar sight in large country houses between the wars. Other guest rooms around the house were known by equally charming and evocative names. The 'Winterhalter Room' was named after an engraving by the artist of Harriet, Duchess of Sutherland, daughter of the 6th Earl of Carlisle, which used to hang in the room; the 'Marigold' and 'Poppy' bedrooms were called after the William Morris wallpapers with which they were decorated; the 'Print' room was born of the fashion for glueing unframed prints straight on to the walls and the name of the 'Goose' room derived from its nineteenth-century Japanese wallpaper, which was patterned with geese. The nurseries, consisting of ten rooms and two bathrooms, were housed on the same floor: and in the attics there were four extra little circular garrets, known as the 'bulls-eyes' in reference to the shape of their windows.

Besides all these rooms there was the Great Hall to be taken into account, to say nothing of the many stairs, corridors and passages, all of which had to be cleaned regularly and cost a fortune to heat and light. It was no longer a feasible proposition for a single family of limited income, particularly in the economic climate of the thirties. Dame Christian Howard, Geoffrey's daughter, who was born in

1916, still lives on the estate and remembers the difficulties of maintaining a house the size of Castle Howard during the Depression. Her recollections explain that the use made of the various rooms was by no means immutable:

'In 1931,' Dame Christian remembers,

my parents realized we needed to economize, so we closed off a number of rooms, including the East Wing, where the family had been living for some time. [And where Simon Howard has his private apartments today.] We all moved into the centre block of the house: my mother took over the bedroom on the South Front which used to be known as the Queen's Room, and had her piano in the High Saloon. My father moved his desk into what used to be the drawing-room, but then he also put the radio and the gramophone in there, so, of course everyone else used it too. The old still room was turned into a kitchen, and in various other ways my parents reorganized the house so as to make it more compact. By reducing the number of rooms in use we saved on heating and electricity, and needed fewer servants.

In 1927 the telephone was installed at Castle Howard – this was comparatively late, but the Howards wanted to wait until they could be guaranteed a private line – and in 1930 the house was converted to electricity, which was manufactured on the premises. 'We had our own generators and stored it in batteries,' Dame Christian explained. 'That meant that you had to be very careful not to use too much – *very* small electric fires. I got to know how to get round the house almost completely in the dark, feeling my way along the walls.'

At the time of her father's death Dame Christian was only eighteen and in the middle of her first 'season'. Castle Howard was put in the hands of 'somewhat absentee trustees', but the young Miss Christian, as she was then known by the staff, decided to take on the management of the house herself – a daunting task, one would have thought, for a girl of that age, but one which she appears to have taken for granted.

My father had sent me into the estate office every morning, even before I 'came out', to learn double entry book-keeping, and it had been arranged even before his death that after my first season I would take over running Castle Howard, while he was busy with his political career. I learnt to study the books and apply the figures to economy.

'I got rid of the housekeeper straight away,' Dame Christian remembered,

because I discovered that it was really the head housemaid who did most of the work. Once a week I would sit down with her and give out the stores – we had an enormous store-room. At that time there were still several different groups in the house – the dining-room, the servants' hall, the nursery, and the kitchen – who were all separate units, and had to be catered for individually. Everybody had to hand in a list of what they needed for the week, be it soap, or sugar, or whatever. The Co-op supplied most things. We economized as much as possible: for example we decided never to spend more than a shilling a day on meat, except on special occasions. And we bought in bulk: we would order a whole side of bacon, with a gammon attached, which was much the cheapest way of buying it. Coffee beans were ordered direct from Hays Wharf in bulk, and Indian tea in 60 lb chests. [Indian tea used to be known as 'servants' tea', because it was so much cheaper than China – regarded as a definite luxury.]

Only fifty years before the young Christian struggled with the housekeeping at Castle Howard, the house had been virtually self-sufficient: but by the late 1930s both the Home Farm and the Dairy had been leased out to tenant farmers, and though the gardens continued to provide vegetables and fruit for the house, everything else had to be paid for in cash. By this time, too, the number of indoor servants employed at Castle Howard had been reduced to four, excluding the nanny and the nurserymaid who looked after Christian's younger brothers and baby sister. Wages had remained more or less static since the previous generation:

But you must remember that this was in the mid-thirties, when there was no inflation and even deflation. And the girls lived in. They got their keep, and their afternoon uniforms were provided as well. At this time a girl who worked in the salt works earned 10s. a week, of which they paid 3s. for their welfare [the pre-war equivalent of National Insurance]. That left take home pay of only 7s. a week – to cover the whole cost of their keep at home. A girl working in a hairdresser at that time was probably paid no more than 7s.6d. a week, either. My point is that the girls in service were probably better off, in terms of what they actually had, than those who went out to work daily. But, on the other hand, it was becoming increasingly difficult to get girls because they wanted more freedom, evenings off and a different kind of life. The local miners' daughters, for example, stopped going into service.

During the economic crisis of 1931, Dame Christian recalled that her father gave all the farmers on the estate a 10 per cent rebate on their rent:

I think he knew just how hard life had become for them. And, also, he wanted to avoid having farms which were leased out being thrown back at him. I remember my father telling me at the time that the owner of a neighbouring estate had had six farms thrown back because the farmers simply couldn't afford to go on. That would have been a total nightmare for us as, by then, there were no facilities for farming left on the estate.

The financial prospect for the Howards was bleak indeed in 1939: one year later Castle Howard was to suffer the worst catastrophe of its entire career.

During the Second World War the trustees decided to lease Castle Howard to Queen Margaret's Girls' School, which had been evacuated from Scarborough. On the night of Saturday 9th November 1940, fire broke out in the South East Wing. Nearly twenty rooms were destroyed, including the Jasmine Room, the Queen's Room, the Colonnade, the Kit-Cat Room, the Canaletto Room, the Long Dining Room, Lady Carlisle's Room, the Garden Hall and the Steward's Room. Worst of all, the fire spread to the great dome: blazing like a beacon, it lit the countryside for miles around – and this was in wartime, when air-raids were a constant threat and blackout compulsory. Molten lead cascaded from the roof into the central hall, and then the dome itself crashed to the ground, leaving the interior an inferno of burning timber and shattered stonework. In all, approximately two-thirds of the South Front was destroyed, and a number of other rooms were seriously damaged by smoke and water. Christian Howard and her brother Christopher organized a salvage operation, with the help of some of the schoolgirls and teachers, before the Fire Brigade arrived. Many of the most important pictures, books and other valuables were rescued and thrown out on to the lawn. One of the pupils in the sixth form of Queen Margaret's wrote a vivid account of the drama:

I was awoken by somebody shaking my shoulder, and I heard the matron telling me, in a high-pitched unnatural voice, to get up quickly and wake the rest of the bedroom. I sat up and listened, but I could hear not a sound; suddenly, however, I happened to glance out of the window, and I saw that the sky was a lurid crimson, and that the woods were lit up by the same brilliant light, and then I saw that flames were pouring from the other side of the house . . .

The girls were sent down to the air-raid shelter at first, and then some of the older ones were asked to come up and help with the salvage work.

We made our way up the stone steps into the corridor which runs straight down the central block and past the form rooms, and here we saw the fire. The far end of the passage was ablaze from floor to ceiling, and dull red smoke poured down the corridor . . . The pictures in this room [the Reynolds Room] were immense portraits, one of which took up nearly a whole wall. There was not time to unscrew the rails on which they were hung, so we just had to tug at them until the wires broke and they crashed on top of us . . . Somebody suggested getting into the studio and trying to rescue the priceless mirrors which hung there. On opening the door, however, we discovered that the fire had already claimed them, and the windows and mirrors were cracked and falling in, while flames licked up the walls . . .

it began to look as though nothing could prevent the fire from consuming everything, and the priceless old books in the Tapestry Room and corridor had to be saved at all costs . . . Red hot timbers were crashing from the roof, and through the haze of smoke and flame, we could see that the studio, Vb. form room, the office, the headmistress's room, and the dining-room, which contained several more mirrors, worth thousands each, priceless Canalettos, and family portraits, were nothing but a smouldering ruin . . . We tried to rescue the tapestries from the Tapestry Room, but we could only reach one. [The rest were, in fact, cut down and saved by the firemen.] The corridor was knee-deep in water, as the hoses had been persuaded to work at last [no fire engine arrived for two hours], so we used our cloaks for carrying the books, and dragged them along the floor when we reached the Long Gallery.

It was by this time about 7.00, and the fire was at its height, when an air-raid warning came through . . . Nothing happened, however. Then, miraculously, breakfast appeared, and plates of steaming porridge were passed down to everyone, for the kitchens were in a safe quarter of the castle . . . We went outside, and from here we saw the blazing exterior of the building. It was a strange sight, for it was only half light, and the whole landscape was dusky with smoke. Above us, 100 feet high, towered the dome, and already flames were licking through the windows; and above the dome, silhouetted against the sky, was a gigantic fireman perched on top of an immense ladder, with his hose concentrated on the dome . . .

The garden was full of stuff which had been rescued from the house, bedding, clothes, carpets, books, pictures and crosses, vases and altar cloths from the chapel lay everywhere. And all this had to be somehow moved again, for it was pouring with rain, and they were all getting ruined . . . Boiling lead splashed all around as the dome finally crashed, and the timbers which constituted its framework were left stark and glowing against the sky, until they, too, fell in.

'The Renaissance of Castle Howard'

Castle Howard today is one of the most popular stately homes in Britain, attracting some quarter of a million tourists every year, and has become known throughout the world as the house where the hugely successful television series *Brideshead Revisited* was filmed. Yet only fifty years ago the whole property had fallen into a state of such desolation that many deemed it beyond repair. The renaissance of Castle Howard and the grounds to their present state of prosperity is entirely thanks to the energy, vision and initiative of George, the late Lord Howard of Henderskelfe. He showed a dedication to the project of restoring Castle Howard comparable to that which fired his ancestor, the 3rd Earl of Carlisle, to build the house in the first place, nearly 300 years ago.

George Howard was born in 1920, the second son of Geoffrey and Kitty Howard, and grandson of the 9th Earl of Carlisle. During the Second World War he was commissioned in the Green Howards and served in India and Burma, where he was wounded. In 1944 both his elder brother, Mark, and his younger brother, Christopher, were killed in action, leaving George, as the sole surviving son, to inherit Castle Howard.

In 1949 he married Lady Cecilia Fitzroy, and in 1952 they decided to move back into Castle Howard. It was an act of tremendous faith. The house had been decimated by fire and most of the living quarters destroyed; the park was overgrown and its buildings were falling into decay; the lakes had silted up and the fountain had ceased to function. The prospect could hardly have been more daunting: nevertheless the Howards moved in and embarked at once upon a massive programme

of restoration which continues to this day. To start with they opened
Castle Howard to the public for the first time on a fee-paying basis –
at 2s.6d. a head. (It had, in fact, always been possible to view the
house by appointment, the visitors being shown round the house by a
senior member of the staff. This was the custom among all but the
most churlish owners of stately homes: the eighteenth- and
nineteenth-century 'tourists', however, tended to be confined to a
very limited number of the educated classes. The concept of the
stately home as a major tourist attraction was not born until after the
last war, when the 4th Marquess of Bath opened Longleat to the
public in 1949: most of the other owners swiftly followed suit.) In
preparation for the opening of Castle Howard, on Thursday 31 July
1952, 5,000 publicity leaflets were sent out to various hotels and
organizations with tourist potential and by midsummer the demand
was such that another 5,000 were ordered. The takings on opening
day came to £15 12s. 6d. and on the first Sunday there were 650
tourists: by the end of the first season 7,495 tickets had been sold.
Castle Howard was back in business and the restoration work could
begin in earnest.

It was decided that the first priority was to save the Temple of the
Four Winds, the lovely building in the park which had been designed
by Vanbrugh in 1726 and which was in imminent danger of collaps-
ing. At the same time it was essential to cover, and weatherproof, the
burnt-out section of the house, which had stood open to the sky since
1940, before anything could be done to restore the interior. Nevertheless, by the end of the decade work was already well under way on
rebuilding the great dome and its golden lantern. No accurate plans
of the original existed, and probably never had, so a technique known
as photogrammetry was employed: the architects used old
photographs of the house to reconstruct the measurements of the
dome, and to make an accurate model from which they could work.
Next, eight new statues were commissioned to replace the stone
figures which had formerly ringed the dome: these colossal busts,
each weighing nearly a ton, were carved by local Yorkshire masons
and then hoisted on to the entablature some eighty feet above the

ground. The Canadian artist Scott Medd was commissioned to reproduce Pellegrini's painting depicting the Fall of Phaeton on the ceiling of the dome; he, too, was obliged to work from a single black and white photograph of the original.

By 1964 the various restorations had cost nearly £120,000 – the equivalent of at least a million pounds in current prices: George Howard had been able to obtain just over £70,000 in grants, notably from the Historic Buildings Council, towards the cost of the work, but even so the expense was crippling and he was forced to retrench for a time. The financial situation recovered in the early 1970s, so work was begun on the restoration of the eighteenth-century stable block – which needed a new roof among other things. This project alone cost a further £181,000, of which £45,000 was contributed by grants. In 1979, however, Castle Howard was picked by Granada Television as the location for the prestigious series *Brideshead Revisited*. George Howard was an influential member of the media Establishment at the time, since he had been made a Governor of the BBC (he went on to become Chairman of the Board of Governors in 1980). The success of the series not only enabled him to rebuild the Garden Hall, but stamped an image of Castle Howard on the public consciousness which has remained in force ever since.

In the case of the Garden Hall it was decided that any attempt to reproduce the original Pellegrini murals exactly could only result in unsatisfactory pastiche: instead, Felix Kelly, a friend of the family, was asked to decorate the room with a series of paintings depicting imaginary Vanbrugh scenes. During the same period work was begun on the enormous task of restoring the mausoleum – which has yet to be completed – and on repairing the Chapel roof. Over the last few years George Howard's son, Simon Howard, has concentrated on the restoration of the waterways on the estate, and in so doing has shown the same kind of energy and dedication to Castle Howard as his father. Both the North and South Lakes have now been cleared and the fountains are once again in working order: the cost of this particular project has already mounted to more than a quarter of a million pounds.

George Howard, however, was concerned not solely with restoration at Castle Howard, but also with making various innovative and personal contributions to the property. One such was the Castle Howard Costume Galleries, launched in 1965 and housed in the newly restored stable block. Today they contain the largest private collection of historic costumes in Britain, with approximately 18,000 items in all, ranging from early Coptic fragments to the present day. The collection includes, among other gems, early eighteenth-century fans, costumes from the Diaghilev Ballets Russes and a replica set of the Crown Jewels. George Howard's other charming innovation at Castle Howard was the creation of an eighteenth-century rose garden, to commemorate the death of his wife, Lady Cecilia, in 1974. It was designed by James Russell, one of the leading landscape gardeners at the time, within the framework of the existing walled garden, and specializes in all kinds of old-fashioned roses. Lady Cecilia's Rose Garden contains, to date, some 900 plants of more than 300 varieties.

On New Year's Eve 1975, 'Une Nuit Blanche' was held at Castle Howard, and for one night the house returned to the magnificence of the eighteenth century. The guests were dressed in silver or white, and the house was lit entirely by candlelight, while flaming torches lined the façade. Once again Cavendishes, Russells, Worsleys and Lascelles danced in the Long Gallery and wandered through the candlelit galleries. As the 'thank you' letters show, the past was a tangible presence . . .

Castle Howard looked truly wonderful that night, glorious ghosts floating everywhere . . . Any ball in such a setting would be memorable, but your hospitality was quite magnificent, the sort of thing which belongs more to the age of Vanbrugh and Capability Brown than to these shabby modern times . . . I shall never forget the magic of the candlelit hallways, passages, galleries and state rooms. As Keats wrote, 'Was it a vision, or a waking dream?'

Sources and Selected Bibliography

SOURCES

The majority of the material used in this book comes from the Castle Howard archives. Other sources include: *The Dictionary of National Biography*, York Municipal Library, the Public Record Office, the Historical Manuscripts Commission, the British Library, the London Library, Bath Public Reference Library, and other local libraries.
Publications include:

> *The Gentleman's Magazine.*
> *The Malton Messenger* and other contemporary local newspapers.
> *The Spectator* 1711–14 (ed. Steele and Addison).
> *The Tatler* 1709–11 (ed. Richard Steele).
> *The Times* (Obituaries, Court Circular, etc.)

SELECTED BIBLIOGRAPHY

Ashton, J., *Social Life in the Reign of Queen Anne* (2 vols.), Chatto & Windus, London, 1900.
Askwith, Betty, *Piety and Wit*, Collins, London, 1982.
Bell, Alan, *Sydney Smith. A Biography*, Clarendon Press, Oxford, 1982.
Bingham, Madeleine, *Masks and Façades*, Allen & Unwin, London, 1974.
Borsay, Peter, *The English Urban Renaissance: Culture and Society in the Provincial Town 1660–1770*, Clarendon Press, Oxford, 1989.
Buck, Anne, *Eighteenth Century Dress*, Batsford, London, 1979.

Cannon, J., *Aristocratic Century*, Cambridge University Press, 1984.

Clarke, John, *George III*, Weidenfeld & Nicolson, London, 1972.

Clay, Christopher, 'Marriage and Inheritance and the Rise of Large Estates in England 1660–1815', *Economic History Review*.

Downes, Kerry, *Sir John Vanbrugh. A Biography*, Sidgwick & Jackson, London, 1987.

Duncan, Andrew I.M., *A Study of the Life and Public Career of Frederick Howard, 5th Earl of Carlisle, 1748–1825*, Ph.D. dissertation, University of Oxford, 1981.

Duncan, Andrew I.M., *A Georgian Country Estate: Castle Howard 1770–1820*, unpublished, 1988.

Fowler, John, and Cornforth, John, *English Decoration in the Eighteenth Century*, Barrie & Jenkins, London, 1974.

Fowler, Marian, *Blenheim – Biography of a Palace*, Viking, London, 1989.

Fowler, Sybilla Jane, *The Stately Homes of Britain*, Debrett/Webb & Bower, London, 1982.

Geduld, H.M., *Prince of Publishers: A Study of the Work and Career of Jacob Tonson*, Bloomington, London, 1969.

George, Dorothy M., *London Life in the 18th Century*, Kegan Paul, London, 1925.

Gibbs, Lewis, *The Admirable Lady Mary*, Alan Dent, London, 1949.

Girouard, Mark, *Life in the English Country House*, Yale University Press, 1978; Penguin, Harmondsworth, 1980.

Grundy Heape, R., *Georgian York*, Methuen, London, 1937.

Henley, Dorothy, *Rosalind Howard, Countess of Carlisle*, Hogarth Press, London, 1958.

Historic Houses – Conversations in Stately Homes, Condé Nast Publications, London, 1969.

The Household Book of Lady Grisell Baillie, 1692–1733, Edinburgh University Press, 1911.

Hussey, Christopher, *English Gardens and Landscapes 1700–1750*, Country Life, London, 1967.

Laver, James, *A Concise History of Costume*, Thames & Hudson, London, 1969.

Lees-Milne, James, *Earls of Creation*, Hamish Hamilton, London, 1962.

Lees-Milne, James, *English Country Houses – Baroque 1685–1715*, Country Life, London, 1982.

LeFanu, William (ed.), *Betsy Sheridan's Journal*, Eyre & Spottiswoode, 1960.

Leveson-Gower, G. (ed.), *Hary-o: The Letters of Lady Harriet Cavendish, 1796–1809*, London, 1940.

Leveson-Gower, Iris, *The Face Without a Frown*, Muller, London, 1944.

Moir, E.E., *The Discovery of Britain. The English Tourists 1540–1840*, London, 1964.

Nicolson, Nigel, *The National Trust Book of Great Houses of Britain*, The National Trust and Weidenfeld & Nicolson, London, 1978.

Oliens, Diana, *Morpeth – A Victorian Public Career*, Ph.D. dissertation, University Press of America, 1983.

Passages from the Diaries of Mrs Lybbe Powys 1756–1808, Longmans, London, 1899.

Porter, Roy, *Health for Sale: Quackery in England 1660–1850*, Manchester University Press, 1989.

Roberts, Charles, *The Radical Countess*, Steel Brothers, Carlisle, 1962.

Saumarez Smith, Charles, *The Building of Castle Howard*, Faber and Faber, London, 1990.

Saumarez Smith, Charles, *Charles Howard, Third Earl of Carlisle and the Architecture of Castle Howard*, Ph.D. dissertation, University of London, 1986.

Smith, Nowell C. (ed.), *Selected Letters of Sydney Smith*, Oxford University Press, 1981.

Stevens, John, *Knavesmire – York's Great Racecourse and Its Stories*, Pelham Books, London, 1984.

Stone, Lawrence, *Family and Fortune. The Howards, Earls of Suffolk 1574–1745*, Clarendon Press, Oxford, 1973.

Stone, Lawrence, *The Family, Sex and Marriage 1500–1800*, Weidenfeld & Nicolson, London, 1977; Penguin Books, 1979.

Surtees, Virginia, *The Artist and the Autocrat*, Michael Russell, 1988.

Waterson, Merlin, *The Servants' Hall*, Routledge & Kegan Paul, London, 1980.

Webb, Geoffrey (ed.), *The Complete Works of Sir John Vanbrugh. The Letters* (Vol. 4), Nonesuch Press, London, 1928.

Wharncliffe, Lord (ed.), *The Letters of Lady Mary Wortley Montagu*, Richard Bentley, London, 1837.

Wilkinson, J. Brooke, *History of Carlisle House, Soho*, London, 1939.

Woodforde, John, *Georgian Houses For All*, Routledge & Kegan Paul, London, 1978.

Index

Index